TOWPATH-TRAILS

A practical guide to walking beside canals

NIALL ALLSOP & MICHAEL PEARSON

PEARSON

British Library Cataloguing in Publication Data
Allsop, Niall
  Towpath trails: a practical guide to
  walking beside canals.
  1. Canals — England — Guide-books
  2. England — Description and travel —
  1971 — Guide-books
  I. Title   II. Pearson, Michael, *1952* —
  914.2'04858   DA632

ISBN 0-907864-33-3

First impression 1986
by J. M. Pearson & Son (Publishers) Ltd
The Midland Railway Grain Warehouse, Derby Street,
Burton-on-Trent, Staffordshire.

Typeset by Harrad Jackson
Curzon Street, Burton-on-Trent.

All rights reserved

© J. M. Pearson & Son (Publishers) Ltd.

Printed by The Matthews Wright Press,
Chard, Somerset.

Cover photographs - front: Great Haywood Junction, meeting place
of the Trent & Mersey and Staffordshire & Worcestershire canals;
rear: Towpath walkers near Chirk on the Llangollen canal.

CONTENTS

Introduction

"Towpath Trails" was prompted by a glut of books, in recent times, all purporting to be the last word in canal walking. Each had its admirable points, but none of them - or so we felt - were very practical when it came to following in their authors' footsteps, and none communicated the sheer fun of towpath walking. From some of these tomes one came away with the impression that canalside walking was something not to be taken lightly; an extramural activity for earnest students of industrial archaeology. Other approaches were more subjective - great for armchair travellers but virtually useless in guide book terms. What was needed, we decided with the easy wisdom of hindsight, was a comprehensive, entertaining, well presented, informative and thoroughly practical volume which would make you just itch to get out there and explore the towpaths of the inland waterways for yourself . . . .

Here it is!

We spent many lamplit hours pouring over maps. Made many an abortive reconnaissance, only to find the towpath petering infuriatingly out, or some public footpath - irrefutably marked on the OS map - blocked by industrial, or more often, agricultural development. In the heady early days of the project we considered covering the whole network of waterways, past and present, navigable and derelict, but rapidly came to the realisation that to adopt such a course would be to bite off more than we could geographically chew. So we compromised and drew up a roster of walks which included virtually all the canals and navigations linked to the presently definable inland waterway system; as well as a number of routes now derelict, or under restoration, once connected to it. We felt that most of the book's eventual users would not argue with our choice, but if they did (and were prepared to quote their credit card numbers) we could produce a guide to the more esoteric waterways later on.

Having arrived at our geographical mix we set about considering what type of walks should be included. Variety was paramount. So there had to be linear routes - by definition - and circular too; not the contradiction in terms at first apparent. We were quite prepared to forsake the towpath and its earnest devotees to add to the appeal of a walk. Indeed, it was important, we believed, that a canal should be seen (both physically and historically) in context as part of the landscape it traverses. In the event, roughly a third of the walks are circular, returning the walker to his or her starting point. The rest involve using public transport (for which we include copious details) always at the outset to eliminate timetable insecurities: take the train on the outward journey and you can stroll relaxedly back, pausing to inhale the fragrance of wild flowers (or abattoirs) and passing the time of day with rustics (or youths with air rifles).

We actually walked well over fifty routes, of necessity rejecting those which didn't meet our criteria by living up to the cartographic potential displayed. On some promising linear routes the complexities of local public transport defeated us; others were too similar to others; the rest were plain boring. We were as hard to please as a casting panel for a children's musical and as susceptible to superficial charm. Those which did pass muster stand here to face the ultimate test - your approval. Over forty walks are featured, and reading between the lines of the encores, you should be able to amuse yourselves by developing itineraries of your own. A good guide book throws down the proverbial gauntlet to its readership. Finally, it is at this point that most walking books offer stern injunctions concerning the wearing of 'stout' footwear, and thermal vests; the carrying of compasses, Primus stoves, and Swiss army knives; and the consumption of Kendal Mint Cake. Bosh! In such matters we were gloriously insouciant: walking in trainers; wearing clothes we would wear to high tea at the mother-in-law's; and trusting to the restorative powers of the local brewery and pie-maker. Extreme, to extreme, we know, but the point is not to overburden yourself, thereby compromising your senses. Tuck this book under your arm, put a Yorkie bar in your pocket, and all the treasures of the Towpath Trails await you . . . .

★   ★   ★   ★   ★

The 43 featured walks are presented alphabetically. Following a brief introduction, start point and access details are quoted. In the case of linear walks the start point is always quoted at the point at which the outward journey by bus or train commences. **Directions** are numbered and correspond to numbers circled on the map. **Points of Interest,** both waterway and general, are prefixed by key letters, again displayed on the map. Details of places to eat and drink or shop for a picnic are quoted under **Sustenance.** For friends or family impervious to the charms of the towpath, convenient places to visit locally are quoted under **Counter Attractions.** Suggested extensions to the featured walk and/or information on other suitable lengths for towpath walking on the canal featured appear under the heading **Encore.** The maps are hand drawn and are generally in proportion. The route is traced by bold lines, broken or solid, depicting lanes and roads and the larger of two dot sizes depicting towpath and footpath. Theoretically one should be able to follow the walk either by reading the directions or referring to the map. Use of both should be foolproof. Unless otherwise indicated all maps face north. Linear walks where the quoted public transport does not run on Sunday are marked thus - ⊠

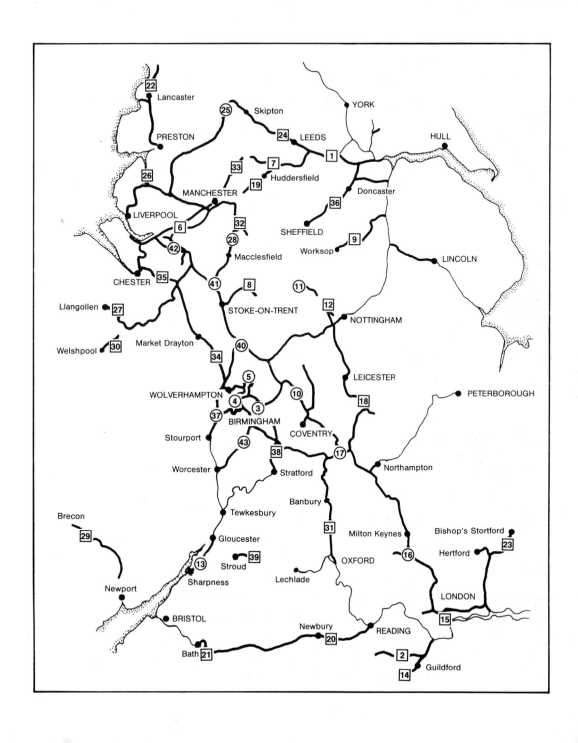

Walk 1

Aire & Calder Navigation
West Yorks.

Knottingley - Ferrybridge   2 miles

A coal laden 'push-tow' passes through Ferrybridge Flood Lock on its way to feed the hungry power station furnaces.

The Walk

The Aire & Calder Navigation might not be Britain's prettiest canal but it is by far the busiest with trade, and if you have an affinity with power stations, working barges and industrial archaeology, then this walk is for you. Coal, chemicals, oil and aggregates are carried on this, the British Waterways Board's premier commercial water highway. However, finding a suitable length of Aire & Calder towpath to explore wasn't an easy exercise. Frequently, throughout the navigation's 34 mile course between Leeds and Goole, industrial infrastructure blocks the way whilst continuity on the river sections is not a strongpoint. But, happily, one of the busiest and most interesting sections, through the town of Knottingley, has been the subject of a laudable towpath improvement collaboration between the doomed West Yorks Metropolitan County Council and the British Waterways Board, and it is this 'Knottingley Canal Walk' that we've chosen to feature here.

Start Point

Ferrybridge, "The Golden Lion".
OS ref: SE 485244.

Access

Train (Knottingley railway station - on the Leeds-Goole line (Tel: Leeds (0532) 448133) is $^3/_4$ mile from the start of the walk), bus (West Riding Services Tel: Leeds (0532) 456308), or car - car parking in lay-by off the B6136 beneath the A1 flyover. Ferrybridge is on the A1, 1 mile north of its interchange with the M62 junction 33.

Directions

1 Catch a West Riding bus 168 (hourly, daily Tel: Leeds (0532) 456308) from the stop adjacent to "The Golden Lion" and ask for Knottingley Common Lane.

2 From Common Lane bus stop proceed a few hundred yards south east to the bridge carrying the A645 Goole road over the canal. Cross the bridge and turn left down the lane to Trundles Bridge.

3 Just short of Trundles Bridge turn right down the track beside chemical works to Bank Dole Lock.

4 After viewing lock return to Trundles Bridge, cross it and turn left on to grassy area. Proceed to Shepherds Bridge.

5 Follow towpath $1^1/_2$ miles to Ferrybridge Flood Lock.

6 Cross lock by footbridge and turn right to join road. You may like to follow this road beneath the A1 flyover to view Ferrybridge's original river crossing.

This walk is so short that, given the interest of the steady procession of commercial craft (at least on weekdays), you might well prefer to walk it in both directions, thereby making it unnecessary to catch the bus out from Ferrybridge to Common Lane.

Points of Interest

A Aire & Calder Navigation
The canalscape in the vicinity of Common Lane is fairly typical of the Aire & Calder in its urban guise. Chemical works, a shipyard and an aggregates depot all with a vested interest in the waterway, combine to create a work-aday atmosphere, to which the ponies in the field between the Goole road and one of the chemical plants provide a welcome antidote. That part of the Aire & Calder featured in this walk was opened as the Knottingley-Goole Canal in 1826. It offered vessels heading from the River Ouse to Leeds and Wakefield a more reliable and shorter route than that via the Selby Canal (of 1788) and the River Aire. Improvements to the River Aire had begun as early as 1700 when a series of 12 locks were constructed capable of taking 15 tonne capacity keels. Various canal cuts were added throughout the 18th and 19th centuries resulting in the present route. During the second half of the 19th and the early 20th century, William Bartholomew was resident engineer on the Aire & Calder and his perspicacity led to the introduction of 'trains' of coal-carrying compartment boats powered by steam-tugs known colloquially as 'Tom Puddings'; a development which enabled the navigation to compete on more than equal terms with the railways.

B Bank Dole Lock
Though barely $^1/_2$ mile from the centre of Knottingley, Bank Dole Lock is an uncannily remote spot at the eastern tip of an island created by the canal and the River Aire. Downstream of the lock the river is navigable for 5 miles to West Haddlesey where boats turn on to the Selby Canal. Prior to 1826, this was the route used by all craft. The river meanders its way across the spirit-level landscape criss-crossed by pylons and horizoned by the huge power stations at Eggborough and Drax. Aggregate carrying barges use a short section of the arm beneath Trundles Bridge to gain access to Steetly Aggregate, but all traffic through the lock itself is of a pleasure variety.

C John Harker
Harker has long been a famous name in waterway circles both as shipbuilders and carriers, though the latter side of the operation ceased in 1976. Knottingley has always been the headquarters of the firm. Shipbuilding and ship repairing is an old industry in Knottingley and the site of the present yard covers an area where in the earlier part of the present century there had been three separate yards engaged in the building of wooden barges. The present site was developed in 1929 by John Harker Ltd., which was a company formed in 1918 for the purpose of carrying tar and petroleum

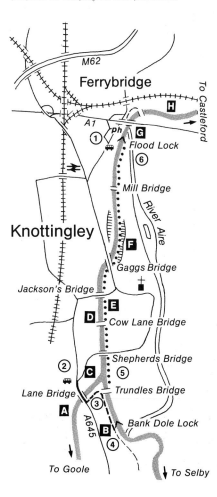

products on the Aire & Calder Canal. The first vessel to be built at Knottingley was a sea-going tanker of 150 tonnes capacity named *"William Kipping"* after one of the founders of the company. This vessel was launched in November 1929 and was the first of 318 vessels to be built at Knottingley, including the most recent delivery, a module type cutter dredger for use in marinas and harbours. Though, sadly, the great Harker trading fleet has been dispersed, a number of their former vessels bearing the suffix 'Dale' are still to be seen at work with other operators.

D Rockware Glassworks
Beyond Shepherds Bridge the canal passes through a built-up, though not ugly area, of industry. A huge overhead gantry on the opposite bank marks the wharves of Rockware Glassworks where many types of bottles are made. Silica sand used in the glassmaking process arrives here by barge from wharves on the River Trent where it has either been loaded directly on to barges from adjacent quarries or, as in the case of Belgian sand used to make clear glass, trans-shipped from sea-going vessels. The contract for carrying sand to Rockware currently belongs to Branford Barge Owners who operate a number of ex-Harker vessels.

E Coal Traffic
The modern successors to Bartholomew's 'Tom Puddings' are much in evidence on the Aire & Calder today in the form of push-tows of 3 compartment craft powered by diesel tugs. On a week day it's unlikely to be long before you encounter one of these distinctive units shuttling between the colliery at Kellingley a mile to the east of Knottingley, and the great Ferrybridge C Power Station. This traffic is operated by Cawoods-Hargreaves using 9 tugs numbered CH101-9. On arrival at Ferrybridge each 150 tonne compartment is hoisted 40 feet out of the water and upended, so that its cargo of coal is discharged into a huge hopper, from which the coal is carried by conveyor belt to the power station.

F Oil Traffic
Negotiating a deep cutting the canal passes the high silos of a flour mill which no longer uses water transport. The proximity of the River Aire suggests that the mill once used the river's power to drive its mill wheels. Emerging through Mill Bridge the towpath runs along a high grassy isthmus between the two water courses. On the opposite bank is a small oil depot which occasionally

receives deliveries by tanker barge. Since the demise of the Harker fleet, all fuel oils are now carried by Whitakers barges and their subsidiary Whitfleet - the former in a distinctive, primarily red livery, the latter in blue. With a capacity of up to 650 tonnes the more modern vessels in these fleets such as *"Humber Pride"* and *"Fleet Enterprise"* are the most sophisticated on Britain's inland waterways, with hydraulic wheelhouses which can be telescoped to pass under low bridges and bow thrusters to aid navigation in restricted waters.

G Ferrybridge Flood Lock
The ranked cooling towers of Ferrybridge's Power Stations occupy the skyline as you approach Ferrybridge Flood Lock. Electrically operated from a neat brick cabin, the lock controls access to the River Aire which the navigation follows as far as Bulholme Lock at Castleford. Beside Ferrybridge Lock is a small BWB maintenance yard.

H Power Stations
The first power station, Ferrybridge A dates from 1927, but this is no longer used to generate electricity. The B power station was opened in 1957. It receives coal by conventional barges, loaded at collieries upstream of Castleford. The giant C power station, served by the push-tow trains, was commissioned in the mid-1960s,

Sustenance
"The Golden Lion Hotel" is handily adjacent to Ferrybridge Lock and does a wide range of food. Across the road stands a modern row of food shops if you are contemplating a picnic.

Counter Attractions
Fairburn Ings - RSPB Reserve, open daily. 1 mile west of Fairburn village off A1 2 miles north of Ferrybridge Tel: (0767) 80551.

Encore
Towpath walking on the Aire & Calder is, as we have hinted severely restricted. However, if your interest lies in watching commercial traffic at work on the waterway, the short section of towpath between Bulholme and Castleford Flood locks, crossed by the A656 on the northern outskirts of Castleford, provides a good vantage point.

Information
Tourist Information Centre, Bus Station, Selby. Tel: (0757) 703263.

Walk 2
Basingstoke Canal
Surrey
Ashvale - Brookwood   7 miles

The Walk
Looking at the map this walk would appear to be surrounded by 'no go' areas, courtesy of the MOD. But not to go would be a mistake, for secreted in Surrey's suburban wasteland between Woking and Aldershot, is one of the most beautiful canals ever cut. Commercially the Basingstoke was a disaster, but in its natural attributes it leaves a unique and lasting legacy - provided of course there are no further mishaps like the one in 1957 when troops, returning from a night exercise, partly blew up one of the Deepcut locks!

Start Point
Brookwood Station.
OS ref: SU 952569.

Access
Bus, train and car. Brookwood Station is on the Waterloo/Woking/Alton line, details on Woking (048 62) 65251. Brookwood too is on the local Woking/Aldershot bus route; Tel: Guildford (0483) 575226. The station boasts a large car park.

Directions
1 Catch a train to Ash Vale Station, turning left out of the station, the canal towpath is less than 100 yards away.
2 Turn left onto the towpath, remaining on it for 6$\frac{1}{2}$ miles.
3 Leave the canal at Sheets Heath Bridge, cross this and follow the road up to the main road.
4 Cross the main road, the station is directly opposite.

Points of Interest
A The Basingstoke Canal
The act to construct the Basingstoke Canal was authorised in 1778, the same year a writer in the "Gentleman's Magazine" observed that, "the inhabitants of a little market town in Hampshire where no considerable manufacture is carried on, have unaccountably conceived the idea that if a navigable canal was made 'some way or other' from there to London, they should emerge from their present obscurity . . .". Surrounded as they had been for years by navigable waterways - the rivers Itchen, Kennet, Wey and Thames - it is hardly surprising that these 'inhabitants' wanted their 'slice of the action'. An original link with the proposed canal between Reading and Maidenhead was shelved when the latter itself never materialised. It was therefore an alternative route to the Wey Navigation at Woodham near Byfleet that was given Parliamentary approval. Thanks to the American War, work did not begin until 1788 and took six years to complete. Not uncommonly, it was a difficult engineering project - in this case the 1230 yd. Greywell Tunnel near Basingstoke - that thwarted earlier completion for there were only 29 locks in its 31 miles. In commercial terms the canal was a failure; it had peaks and troughs but in Hampshire, which is an agricultural rather than an industrial county, the coming of the canal did not itself generate the new industries of the Industrial Revolution. Bedevilled by a succession of negligent owners and its fair share of bankruptcies, trade to Basingstoke ended in 1910, to Aldershot in 1921 and to Woking in 1949. Now under the aegis of the Surrey & Hants Canal Society the canal looks forward to a better future, as a once heavily silted channel and its derelict locks are slowly returned to their former glory, albeit with a quite different market in mind.

B Ash Vale
From the early part of the century the Ash Vale Boat House was run by A. J. Harmsworth. Initially it was a pleasure boat business but he soon extended his operations to carrying, trading mainly in bricks from Nately Brickworks near the western end of Greywell. In 1913 one of the company's boats, the

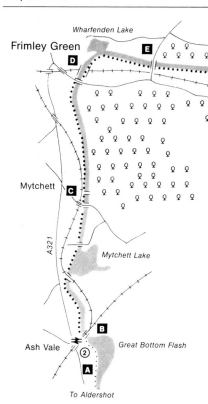

narrow boat "Basingstoke", left Ash Vale to work through to Basingstoke in an attempt to prove that the waterway was a Statutory Navigation under the meaning of the Railway and Canal Act of 1888 - such tactics being necessary to avert possible closure of the canal over a dispute about who should pay for the repair of bridges in the Woking area. "Basingstoke" made it as far as Basing Wharf where it ran out of water. Today the "Basingstoke" lies rotting across from the Boat House in Great Bottom Flash.

C Mytchett and Frimley Green
This stunningly beautiful wooded walk which begins at Ash Vale sets the pattern for much of the six plus miles to Brookwood. Oak, beech and assorted conifers display their green and golden magic to the cut as it heads north past Mytchett to Frimley Green. Mytchett Lake on the offside is MOD property and is believed to have been a natural hollow which in turn became a convenient reservoir

for the canal. In behind is Mytchett Place where, during the early years of the war, Rudolph Hess was kept in custody for some time. The new pub, "Potters", and the moorings on the offside are the brainchild of a local entrepreneur who is also responsible for the "Lakeside Country Club" further north at Wharfenden Lake. Frimley Green itself is west of Kings Head Bridge where the towpath changes sides. There is a pub down the hill, but, if you can resist the temptation, have a break instead on the bridge itself and survey the scene. The house to the right looks as though it should have canal connections but is in fact Frimhurst Lodge, on the approach lane to "Frimhurst" (House); on the left is the Boat House where pleasure skiffs were once available for hire.

D Frimley Aqueduct
As the lane at the side of Frimhurst Lodge becomes towpath, the canal enters a tidy brick-lined channel; what is not immediately obvious, is that this is an aqueduct. Frimley Aqueduct did not start life as such for it was only after the coming of the London & Southampton Railway in the 1830s that a need to burrow under the canal arose. The exercise was repeated early in this century when the then London & South Western decided to quadruple the tracks, which in turn caused it to complain in the 1920s when water started to leak through the 'join' and was, seemingly, putting out the fires of the engines passing underneath! A. J. Harmsworth again came to the rescue by diverting the channel via a wooden trough while it was relined with lead. (For the best view of the aqueduct walk back to the main road and down to where the railway goes under it.) Ethel Smyth the Victorian composer and concert pianist was brought up in "Frimhurst" and in "Impressions that Remained" recalls that the Railway Company complained about local boys hurling stones onto the train from the parapet; the local bobby was called in, hid behind a hedge to watch and the culprit was duly caught . . . herself!

E Deepcut
What follows is the mile long Deepcut. Borne of a scar across the wooded landscape, the healed wound has matured into a unique and intimate tunnel of trees. Deep rooted beech and Spanish chestnut have, for too long, watched over a decaying ditch; the water is deep and clear now and Deepcut is poised to enrich all who walk or boat this way.

F Deepcut Locks
The cutting ends at Lock 28, the first of 14 that drop the canal down 97 ft. in two miles to Brookwood. This was the site of a former wharf and dry dock, the latter and the lock have been restored, the gates and all the locks having been made in the adjacent workshops. Dock and locks are now restored and the standard of work can only be marvelled at - as can the setting, for what follows is a stepped version of Deepcut itself, black and white jewels set in a green crown.

G The Railway and the Army
Halfway down the flight the commanding rhetoric of the army at play on the one hand competes with the rattle of the railway on the other. Curiously both were responsible for peaks, albeit short-lived, in the canal's fortunes. When work began on the railway the canal's trade increased mainly as a direct result of the lucrative contracts to carry sleepers for the railway! Likewise, the building of the Aldershot Army Camp between 1854 and 1859 involved the canal company in the transportation of large quantities of building materials and related commodities.

H Brookwood
Civilisation intrudes temporarily around Purbright Bridge. Just before the lock are the brick abutments of the steel viaduct that carried a branch line between Brookwood Station and Bisley Rifle Ranges to the north-east. But with the A321 (where the towpath changes sides) behind, the last leg to Brookwood blossoms with the best of suburbia. The tidy canalside gardens on the offside complement the softness of the

Restoring the Basingstoke Canal - bank piling at Mytchett.

spinney opposite - even the old war-time pill box doesn't seem out of place. A perfect ending to an inspiring walk.

Sustenance

Brookwood and Ash Vale have a lot in common, a few pubs, a few shops. The handiest hostelry en route is the "Kings Head" at Frimley Green, but for real character the "Station Hotel" at Brookwood is a must. Here too there is a gem of a home-made-bread-et-al shop.

Counter Attractions

● Farnham Castle, Farnham, Surrey. Open mid-Mar/mid-Oct, Mon-Sat, 9.30am-6.30pm; Sun 2pm-6.30pm. Mid-Oct/mid-Mar, Mon-Sat, 9.30am-4.00pm, Sun 2pm-4pm. Admission charge. Tel: Tunbridge Wells (0892) 24376 ext. 2. Originally built in 1138, it took the usual form of an earthmound with a rectangular stone keep on top. Damaged in 1155 but rebuilt later in the 12th century when the original mound was tightly enclosed by a shallow shell keep.

Encore

Walking the western end of the Basingstoke is hampered by its incessant wanderings and the reluctance of public transport to follow the same route. That said it is possible to get to - and from - the eastern portal of Greywell Tunnel, a 2^1/$_2$ mile walk along the canal from the A287 near Odiham, though you will need to retrace your steps for about a mile to catch a return bus at North Wanborough. The reward is, of course, the tunnel which is also one of the major obstacles to further restoration through to Basing Wharf. The technology, it seems, is not the problem, it's just the bat colony inside and the fact that the National Conservation Council wish to make it a Site of Special Scientific Interest.

Information

Tourist Information Centre, County Library, Tynehurst Avenue, Farnborough, Hants. Tel: Farnborough (0252) 513838.

Walk 3

Birmingham Canal Navigations
West Midlands

Central Birmingham   **8 miles**

The Walk

Gas Street Basin is synonymous with working narrowboats past and present, and so a thoroughly appropriate starting point for this exploration of Birmingham's city centre canals. No less than 5 distinct routes are encountered in this 8 mile circuit: the Birmingham Canal Navigations 'main line'; the Birmingham & Fazeley Canal; the 'Saltley Cut'; the Grand Union Canal; and the Digbeth Arm. Furthermore, in spite of recent improvements by the doomed West Midlands County Council, who have recently rebuilt towpaths and opened out these once largely inaccessible waterways, these are still under-walked and under-boated canals, waiting to be discovered by a new generation of "Birmingham Lads" - the title of an 18th century song about Birmingham's new canals.

Start Point

Gas Street Basin.
OS ref: SP 063866.

Access

Gas Street is situated off Broad Street adjacent to the city centre and only 5-10 minutes walk from New Street railway station. A door in the wall on the east side of the street, 200 yards from its junction with Broad Street, is always open. A limited amount of 4 hour meter car parking is available in Gas Street but there are numerous unrestricted city centre car parks within easy walking distance.

Directions

1 Proceed north-westwards from Gas Street Basin beneath Broad Street Tunnel to

Farmer's Bridge Junction.

2 Bear left over Oozell's Street Loop roving bridge, then immediately right over main line roving bridge, then right again down onto towpath - proceed eastwards to Cambrian Wharf.

3 Proceed down Farmer's Bridge flight to Aston Junction.

4 At Aston Junction the towpath changes sides. Continue down Aston flight to Salford Junction. (There is access from Thimble Mill Lane bridge to nearby Aston station should you wish to shorten the walk by returning to New Street station).

5 Keep to the towpath turning right under two roving bridges to join 'Saltley Cut' signposted "Warwick". Proceed to Bordesley Junction. (There is access from bridge 106 to Duddeston station offering another opportunity to shorten your walk).

6 Turn right under roving bridge and proceed to Warwick Bar.

7 Turn right under roving bridge and proceed through tunnel under railway up Ashted flight back to Aston Junction.

8 Cross roving bridge and retrace route to Gas Street.

Points of Interest

A Gas Street Basin

The atmosphere of working boat days is still very tangible at Gas Street where a number of narrowboats, lovingly preserved in their commercial guise, are usually to be found. An isthmus separates the once distinct basins of the Worcester & Birmingham Canal and the Birmingham Canal. Until 1815 no agreement could be reached by the two companies regarding tolls and all through goods had to be laboriously trans-shipped at this point; subsequently a stop lock was inserted. Passing beneath Broad Street Tunnel, Farmer's Bridge is reached through a corridor of deserted factories. An adjoining brewhouse is in the process of being restored.

B Farmer's Bridge Junction

Recent towpath improvements are everywhere in evidence, with neat two-tone brick courses running up and down the ramps of three iron roving bridges that span routes radiating from this once busy junction. The Oozell's Street loop formed the original tortuous 'main line' of the Birmingham Canal designed by Brindley and opened through to Wolverhampton in 1772. Telford's straighter, more immediately imposing 'main line' of 1827 goes off to the left and you must cross

it in order to reach the Birmingham & Fazeley Canal, signposted: "Fazeley 15 miles, 38 locks." The actual junction of the BCN and B&F is at Cambrian Wharf, so that for a short distance beneath Tindall Street bridge you are beside the Newhall Arm of the Birmingham Canal which ran into the very heart of the city, though all trace beyond the basin by "The Longboat" public house has disappeared.

C Cambrian Wharf and Farmer's Bridge Flight

High rise flats dominate the skyline as the B&F commences its descent through 13 locks beneath central Birmingham. To walk, let alone boat down this flight is an unforgettable experience. So closely gathered together are the chambers, that the restricted intervening pounds are extended sideways to ensure adequate water supply. Water can be heard constantly, and noisily passing down the spill weirs and foaming up from the sluices at the foot of each chamber. Encircled by the high canyons of industry and commerce, the towpath permits only occasional glimpses of Birmingham going about its business.

D Aston Junction

Presently, the locks are left behind and you emerge onto a more open section of waterway. A series of switchback roving bridges indicate once numerous water passages to subterranean wharves. Then you pass under the giant concrete edifice of Aston Expressway to reach Aston Junction which has been pleasantly landscaped. Here the Digbeth Arm branches off to the south - a route you'll return along later in the walk. Descending the Aston flight of 11 locks a subtle change comes over the surrounding industry. The sense of dereliction increases. No-one is to be seen. Researching this walk on a winter weekday we felt like the survivors of some enormous catastrophe. One canalside factory in particular, with broken windows and curtains sucked by the wind, resembled the hideous aftermath of a nuclear explosion. As we hinted, the walk is an unforgettable experience!

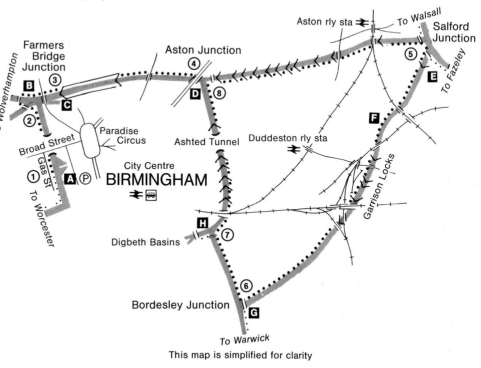

This map is simplified for clarity

Gas Street Basin, Birmingham.

E Salford Junction

Spaghetti Junction begins to fill the horizon - tier upon tier of uniformly dreary concrete; what will future industrial archaeologists have to say of this? The more modest, but hardly less significant in its own time, Salford Junction, is the meeting place of three canals: The Birmingham & Fazeley; the Tame Valley Canal of 1844; and the Birmingham & Warwick Junction Canal (or 'Saltley Cut') of the same year. Monstrously compromised by Man, the river Tame churns sadly through brick-lined channels beneath subsequent generations of engineering. In imagination you can peel back the layers of time to when the river wound between untainted water meadows. On the opposite bank of the junction one is chagrined to see T. S. Element - once operators of a proud fleet of narrowboats - making their living with rubbish skips.

F The Saltley Cut

Abandoned power stations, gas works and scrapyards characterise the 'Saltley Cut', though the bullrushes of Saltley's silted reservoir provide token greenery. Railways make their presence felt, criss-crossing the canal as lines converge on New Street. Between bridges 106 and 105 Saltley engine sheds lie beside the canal, and the Midland Railway once had a carriage and wagon works of some size here. Besides the stop lock at Salford (no longer in regular use), there are 5 chambers in the Garrison Flight. Beyond the final railway bridge a sequence of eight brick overbridges span the waterway like a recurring dream of diminishing perspective. The red hatches on the parapets are fire doors enabling hoses to be fed by the canal in the event of a fire. An evocative description of this stretch of canal in its last days of use by working boats appears in David Blagrove's "Bread Upon The Waters".

G Bordesley Junction

At Bordesley the 'Saltley Cut' meets the Grand Union Canal heading northwards to its city terminus at Warwick Bar. The upper decks of West Midlands buses loom over the perimeter wall of an adjacent garage forecourt and the six locks of the Camp Hill flight commence their ascent to the south. This section of canal was opened as the Warwick & Birmingham in 1800. The short walk to

Warwick Bar is full of interest: Great Barr road bridge is a cast iron structure of unusual design; a lofty dissected blue brick viaduct remains from a loop line between the LNWR and GWR companies' lines but never used; and Fellows, Morton & Clayton's huge 1930s warehouse stands beside the canal where it crosses the river Rea on a short aqueduct.

H Warwick Bar & Ashted Flight

Beneath the roving bridge at Warwick Bar the Digbeth Arm of the Birmingham & Fazeley Canal proceeds through to the terminal basins beyond the road bridge on your left - there is no public access. On the opposite bank stands the Birmingham Gun Barrel Proof House (though its ornate entrance door can best be appreciated from a slow moving train approaching New Street station) whilst, peeping above and beyond the embankment, is the huge Ionic bulk of the original London & Birmingham Railway's Curzon Street Station. A dark, curving tunnel leads beneath massed railway tracks to the foot of the Ashted flight of 6 locks. Ashted tunnel is exaggeratedly claustrophobic and the broken balustrade in mid-bore provides an unwelcome element of danger. Beyond the tunnel you return to Aston Junction passing the high tech architecture of Aston Science Park.

Sustenance

The only convenient canalside pub at present is "The Longboat" at Cambrian Wharf, an Ansells house with canal theme decorations despite the misnomer; a new pub development is taking place at Gas Street Basin. There's a useful row of shops uphill from bridge 106 on the 'Saltley Cut'.

Counter Attractions

Birmingham Botanical Gardens - Westbourne Road, Edgbaston. Open daily 9a.m. to dusk or 8p.m. 12 acres of ornamental gardens, tropical houses and aviaries. Admission charge. Tel: (021) 454 1860.

Encore

The Birmingham & Fazeley can be encountered in a more rural setting in the vicinity of Kingsbury Water Park, near Tamworth, where at least one of the nature trails incorporates part of the towpath on the Curdworth flight of locks.

Information

Tourist Information Centre, 2 City Arcade, Birmingham. Tel: (021) 643) 2514.

Walk 4
Birmingham Canal Navigations
West Midlands

Tipton   **4½ miles**

The Walk

A walk in the Black Country does not instantly open up the mind to images of green pastures and wooded valleys . . . and rightly so. But the beauty of the countryside is not what canals were about, much of the scenery we revere today was a by-product of the link between two or more centres of (largely) industrial activity. The epicentre of this activity was the Midlands. The tentacles of the canal network, like the railways and more recently the motorways, converge in and around Birmingham; not surprisingly there are more miles of navigable water here than in Venice! This short walk explores one aspect of the Birmingham Canal Navigations (BCN), the two levels of the Old and the New Main Lines, and it is by no means all grit and grime, for these man-made edifices have their own lasting and unique charm.

Start Point

Tipton Station.
OS ref: SO 956926.

Access

Bus, train and car. There is an hourly service to Tipton on the Birmingham New Street/ Wolverhampton line - information from 021-643 2711. Four West Midlands bus services 244, 266, 301 and 545 pass through Tipton; Tel: 021-236 8313 for details.

Directions

1 Join the canal by Tipton Station, turning right (west).
2 Cross the canal to the left above the locks onto the Wolverhampton level (the Old Main Line), remaining on the towpath for 2 miles.
3 Descend on to the Netherton Tunnel Branch and proceed up to the tunnel mouth before retracing steps and continuing towards Dudley Port Junction.
4 Cross back onto the Birmingham Level (the New Main Line) via the two iron bridges -

continue along the towpath westwards for the 1½ miles back to the bridge by the station.

Points of Interest

A The Main Line

The Main Line is the name given to the most direct link between the connecting waterways of the north-west Midlands, the Staffs & Worcs and the Shropshire Union Canals. It all started with the Birmingham Canal, completed in 1772, which was a meandering 22½ mile cut that supplied coal to the (then) small town of Birmingham. 'The Canal Age' was in full swing and it was not long before loops and branches broke off from the Main Line and rival canal companies wanted to hustle in on some of Birmingham's action. In this, they were eventually successful - despite the original Birmingham Canal Company's reluctance to share their water, let alone their trade, with anyone. But traffic did increase and gradually, like the roots of a tree, a network of man-made cuts spread in all directions to become the life-blood of the Black Country.

B The New Main Line

By the 1820s the arteries were becoming choked. Traffic was ever-increasing and would increase still further when the Birmingham & Liverpool Junction Canal (now called the Shropshire Union Canal) was completed. In 1824 Thomas Telford was called in with the brief of shortening the Old Main Line route and at the same time creating an alternative line between Wolverhampton and Birmingham. The new canal, nicknamed the 'Island Line', because it cuts through the high ground at Smethwick of the same name, was completed in 1837, cutting some seven miles off Brindley's original route. Joining the canal at Tipton, the New Main Line stretches almost in a straight line to the east where we will join it later in the walk. But for the moment we head west from Three Furnace Bridge towards its junction with the Old Main Line above the three Factory Locks.

C Factory Locks

Like much of the BCN the Factory Locks have had a face-lift. The area generally shows the inevitable signs of urban decay, in the midst of which the locks stand out as an attractive alternative to letting things go. The tail of the bottom lock is spanned by a fine cantilevered bridge, its mini-span not quite stepping across the cut - stopping short to facilitate the passing of the towrope. There was once a coal wharf at the next lock but lock 3 is by far the most interesting. Here on the left was the old BCN Gauging Station where each boat's cargo was gauged to determine the toll payable. New boats had their freeboard (the distance between the water line and the top edge of the 'hold') measured at four points - empty and when loaded with weights. Toll collectors would know each boat's 'dry inches' corresponding to particular tonnages and thus easily check the weight of any given cargo with a gauging rod.

D The Boatman's Mission

Above the third lock on the right before the bridge is an insignificant red-brick building, a little worse for wear from modern industrial usage. The building's foundation stone was inscribed thus: TO THE GLORY OF GOD and for all the good of the souls of those who pass on the canal THIS STONE IS LAID Novr 26 1892. This was one of five Boatman's Missions that served the boating community on the BCN. Three of these, at Birmingham's Worcester Wharf, at Hednesford Basin and at Walsall were run by the Incorporated Seamen & Boatmen Friends Society, while those at Wolverhampton and here at Tipton were run independently though along similar lines. During the week the missions were often known as 'coffee rooms' and not only provided boatmen with the basics of food and non-alcoholic drink but also washing facilities, newspapers and games such as chess, draughts and bagatelle. In this way, they strove indirectly to save the souls of the boatmen. Sundays saw a more direct approach with up to four services, including a Sunday School for the boat children. Those who didn't make it to the mission would be enticed to take part in wharfside services to the accompaniment of an accordion or portable organ.

E The Old Main Line

At Factory Junction, we join the Old Main Line coming in from Wolverhampton in the west to head south towards Dudley. For obvious reasons, it is also known as the Wolverhampton Level while the New Main

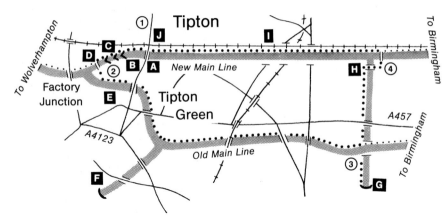

Line, 20 ft. below, is the Birmingham Level. The unique, ornate, iron, lifting Factory Bridge has been removed and preserved in the Black Country Museum less than a mile away. From Factory Junction, the "Euphrates Packet" ran to Birmingham in two hours 'for the accommodation of passengers and conveyance of parcels', the first class fare being a mere 1/6d (7$\frac{1}{2}$p). On the offside is the restored malthouse stable block, the sole survivor of what was a busy row of canalside buildings. Many such buildings, having ceased to be part of a working canal, have fallen into disrepair as a prelude to just disappearing. Here and there modern industry has reclaimed the site, but many of these have in turn fallen by the wayside - the stable block for example, was a derelict shell when the council took it over; it now lives on as a canalside centre.

F Dudley Tunnel

The canal swings round to and under Owen Street Bridge with the "Fountain Inn" to the left, the erstwhile headquarters of the so-called 'Tipton Slasher', an old boatman-turned-boxer. The building is listed and, as well as housing the canal company's stables at the back, it's one of those hostelries where you are made to feel at home and treated to some fine yarns in that broad Black Country accent. Behind the trees on the offside a 'fine' example of high-rise madness contrasts sharply with an imaginative housing development on the left. This not only blends in with the canal but sits atop another New Line/Old Line link, the Tipton Green and Toll End Communications Branch, closed in 1960. Beyond the next bridge, in the shadow of Dudley Castle, an arm to the right leads down to the Black Country Museum, Dudley Tunnel

and the Dudley Canals. The 3172 yard tunnel was cut as a private branch to carry boats into the Earl of Dudley's limestone mines beneath Dudley Castle to the Birmingham Canal. By 1792 it had been extended to connect the main line to the Southern Staffs & Worcs via the Stourbridge Canal. In recent years it has had a chequered history in terms of being or not being navigable. Inside there is a vast network of natural caverns and mines, one of which, the 'Singing Cavern', has recently been re-opened, via a new tunnel, into a veritable wonderland. Details of public trips are available from the Black Country Museum (see below).

G Netherton Tunnel

The Old Main Line continues under the railway and into a derelict wilderness, an industrial hinterland that industry has forsaken; wharves and warehouses have come under the hammer, their proud brick and stone edifices auctioned off in the name of progress. The line then strides across the Netherton Tunnel Branch from the New Main Line, for once again we join the Birmingham level. On the southern end of the extensions to Tividale Aqueduct's central arch is the turbine house that once generated electricity for lighting the tunnel (it originally had gas lighting). The pipes from the Wolverhampton level that drove the turbines are still in situ. The narrows either side of the arch were, like Factory Locks, gauging points for calculating tolls. The 3027 yd. tunnel, completed in 1858 was built to relieve the congestion on the Dudley Tunnel route; it was the last canal tunnel to be built, hence the luxury of gas lighting and a towpath along each side. Despite its more modern image it has, like Dudley, suffered from occasional closure.

H Dudley Port Junction
The industrial canalside between Tividale Aqueduct and Dudley Port Junction is in a state of disarray. There is, therefore, relief in the ordered simplicity of the two iron turnover bridges, each inscribed 'Toll End Works', that span the branch and the main line. More than anything else such iron bridges, cast either by Horseley Ironworks at Tipton or the rival Toll End Works, personify the BCN; their functional latticework often bringing a stark beauty to otherwise drab surroundings. East and west of the second bridge, the new Main Line embankment stretches for a straight mile in both directions. It was a short distance to the east that the Dudley Port 'disaster' occurred in September 1899. The canal breached into an adjacent marlhole (or clay pit) of the Rattlechain & Stour Valley Brickworks, carrying with it several boats. Six miles of water drained into the breach leaving a scene of total devastation. One boatman leapt to the towpath when his boat suddenly overtook the horse and managed to tie the towline around a telegraph pole to save both horse and boat being drawn down into the chasm.

I Horseley Ironworks
Heading west on the northern towpath, with the railway on one side and Tipton spreading below on the other, the embankment crosses two roads and a railway on aqueducts. The first is a modern concrete affair replacing one originally built by Telford; beyond the third, Puppy Green Aqueduct, the short Dixon's Branch to the north once linked the Horseley Ironworks with the New Main Line. It was here that many of the BCN's bridges were cast; some went further afield too. For example the Grand Union, where what is believed to be the oldest surviving bridge spans the cut just above Brentford (see Walk 15). The company also built the world's first iron steam ship, the "Aaron Manby" in 1822, its giant paddle wheels driven by a 30hp steam engine. Here too was the junction (known as Watery End) from the Old Main Line with the 3 lock Tipton Green and Toll End Communication Canal (see above). Though most of this mouthful has been filled in, a landscaped footpath at Tipton Green runs through the still intact chamber of lock 2 (OS ref: SO 954922).

J Three Furnace Bridge
With the trains alongside slowing down for or accelerating from Tipton Station, the present reasserts its authority in the form of Tipton. But there is one final and inescapable remnant of the past just before we leave the canal at Three Furnace Bridge. Here a small boatyard occupies the site of a former railway interchange basin. Unlike most of the rest of the inland network, the marriage between railways and canals on the BCN was to their mutual benefit and such interchange basins were not uncommon.

Sustenance
The area on both 'lines' east of Three Furnace Bridge and Tipton Junction is virtually devoid of watering holes. To the west, however, there are several pubs and take-aways as well as a good general shopping area. As already indicated, the "Fountain Inn" is well worth a visit.

Counter Attractions
Black Country Museum, Tipton Road, Dudley, West Midlands. Open daily Mar–Jan, 10am–5pm (or dusk). Admission charge. Tel: 021-557 9643. Sights and sounds of the past echo from buildings and machines that create a living tribute to the skills and enterprise of the people of the Black Country. Workers' homes, shops, narrowboats and even a pub are authentically recreated to bring the past alive. Boat trips are run into Dudley Tunnel and the Singing Cavern.

Encore
Another circular walk, that not only puts the relationship between the Old and New Lines into perspective but also includes some of the most spectacular bridges and aqueducts across the New Main Line, can be found between Bromford Junction and Smethwick Junction. The walk also takes in Spon Lane and Smethwick Locks, the Engine Branch and Smethwick Pumphouse. Both Smethwick Rolfe Street and Sandwell & Dudley Stations (on the New Street/Wolverhampton line) are good starting points.

Information
Tourist Information Centre, 39 Churchill Precinct, Dudley, West Midlands. Tel: (0384) 5033.

Iron roving bridges at Dudley Port Junction on the BCN.

Walk 5

Birmingham Canal Navigations
Staffs/West Midlands

Chasewater   9 miles

The Walk

This is an exploration of the remoter reaches of the Birmingham Canal Navigations, and if 'Birmingham' conjures visions of an overtly industrial and urban landscape, little could be further from the truth. Only one town, Brownhills, is encountered, for the rest you are out on the windy heathlands on the perimeter of Cannock Chase. Industry there was, in abundance, but collieries and ironworks have fled the scene of the crime. And in an age obsessed with leisure, reclamation is applying cosmetics to an emasculated region bravely trying to cope with an understandable identity crisis.

Start Point

Chasewater Leisure Park.
OS ref: SK 035070.

Access

Bus (Midland Red North service 156, hourly weekdays, bi-hourly Sun, between Birmingham and Cannock) Tel: Cannock (05435) 78124, or car parking at leisure park, approached off eastbound carriagway of A5, 8 miles east of M6 junct 12.

Directions

1 Leave car park in a westerly direction. At Go-cart circuit bear left on to shale track towards preserved railway.
2 Cross bridge over disused railway and go through kissing gate onto road.
3 Turn left onto Hednesford Road, then immediately bear right at pub onto Wilkin Road.
4 Turn right at roundabout onto A5 (pavement provided).
5 At railway bridge go down steps onto disused trackbed and turn left under bridge proceeding ½ mile along route of old line.
6 Turn right across bridge over brook and follow track, keeping right at next fork.

7 Cross road beside kennels and just before "Dangerous Bridge" sign turn down to towpath, proceeding 1¼ miles to Pelsall Junction.
8 Turn left at Pelsall Junction and proceed along Wyrley & Essington Canal 3 miles to Catshill Junction.
9 Turn left at Catshill Junction and proceed 1 mile to Ogley Junction.
10 Continue 1½ miles to Anglesey Basin.

11 Continue along cinder track to end of canal. Turn left up lane to top of reservoir embankment and return to car park.

Points of Interest

A Chasewater Reservoir
Sometimes known as Cannock Chase Reservoir, Chasewater was constructed in 1800 by the Wyrley & Essington Canal Co. to reinforce their hitherto inadequately supplied main line. It fulfils the same function today, as well as being used as a source of domestic water supply, though its builders could scarcely have envisaged its recreational use by power boats, yachts, water skiers and the motorists who come just to look morosely at it through their windscreens.

B Watling Street
The A5 follows the route of the Roman's 'Watling Street' which ran from Dover, through London to Wroxeter, near Shrewsbury. It is also known as the Holyhead Road and was rebuilt by Thomas

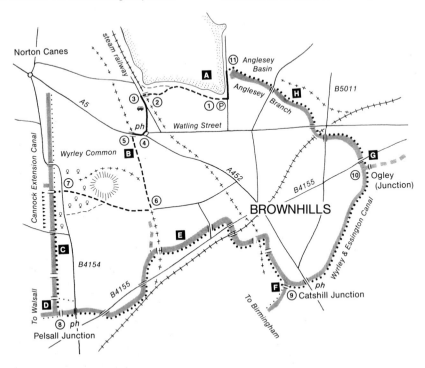

Winter's day at Friar Bridge, Pelsall on the Cannock Extension.

Telford in 1830, though the latter route diverted through the Black Country between Daventry and Oakengates. The disused railway line was once part of a dense network of mineral lines which enmeshed the Cannock coalfield. It was opened in 1858 and saw use for 106 years, in its heyday being part of the London & North Western Railway. A lane crosses Wyrley Common which could be deep in the pretty heart of Cannock Chase itself were it not for the scars of former spoil tips. You reach the canal opposite the old loading basins of the Brownhills Colliery 'Grove Pit'. The basin is now used for moorings, though old colliery buildings retain the workaday ambience and it's not difficult to imagine convoys of horse-drawn Joey boats turning on to the main line on their way to the hungry furnaces of the Black Country.

C Cannock Extension Canal
There could hardly be a straighter waterway than the Cannock Extension Canal, the last branch of the BCN system to be built, being completed in 1863. It was once a through route, passing beneath the Watling Street at Norton Canes and linking up with the Hatherton Branch of the Staffs & Worcs Canal. Today, an aquatic *cul de sac* since subsidence brought about abandonment beyond the A5 in 1963, the branch remains busy with boats making for the two boatyards at its terminus. The canal retains a sense of purpose despite the surrounding decay: "Utopia" blue engineering bricks line the channel; BCN concrete fencing posts peep through the undergrowth; and hefty nameplated, brick bridges - more railway like than canal - parenthesise progress to Pelsall.

D Pelsall Junction
There is a melancholy ambience about Pelsall Junction. Two cream-washed cottages, numbered 211 and 212 in the BCN sequence, adjoin the massive proportions of Friar Bridge. Opposite are the old stables which, though doorless, retain the framework of the stalls. One can easily picture the boat horses champing in the frosty air of a winter dawn as they awaited the boats coming down from the Cannock pits. Wasteland extends westwards across Wood Common, the site of a huge ironworks. In the opposite direction a miry path reaches over to a regimented line of poplars on Norton Road. One of the distinctive Horseley Iron Works bridges spans

the junction itself.

E Wyrley & Essington Canal
Eastwards from Pelsall the Wyrley & Essington becomes a watery corset, keeping at bay the burgeoning housing estates of Walsall's suburbs. Only occasionally does the 'whalebone' give way as industry spills across the cut. The tortuous main line of the Wyrley & Essington Canal was opened throughout between Horseley Fields, near Wolverhampton, and Huddlesford on the Coventry Canal near Lichfield by 1797. Unsurprisingly, coal was its mentor, though a good deal of general merchandise was carried as well. Amalgamation with the BCN took place in 1840. Throughout the walk to Brownhills numerous abandoned arms which once served collieries, lime kilns and iron-works can be discerned. Two more railways cross the canal, and then each other: the first, the former South Staffordshire Railway's Walsall-Wychnor line, is now barely used; the second, marked by huge blue brick abutments beyond the unusual Cooper's Bridge, was the Midland Railway's branch from Aldridge to Brownhills 'Watling Street' closed to passengers as early as 1930.

F Catshill Junction
Suddenly the canal turns sharply to the south-east and passes a hypermarket provided with a neat brick jetty for pleasure boaters. High Street runs parallel to the canal and can be reached over a green painted footbridge. A busy market is held beside the canal on Tuesdays. With a parcel of reclaimed land to your right you reach Catshill Junction. The Daw End branch heads south to Aldridge and beyond. Tower blocks overlook the junction and solitary men trudge the towpath - unemployment is something you don't share with your mates.

G Ogley Junction
Ogley Junction sounds as though it's escaped from a J. B. Priestley story and it must surely have flummoxed quite a few self-professed pundits at waterway society quiz meetings. But it was here, until abandonment in 1954, that the main line of the Wyrley & Essington continued eastwards, climbing through first a flight of 8 locks, then 4 more, by way of Muckley Corner to Huddlesford, 7 heavily locked miles away. Loss of this through-link to the canals of the East Midlands was particularly unfortunate and

unwarranted. The junction itself, spanned by one of the ubiquitous Horseley Ironworks bridges, is gained through a shallow sandstone cutting of bracken and broom. It is brooded over by a chimney-topped foundry and a BCN cottage marooned beyond the water's end; altogether a very satisfying spot to be on a fighting cold December afternoon!

H The Anglesey Branch

At the outset simply a feeder channel from Chasewater, the Anglesey Branch was opened to navigation in 1850 following the development of a number of pits in the vicinity. Soon after leaving Ogley Junction the branch crosses the railway upon a short aqueduct with high iron, graffitied parapets, then passes beneath the Watling Street. With housing (interrupted by an unlikely scrapyard) to your left and abandoned sandpits to your right, the canal heads for its destination at the foot of the Chasewater dam. Beyond the last bridge contorted rusting metal remains were once the loading machinery for coal exported from here up until 1967. Nature has all but reclaimed this final bastion of coal traffic on the BCN, a chastening thought for you to cogitate upon as you return to your starting point.

Sustenance

Three pubs are encountered early on in the walk. More conveniently near the middle, at a point where you may be considering a rest, is the "Royal Oak" near Pelsall Junction, an Ansells house which does food. Brownhills has fish & chip bars, shops, pubs and cafes. Finally, there's "The Anchor" (Banks's beer and bar food) beyond Catshill Junction.

Counter Attractions

Wall Museum of Roman remains. Located on A5 3 miles east of Chester. Tel: Shenstone (0543) 480768.

Encore

It was a toss of the coin whether we featured the W & E around Brownhills, as we have done, or walked it from Wolverhampton to Walsall. So we think the latter provides a natural encore if you've enjoyed this sample of the canal's distinctive charms. West Midlands PTA service 529 between the two towns is frequent, daily (Tel: Wolverhampton (0902) 20018) and there are rail connections at both ends - Tel: 021-643 2711. Highlights are the restored boat dock at Horseley Fields. The remains of the Bentley Canal at Wednesfield Junction, the adjoining nature trail at Rough Wood, BWB's

maintenance yard at Sneyd and the Walsall Branch down into the town from Birchalls Junction; total distance 10 miles.

Information

Tourist Information Centre, 9 Breadmarket Street, Lichfield. Tel: (0543) 252109.

Walk 6

Bridgewater Canal/ Manchester Ship Canal

Cheshire

Warrington Area   8 miles

The Walk

Warrington is famous for Vodka, Rugby League, Eddie Shah, and for being in a quandary as to whether its allegiance belongs to Manchester or Liverpool. Warrington is not as famous for its waterways. But once they were there in abundance - rivers, navigations, and canals - busy trade routes carrying commodities to and from the breweries, wire works, paper mills and soap factories that flourish hereabouts. But the waterways of the north-west, unlike their Yorkshire counter-parts, have not contrived to keep their trade. Even the mighty Manchester Ship Canal is currently threatened with closure above Runcorn. Nevertheless, as commerce retreats, leisure colonizes the 'cuts'. The early Bridgewater Canal has long been part of Cheshire's cruising ring and new develop-ments in the Warrington area have seen sections of the Sankey Brook Navigation, the Runcorn & Latchford Canal and River Mersey towpaths opened up to the general public. So this itinerary sets out to explore Warrington's towpaths in transition, and, as a bonus, includes the only boat ride officially included in any of the itineraries featured in this book!

Start Point

Warrington Bus Station.
OS ref: SJ 605884.

Access

Train (Tel: Warrington (0925) 32245), bus (Tel: Warrington (0925) 34296) and car - Warrington is 4 miles north-west of junction 20 on the M6 and junction 9 on the M56.

Directions

1 Catch a bus to Stockton Heath (7 buses per hour Mon-Sat, $1/2$ hourly Sun). Alight on London Road and proceed to London Bridge over the Bridgewater Canal.

2 Access to the canal is by way of Mitchell Street and an opening beside Thorn Marine. On reaching the canal, turn left beneath London Bridge and proceed $1^1/2$ miles to Stanney Lunt Bridge.

3 Pass beneath bridges and climb somewhat awkward steps up to roadway. Cross bridge and follow road (with pavement) into Grapenhall Village.

4 Bear left along Church Lane through village, rejoining canal at Grapenhall Bridge.

5 Proceed along towpath for 1 mile to Thelwall Aqueduct.

6 Cross aqueduct and turn immediately left down steps to roadway. Turn right beneath railway, cross main road and proceed down Bell Lane (signposted "Thelwall $1/2$ mile") to village, bearing left at village cross.

7 At left turn in road by "Pickering's Arms" and Thelwall Post Office, continue straight down Ferry Lane to Ferry Landing Stage.

8 The ferryman is usually on duty in his brick hut to the left of the landing stage or can be summoned from his house, approached through a makeshift gate adjacent to the landing stage. But do note that the ferry only operates between the official hours of 7-9 (ex Sun.) 12-2, 4-7. At the time of writing, the single fare is 11p.

9 Turn left and follow the track beside the Manchester Ship Canal to Latchford Locks.

10 There is a public right of way across Latchford Locks by way of the lock gates.

Once across, turn right along Thelwall New Road as far as Knutsford Road swingbridge.

11 Turn left up Knutsford Road, then bear immediately right along Hunts Lane. This becomes Ackers Road and presently arrives at a 3-way junction. Take the middle road uphill across the Cantilever Bridge over the MSC.

12 Turn left along Station Road signposted "A50 town centre". Beneath the railway this becomes Wash Lane.

13 Turn left along Halla Way onto Knutsford Road. Immediately over old bridge, turn left down on to metalled path along bed of old canal. Pass under bridge and proceed for $^1/_2$ mile to site of Manor Lock.

14 Turn left along river bank.

15 Cross suspension bridge. On far bank, turn right and pass beneath bridge following riverside walkway. This becomes Wharf Street. Continue along riverside back to Warrington Bridge and then to town centre.

Points of Interest

Warrington's Waterways

It is worthwhile getting the gist of Warrington's complex waterway history at the outset. During the 17th century the River Mersey was navigable as far upstream as Bank Quay, Warrington. In 1736, the Mersey & Irwell Navigation opened up the river by way of a series of locks through to Manchester. By 1773 the Canal Age had dawned and the pioneering Bridgewater Canal was opened between Runcorn and Manchester, taking much of the river trade. In retaliation, the Mersey & Irwell Company opened the Runcorn & Latchford Canal in 1804, by-passing the trickiest parts of the river. Then at the turn of the century came, in the most ambitious scheme of all, the Manchester Ship Canal. Opened in 1894, it was constructed to permit sea-going vessels to trade up to Manchester itself without recourse to trans-shipment at Liverpool, Birkenhead or Runcorn. Its advent had a significant knock-on effect on the existing waterways of Warrington. The new route cut across the Runcorn & Latchford, which was subsequently abandoned to the west, although a short section which became known as the 'Black Bear Canal' was retained to permit access to riverside wharves on the non-tidal section above Howley Weir in the centre of Warrington. A new lock was built at Walton giving access to the tidal river below Howley Weir; this development included a new cut to replace the old Wilderspool Loop. Walton Lock remained in commercial use until 1984, when imports to Fairclough's Mill at

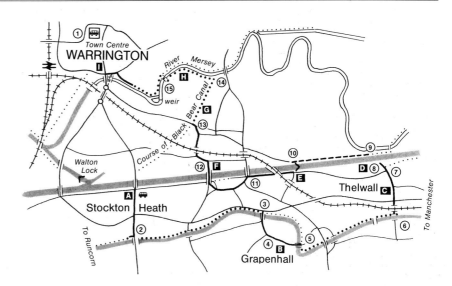

Bank Quay ceased, bringing to an end the local use of Warrington's waterways by commercial traffic.

A Stockton Heath

The short outward bus journey takes you over the Northwich Road swing bridge spanning the Manchester Ship Canal. It is a good idea to alight at the first stop beyond the bridge and walk back to view the waterway scene at this point. Immediately below the swing bridge there was a lock into the Black Bear Canal obliterated in 1978; you will be following part of its course later on. To the west, beyond Greenall Whitley's brewery, an arm leads off the Ship Canal and doubles back to Walton Lock. Take another look at the Ship Canal and keep its dimensions in mind as you make the short walk up through Stockton Heath to the Bridgewater Canal. What a difference! Britain's first and last canals have everything and nothing in common. Separated by 120 years of engineering progress, they encompass the whole history of canals in this country. The Bridgewater reached Stockton Heath in 1771 and a packet boat service operated to Manchester. The circular steps down which passengers descended from their coaches to board the packets can still be seen clearly through the arch of London Bridge on the southern bank. On the towpath side, a green coloured crane, with attendant wooden

planking, is used to create a dam at the bridge hole should a breach occur or a section of canal need to be drained. At the outset, the canal is suburban in character, but soon an embankment is reached with the first of the three 'underbridges' that are encountered on the way to Thelwall.

B Grappenhall

With suburban Warrington to the north and farmland to the south, the Bridgewater sweeps in an arc around Grappenhall and we recommend a diversion along the village's cobbled street to see the old stocks. The whole of Grappenhall seems caught in a time warp. The image of a Cheshire cat leers down from the tower of St. Wilfred's Parish Church. A neat row of almost colonial looking cottages separates the two pubs; it is hard to resist lingering here, but remember that the ferry runs to a timetable and that you still have about half an hour's walking to go.

C Thelwall

Passing beneath the new Knutsford Road, the canal crosses the original road beside a disused tannery. Soon Thelwall Aqueduct is reached and it is time to leave the Bridgewater. The adjacent railway was closed in 1985; the rusting tracks were still there when we researched the walk but may well have been lifted since. The line was opened as the Warrington & Altrincham Junction

Who pays the Ferryman? - Thelwall on the Manchester Ship Canal.

Railway in 1853, passenger services ceased in 1962; though Thelwall Station, which once won prizes for its platform gardens, had closed 6 years earlier. Thelwall itself is an ancient place dating back a millennium. Edward the Elder, son of Alfred the Great, built a settlement here in 923, an event inscribed on the gable-end of the timber-framed "Pickerings Arms", itself of 17th century origin.

D Thelwall Ferry
Ferries on inland waterways are an endangered species, and the world is a smaller place for their disappearance. So it comes as a wonderful surprise to find one flourishing under unlikely circumstances. Thelwall Ferry even has a local preservation society determined that it should be retained no matter what the future of the Ship Canal. The ferry itself is an open, clinker-built boat licensed to carry up to 9 passengers. The ferryman dexterously sculls it with a single oar athwart the stern. To the east the motorway crosses the canal on the long Thelwall Viaduct, and you are left in no doubt as to who has the better deal! The ferryman told us that little more than three or four ships per week use this section of the canal now; small wonder that its owners want to close it to navigation above Runcorn. The expense of keeping the channel open can be witnessed by the dredgers and mudhoppers which ply to and from the slurry beds on either side of the ferry.

E Latchford Locks
If you are fortunate enough to see a ship negotiating the huge locks at Latchford, then you are in for a memorable experience. There is something extraordinarily satisfying about a huge vessel, with its crew leaning over the rail exchanging oaths in a foreign tongue, momentarily captured in an English lock in full knowledge that later that day it will be on the high seas. Sadly, it is an event you are increasingly unlikely to encounter - even the giant 'Trader' barges have ceased working from Seaforth to Manchester. Nevertheless, you will want to spend some time exploring the two chambers; the larger measuring 600 x 65 ft.

F Ship Canal Bridges
Below the locks, the canal is semi-tidal and is crossed in swift succession by three distinctive bridges. The first is a steel girder bridge with immense blue-brick piers and a span of 250 ft. at a height of 75 ft. This carries the now closed Warrington & Stockport line already encountered at Thelwall, so the bridge's future must be in as much doubt as the Ship Canal itself. The next bridge is one of three giant swing bridges; frustrating

obstacles for generations of Warrington motorists when the canal was busier than now. All three bridges - carrying respectively the Knutsford, Northwich and Chester Roads - are operated hydraulically. Thirdly, and our chosen route back across the canal, comes the magnificent Latchford high level bridge - known locally as The Cantilever. Iron built, with brick approaches, it has a centre span of 206 ft., again with a height above the Ship Canal of 75 ft. The view from its span is tremendous and particularly dramatic if you are lucky enough to find a sea-going vessel passing beneath you.

G Black Bear Canal
The rather over-ornate Black Bear Bridge dates from 1925 and replaced a more typical stone arch. Barges last used the Black Bear Canal to reach Howley Quay in the early 1970s, thereafter the canal fell into decay and was regarded as a danger to local children. It was filled-in in 1978 and has been 'landscaped' as a linear park. At Manor Lock (originally known as Latchford until the name was transferred to the new locks on the MSC) the gates remain, peeping out of the infilled chamber, as does a swing bridge at the head of the lock. An interpretative board supplies further details if you can penetrate the graffiti. Beyond the lock flows the lugubrious Mersey.

H River Mersey
The moon's influence over the Mersey extends to Howley Weir. The Mersey & Irwell Navigation Company constructed a lock here, to gain access to the upper river. This lock fell into disuse between the wars, though the chamber remains in good condition. The old wharves at Howley Quay are enjoying a revival with a boating centre, trip boat operation and a restaurant and pub called "The Old Quay Tavern" which has opened in a former warehouse. To reach the opposite bank you cross the 175 feet span of Howley Suspension Bridge, built in 1912 to provide Warringtonians with easy access to Victoria Park. A not unattractive modern walkway leads round past hi-tech business units into Wharf Street which was the site of Bishop's Wharf. Trade continued here, via Walton Lock, until the early 1970s. Old photographs depict bustling scenes with the local 'Mersey Flats', a type of sailing barge, much in evidence.

I Warrington Bridge
The walk 'proper' ends at Warrington Bridge. The present structure was opened in 1915 and marked the sixth crossing of the Mersey at this site; the earliest being in 1285. The present bridge's daring use of concrete, so early in the 20th century, was regarded with much admiration in civil engineering circles. Just to make sure, they tested it before opening day by leaving five tramcars and two steam-rollers in the centre of the span, watching from a suitable distance to see if the bridge could cope. It did, and it has ever since, despite the burgeoning traffic demands of our times. Reinforcements, however, are on the way, in the shape of the new road bridge to the east which will carry south-bound traffic out of the town centre.

Sustenance
Two pubs vie for your custom at Grappenhall: "The Rams Head" and "The Parr Arms". Both are Greenall Whitley houses and both do bar food; likewise "The Pickering's Arms" at Thelwall. The new development at Howley is "The Old Quay Tavern" - ubiquitous Greenall Whitley again.

Counter Attractions
Dunham Massey Hall - 13 miles west of Warrington off the A56, near Altrincham. 18th century house owned by the National Trust, grounds include deer park and Elizabethan mill. For further details Tel: 061-941 1025.

Encore
The Bridgewater Canal, Manchester Ship Canal and River Mersey can again be combined at Runcorn where the local authority have mapped out a 6 mile circular walk incorporating much of historical interest interpreted in a booklet available from the local Tourist Information Centre: 57 Church Street, Runcorn. Tel: (0928) 76776.
In fact, the Bridgewater towpath is in good condition throughout and is being developed as part of the Cheshire Ring circuit. Its original mainline, between Water's Meeting and Worsley - including the impressive Barton Swing Aqueduct over the Manchester Ship Canal - also offers fascinating walking territory. Whilst in the Warrington area, the St. Helen's Canal has perambulating potential to the west of the town. Dating from 1757, and regarded as the doyen of inland waterways, it closed in 1963, but though partially infilled it has recently been landscaped and opened up to the general public. Descriptive leaflets are available from: Sankey Valley Park Rangers Service - Tel:

Warrington (0925) 571836. Yet another exciting development in the area is the 'Mersey Way' the new system of footpaths following the course of the river. Further details are available from: The Mersey Valley Partnership, Camden House, York Place,

Runcorn, Cheshire WA7 5BD. Tel: Runcorn (0928) 73346.

Information
Tourist Information Centre, 80 Sankey Street, Warrington. Tel: (0925) 36501.

Walk 7
Calder & Hebble Navigation/ Huddersfield Broad Canal
Yorkshire
Brighouse - Huddersfield   **8½ miles**

The Walk
This walk explores the valley of the river Calder and the river Colne and in so doing encapsulates the characteristics of two distinctive waterways, the one a canalised river navigation, the other a totally man-made cut. It is, therefore, a walk of contrasts and yet one which starts and finishes in similar surroundings, Brighouse Basin and Aspley Basin - an opportunity to compare how each has coped with the 'new order'.

Start Point
Huddersfield Bus Station.
OS ref: SE 142164.

Access
Bus, train and car. Huddersfield has excellent rail and bus connections with all parts of the country. Information from Huddersfield (0484) 26313 (buses) and (0484) 31226 (trains). The bus and railway stations are about ¼ mile apart, the former has an adjacent multi-storey car park.

Directions
1 Catch a bus (service 380 or 382) to Brighouse.
2 Alight in Brighouse at the stop just beyond where the road crosses the river and the canal.
3 Cross the road and join the canal by the side of the bridge, following the towpath east to Brighouse Basin.
4 Leave Brighouse Basin (having explored the area) by the exit on the left just beyond the top lock and turn right into Mill Street.

5 Take the 4th turning on the left (Huntingdon Road) and cross the bridge over the river.
6 At the T-junction, turn left into River Street which becomes the towpath just before Anchor Pit Lock - remain on the towpath for the 2 miles to the A62 bridge.
7 View the Calder & Hebble Navigation and the Huddersfield Broad Canal from the bridge. Join the Huddersfield Broad's towpath for the 4 miles to Aspley Basin.
8 Follow the basin round to the left and leave it by turning right on to St. Andrews Road.
9 Turn right at the traffic lights on to the Wakefield Road and cross just to view the other end of the canal on the bridge.
10 Continue up the hill to the roundabout, cross this and take the 2nd exit on the left - King Street, continuing for nearly ¼ mile up through the pedestrian precinct and across New Street to the T-junction at the top.
11 Turn left here, the bus station is about 100 yds. along on the right.

Points of Interest
A The Calder & Hebble
The Calder & Hebble Navigation grew out of a desire to extend the existing navigable waterways of the north-east. The Calder was navigable to Wakefield as early as 1702 (as part of the Aire & Calder Navigation) but it was not until 1770 that the Calder & Hebble cuts opened up the Calder Valley to the eastern seaboard by linking Wakefield and Sowerby Bridge. Cheap transport was thus provided into the Upper Calder Valley to the immediate benefit of the local coal and textile

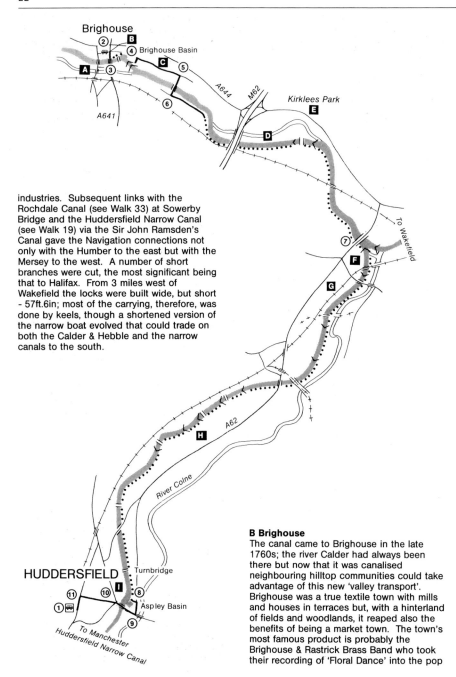

Brighouse
Brighouse Basin
A644
M62
Kirklees Park
A641
A62
River Colne
HUDDERSFIELD
Turnbridge
Aspley Basin
To Manchester
Huddersfield Narrow Canal
To Wakefield

charts in 1977. The short walk to Brighouse Basin from the A641 is flanked by the tall Victoria Mill rising straight from the water. The entrance to the basin, once the end of a colliery railway, is via a graceful turnover bridge. Though at one level pleasure craft dominate the wharves, the backdrop gives a vivid image of how it once was. The six miles from Sowerby Bridge to Brighouse are all man-made cut but, leaving Brighouse Basin, the Navigation drops through two locks to join the broad Calder for the first time. By the lower lock is the attractive lock-keeper's cottage which, despite the seemingly elevated position, has suffered from the river flooding, notably so in 1866 when it rose 14 feet above its normal level. The Calder's towpath is on the southern side, but alas the bridge across is long gone and you can only rejoin by crossing further downstream.

C The Calderdale Way
The walk from Huddersfield Road via the Basin to Mill Street is also part of the 50 mile Calderdale Way, a long distance recreational path that runs along the two sides of the Calder Valley. The western end of the way is near Todmordon (see Walk 33) while Brighouse is at its eastern extremity. Opened to walkers in 1978, the route utilises old pack-horse ways high on the valley sides as it traverses the contrasting features of this grit-stone landscape. The entire route is readily accessible by public transport up the intersecting valleys and via 'link' paths through to the main Calder Valley. An excellent booklet 'The Calderdale Way', is available from all local Tourist Information Centres.

D The Kirklees Cut
As the Calder heads east towards Anchor Pit Flood Lock it is overshadowed by the mighty span of the M62, the trans-Pennine motorway, as it boldly strides across the river valley. But unlike many of the 20th century's other contributions to the landscape there is something majestic, something pleasing to the eye about this concrete megalith. By the Flood Lock's attendant cottage, a stone boundary post, bearing the letters LYR recalls the leasing of the Navigation in 1843 to the adjacent Manchester & Leeds Railway, later to become the Lancaster & Yorkshire Railway. Anchor Pit marks the beginning of the Kirklees Cut; here ferns and oaks, young and old, roll down to the towpath while across the Calder is the wooded escarpment of Kirklees Park. A kink, discernible in the line of the canal below Kirklees top lock, is the sole surviving evidence that the original line used

industries. Subsequent links with the Rochdale Canal (see Walk 33) at Sowerby Bridge and the Huddersfield Narrow Canal (see Walk 19) via the Sir John Ramsden's Canal gave the Navigation connections not only with the Humber to the east but with the Mersey to the west. A number of short branches were cut, the most significant being that to Halifax. From 3 miles west of Wakefield the locks were built wide, but short - 57ft.6in; most of the carrying, therefore, was done by keels, though a shortened version of the narrow boat evolved that could trade on both the Calder & Hebble and the narrow canals to the south.

B Brighouse
The canal came to Brighouse in the late 1760s; the river Calder had always been there but now that it was canalised neighbouring hilltop communities could take advantage of this new 'valley transport'. Brighouse was a true textile town with mills and houses in terraces but, with a hinterland of fields and woodlands, it reaped also the benefits of being a market town. The town's most famous product is probably the Brighouse & Rastrick Brass Band who took their recording of 'Floral Dance' into the pop

Runner on the Huddersfield Broad..

to cross the fields and join the Calder near the present motorway junction. Should a boat be working through any of the locks, take a closer look at the paddle gear; unlike the majority of the waterways network, these are operated by use of a removable 'handspike' and not the conventional windlass.

E Kirklees Park

Back on the river, Kirklees Park still dominates the view. Its history goes back to prehistoric times but it is for events from a relatively more recent era that the park is perhaps best known. The prioress of Kirklees Cistercian Priory was, reputedly, the mother of the legendary 'Robin Hood'; somewhere over there beyond the sewage farm, the scrapyard, the railway and the road, a mere arrow-shot away amid a cluster of rhododendrons is, according to legend, the last resting place of the outlaw.

F The Huddersfield Broad Canal

At Cooper Bridge we leave the Calder & Hebble to wend its way east to Wakefield and beyond, and join the valley of the Colne and the Huddersfield Broad Canal. The canal is more properly known as Sir John Ramsden's Canal, for it was the Ramsden family, eager to reap the advantages for themselves and Huddersfield, who petitioned for the link with the Calder & Hebble. The short 3³/₄ mile canal with its nine broad locks was opened in 1776 thus creating a lifeline for the expanding textile industry of Huddersfield. With the completion of the Huddersfield Narrow Canal in 1811 Huddersfield also had a direct link to Manchester and the western seaboard. Looking east from above the first lock at Cooper Bridge the confluence of the Calder and the Colne can be seen and, beyond, Cooper Bridge Lock on the Calder & Hebble. As the two rivers and the two navigations go their separate ways, the landscape changes, and the gentle hills of the Colne Valley shake off the bustle that seems to draw itself to the Calder.

G Railways

Originally three railways crossed the canal at its northern end - in a sense they still do, but only the first, the Huddersfield-Leeds line, is still active. The others cross the cut on impressive viaducts that dominate the land-

scape. The first of these, just before Ladgrave Lock, was once part of the Midland Railway extension to Huddersfield; it was only completed in 1910 and never saw full service, the track being lifted in 1937. The second, just after Longlands Lock, carried the former L&NW Huddersfield-Kirkburton branch line; during its construction one of the seven arches fell into the canal which delayed the opening of the line for a year. The 'Kirkburton Dick' - as the service was nicknamed - survived only until 1930. The ordered simplicity of these brick viaducts contrasts sharply with the chemical works in between and the assorted tangle of a decaying canalside industry. Some of the chimneys still belch forth signs of life . . . curious how the people who create all that steam and smoke are invariably unseen, shadowless guardians of what remains of an industrial heritage.

H Anyone for tennis?

Despite that brief flirtation with a less dignified aspect of canal 'architecture', Leeds Road Bridge heralds a more rural aspect. A mill stands by the bridge, its central loading doors, now converted to a window, telling their own tale. The climb quickens with four locks in rapid succession; the terrain is fairly open with screening trees here and there and

the brick bulk of erstwhile textile mills on the skyline. But above - or rather below - all else, there are playing fields galore: football, cricket, rugby, hockey, tennis, they are all catered for - teams all white and bright partaking of some ritualistic rite. It mostly ends at the last lock, Red Doles; here the canal's resident keeper lived and here too are the old, still reclaimable, stables that must have seen busier times.

I Huddersfield

One final outpost of man's sporting inclinations gives way to the unmistakable paraphernalia of urbanisation. For a time two chimneys dominate the cut, one brick and one concrete, ambassadors of two different eras that speak a silent message. The final approach to Huddersfield boasts many fine stone and brick buildings, one of these a church and most crying out for renovation; their canalside doors might never re-open but surely such proud structures still have a useful life to live? Heath Robinson seemingly was not a Huddersfield lad though that first encounter with Turnbridge might well make you wonder. It is a gloriously unique contraption, a lift bridge whereby the deck, operated by a series of wheels and chains, rises parallel to the water . . . every canal should have one! Enough of the Aspely

Basin complex survives to piece together the rest and mentally create a picture of the bustling activity around the warehouses and wharves. It was here that the wide boats of the Huddersfield Broad and the narrow boats of the Huddersfield Narrow exchanged cargoes - the standard narrow boat length was too long for the Broad Canal's locks. The junction of the two canals is about 200 yards south of the Wakefield Road Bridge and is accessible should you feel like a short detour. If not, the other side of the Broad Canal and a particularly fine stone warehouse and hand-operated crane can be viewed from the bridge.

Sustenance

If you haven't tasted Yorkshire chips, you haven't tasted chips and Brighouse is as good a place as any to start your re-education; Huddersfield too has hostelries and restaurants aplenty. En route, the most convenient 'halfway house' is the "White Cross Inn" on the Leeds Road just south of Cooper Bridge. Egon Ronay recommends "Bertie's Bistro" in Elland about 3 miles west of Brighouse.

Counter Attractions

● Jubilee Tower, Castle Hill, Almondsbury, Huddersfield, Yorks. Open Easter, May Hol., Spring Hol, mid-Sept, 1pm-5pm. Admission charge. Tel: Huddersfield (0484) 30591. Opened in 1899 to commemorate Queen Victoria's Diamond Jubilee, the tower offers breathtaking views of the Colne & Holme Valleys. Built on the site of iron-age and medieval fortifications, of which there are still remains.
● Calderdale Industrial Museum, Central Works, Square Road, Halifax, Yorks. Open Tues-Sat, 10am-5pm; Sun 2pm-5pm. Admission charge. Tel: Halifax (0422) 59031. A new project featuring many working exhibits from the Industrial Revolution - including oil and steam engines, carpet looms, toffee wrapping machines and even washing machines. A chance to experience Halifax in the 1840s - complete with authentic smells.

Encore

So far the 'Hebble' part of the Calder & Hebble Navigation has not had a mention. Halifax spreads across the Hebble Valley and the three mile walk from Elland to Sowerby Bridge includes the entrance to the short arm up to Halifax where the Hebble Brook joins the Calder. The walk features an attractive wooded cutting above Elland and the three

Salterhebble Locks, one of which has a unique guillotine gate, and ends with the junction of the Rochdale Canal at Sowerby Bridge. A regular bus service links Elland and Sowerby Bridge, Tel: Huddersfield (0484) 26313.

Walk 8

Caldon Canal
Staffordshire
Cheddleton - Leek   **5¹/₂ miles**

The Walk

It would be difficult to overstate the appeal of this walk. Once it has shaken free of the Potteries, the Caldon Canal pursues an introverted and surprisingly beautiful course to its twin termini of Froghall and Leek. The walk down the remote Churnet Valley from Cheddleton to Froghall (part of the "Staffordshire Way") might have been the obvious choice to feature here (see Encore) but, quixotic to a fault, we're leading you in the opposite direction to encounter the fascinating split level junction at Hazelhurst.

Start Point

Leek Bus Station
OS ref: SJ 986564.

Access

Bus or car (Pay & Display parking available adjacent to Leek bus station, but note 3 hour limit!). Leek is served by PMT bus services from Hanley (Stoke-on-Trent) Tel. Stoke (0782) 48284.

Directions

1 Catch a Berresfords bus (services 16 or 106, half hourly Mon-Sat, hourly Sun. Tel. Wetley Rocks (0782) 550240) from Leek bus station and alight at the first bus stop in Cheddleton.
2 Proceed to the canal and join the towpath adjacent to bridge 42.
3 Turn left to view lock 13.
4 Retrace steps to bridge 42 and follow towpath north-west for 2 miles to Hazelhurst Junction.

Information

Tourist Information Centre, 3-5 Albion Street, Huddersfield, Yorks. Tel: Huddersfield (0484) 22133, extension 313/685; 32177 (Sats).

5 Cross canal on iron footbridge and take the Leek Branch towpath 2¹/₂ miles east to end of canal. (At Leek tunnel follow the old horse path directly up and over the hill).
6 Follow path signposted "Leek" from aqueduct through Barnfields Industrial Estate to A53 and turn right, uphill back to town centre.

Points of Interest

A The Caldon Canal
The Caldon Canal - more properly the Caldon Branch of the Trent & Mersey Canal - had its origins in the need to supply water to the 'main line' at Etruria (Stoke-on-Trent) and as a means of transporting limestone mined in the Churnet Valley. The original 17¹/₂ mile section from Etruria to Froghall opened in 1779, and despite being taken over by the North Staffordshire Railway in 1847, remained busy with trade for almost 150 years. After the Second World War the canal fell into disrepair and was unnavigable beyond Hazelhurst. But the Caldon became one of the success stories of the canal revival and was re-opened in 1974. The Caldon Canal is virtually the only narrowbeam inland waterway retaining commercial traffic, in the form of a trio of purpose built narrowboats which trade at the lower end of the canal between depots of a pottery manufacturer in Hanley.

B Cheddleton Flint Mill
Cheddleton Flint Mill is open to the public on Saturdays and Sundays throughout the year. Two large waterwheels, powered by the swift waters of the Churnet, drive a collection of

restored machinery. How agreeable it is to derive power from the elements, a watermill has the appeal of sail over internal combustion. In its working days this mill was used to grind flint for the pottery industry. The canal transported raw materials to and finished product from the mill so an important exhibit is the narrowboat *Vienna,* moored outside the mill. Typical of the working craft which traded on the Caldon in its heyday, this restored horsedrawn boat was built at Saltley, Birmingham in 1911. It is 72ft in length by 7ft beam and could carry 25 tons of cargo; about the same as a medium size lorry. During the First World War the boat's name was changed to *Verbena* as the Austrian association was no longer considered suitable!

C The River Churnet
The canal borders the marshy purlieus of the river Churnet which rises on the moors behind Leek and joins the more famous, yet hardly more beguiling river Dove near Rocester. Downstream from Cheddleton, where the river was once harnessed to drive the machinery of a large paper making works, canal and river combine briefly between Oakmeadow Ford Lock and the splendidly

isolated community of Consall Forge where the well known "Black Lion" pub flourishes far from the nearest road.

D Flood Weir
Beyond bridge 41 steep pastures spill down to the opposite bank, whilst to the east stands the huge Leekbrook mental hospital with its grim Victorian water tower. The towpath crosses a waste weir built to cope with excess flood water which might otherwise cause the canal bank to burst. The long sill is barely inches above the usual water level so that any sudden flood is

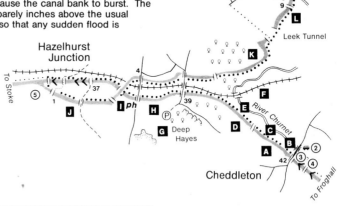

creamed off and discharged into the nearest drainage channel. Wooden planking and a support rail are thoughtfully provided to save foot travellers from wetting their feet at such times!

E Mile Post
A number of the original cast iron mileposts survive on the Caldon Canal but the ones you'll see on this walk are replicas provided by the Caldon Canal Society in recent years. You may be surprised to see the distance quoted to Uttoxeter, but although the original and present terminus is at Froghall, between 1811 and 1845 an extension to Uttoxeter was in operation.

F The Railway
The parallel railway was part of the fiercely independent North Staffordshire system, affectionately known as 'The Knotty'. The line opened in 1867, linking Leek with the six towns of the Potteries. Though closed to passengers as early as 1956, the route is still

The charm of Hazelhurst Junction.

used by freight trains carrying sand from Oakamoor and limestone from Cauldon Low.

G Country Park
Deep Hayes Country Park was once a quarry but has now been turned into an attractive series of waymarked nature trails and a picnic area. There are public toilets and an Information Centre is open at peak times. A shorter 'figure of eight' walk could commence at the car park here.

H Lift Bridge
With woodland to your left and lines of moored craft along the Leek branch above you to your right, a lift bridge comes into view. There are a number of these structures on the Caldon Canal, though this one appears to be rarely, if ever used. Lift, or draw, bridges were a cost cutting alternative to full masonry structures.

I Hazelhurst Junction
Reaching a terraced row of housing - the end building of which proves to be the "Hollybush Inn" - the canal turns sharply to the right and passes under an imposing aqueduct dated 1841, a date which marked the final stage in a series of layout changes at this point. When first built the canal had descended to the valley floor at Endon, some two miles to the west, but with the construction of the feeder from Rudyard (the Leek branch) which had obviously to enter the canal at the summit level to be of any use as a water supply, a new route on higher ground was built. This new line came down through a 'staircase' of three locks which stood in the present garden of the house opposite the aqueduct; the feeder coming in beneath bridge 3 on the Leek branch. In the event this staircase lock was a bottleneck to traffic and so a third and final variation was constructed, the main line leaving the branch at Hazelhurst Junction and descending through three single locks before running under the branch beneath the newly constructed aqueduct. Your route follows this solution to the problem as you head for Hazelhurst. A solitary, whitewashed junction house - powered by its own generator, being isolated from both road and other services - stands possessively by the top lock. A cast iron footbridge carries the towpath over the Leek branch. There is no more sublime a meeting of ways on the Canals.

J Bridge Contrasts
Returning in the same direction, but at a higher level, it is interesting to contrast the construction of bridges 2 on the branch and

37 below on the main line. The former, earlier structure is in local stone, the latter was built some 60 years later, of by then more readily available brick. At bridge 3 the towpath changes sides and it's worth lingering to imagine the earlier layouts at this point again.

K The Leek Branch
Passing some delightful waterside properties, the Leek branch moves into a lovely belt of mixed woodland above the widening valley. Presently the view opens out towards the high flanks of the Morridge rising to 1,300 feet in the east. Suddenly the canal twists away to reach a remote pool surrounded by an enclave of low hills. The canal builders had no alternative but to dig a tunnel through to reach Leek. The confined 130 yards bore is fronted, on the southern side at least, by an imposingly ornate portal of red sandstone. The tunnel, closed for some years, was formally re-opened on 30th April, 1985.

L Rennie's Aqueduct
Beyond the tunnel less than a mile of canal remains in water, the final turning point for boats being just through bridge 9. The narrow feeder comes in from Rudyard some 3 miles to the north (a public footpath follows it throughout and there's an infrequent PMT bus service back to Leek). An aqueduct, dated 1801, once carried the canal over the Churnet to reach a terminal wharf in Leek, but this arm was sadly infilled and walkers are faced with a bleak trudge through an industrial estate to regain the town centre.

Sustenance
There are two pubs, a restaurant (The Flintlock - Tel. Churnetside (0538) 361032) and a general stores (EC Sat, open Sun am) at Cheddleton. The "Hollybush Inn" at Denford, adjacent to bridge 38, does light bar snacks and children are welcome. All facilities are available in Leek.

Counter Attractions
● Brindley Mill, Mill St, Leek. Open Easter to Oct. Sat, Sun & Bank Hol. Mons., plus Mon, Tue & Thur during July & Aug. From 2-5pm. Tel. Leek (0538) 384195. Admission charge. Restored water mill built by James Brindley of canal fame.
● North Staffordshire Steam Railway Centre, Cheddleton. Station open Mon-Fri during Summer. Steam train rides on Suns. and Bank Hol. Mons. "Churnetrail Scenic Cruises" on some summer weekends. Full details from: Churnetside (0538) 360522.
● Froghall Wharf Passenger Service. Horse-drawn trips by narrowboat along the Caldon

Canal from Froghall (on A52 10 miles east of Stoke-on-Trent). 2½ hour public excursions on Summer Thur. and Sun. afternoons. Tel. Ipstones (053871) 486.

Encore
Cheddleton-Froghall, 5 miles. Another walk of exceptional beauty through the bosky Churnet Valley. Highlights include the river section, secluded settlement of Consall Forge and unusual Cherry Eye bridge. Picturesque wharf and picnic site at Froghall where horse boat passenger service operates with crew in period costume. PMT operate a regular service between Leek and Froghall, though not via Cheddleton, so it's necessary to catch a Berresford bus as well; unless, that is, you go the whole hog and combine Froghall-Cheddleton with the featured walk.

Information
Tourist Information Centre, Bethesda Street, Hanley, Stoke-on-Trent. Tel: Stoke (0782) 281242.

Walk 9
Chesterfield Canal
Nottinghamshire
Retford - Worksop $10^1/_2$ miles

The Walk
For boaters, the Chesterfield Canal is an out-of-the-way place, attainable only by navigating the tidal Trent. Walkers have no such restrictions and, as might be expected, this is a quiet unassuming waterway, a canal that to a great extent remains untouched by the paraphernalia of the leisure boating industry. The walk between Retford and Worksop is through delightful rolling farmland, a remote meander away from the hurly burly of the 20th century where locks, cottages and pubs are exciting interludes.

Start Point
Worksop Station.
OS ref: SK 586798.

Access
Bus, train and car. Worksop is on the Sheffield/Cleethorpes line - timetable enquiries from Worksop (0909) 472017. It also has excellent East Midlands local and national bus connections - tel: Worksop (0909) 472433. The station has a car park.

Directions
1 Catch a train to Retford.
2 Leave the station, proceed left and immediately right for $1/_4$ mile to the T-junction.
3 Turn right into Albert Road. Proceed for $1/_4$ mile to the traffic lights.
4 Turn left and join the canal where it crosses under the road and proceed west for the $10^1/_4$ miles to Worksop.
5 Leave the canal just before the Pickfords warehouse and proceed up Church Walk to the left.
6 Turn right across Worksop Bridge and proceed up Carlton Road (signposted to Doncaster) - the station is $1/_4$ mile on the left.

Points of Interest
A 'The Cuckoo Dyke'
How - even if - the Chesterfield Canal became known as the 'Cuckoo Dyke' remains something of a mystery. Carrying continued on the canal until the 1950s and even surviving boatmen seem to disagree on the matter; clearly it all hangs on whether or not the horse-drawn narrow boats particular to the canal were actually called 'cuckoos'. The line of the canal was surveyed by James Brindley in the late 1760s and eventually completed in 1777; it was thus one of the earliest canals and not surprisingly tends to wander, river-like, following contours rather than indulging in cuttings and embankments. One of the most well-known cargoes that was carried down to the Trent was the stone used to rebuild the Houses of Parliament in the late 1830s . . . sadly it didn't stand up to London's atmosphere and has gradually been replaced.

B Retford
Retford, one of the oldest boroughs in England, has many interesting features, including a market place with an assortment of Georgian buildings. In front of the town hall stands the Broad Stone; during the worst years of the plague, cash transactions between villagers and townspeople would involve coins passing through the stone's vinegar-filled hollow - a sort of disinfecting process. In front of the battlemented Church of St. Swithin stands a cannon that was captured at Sebastapol during the Crimean War, one of the few that was not melted down to be restruck as Victoria Crosses.

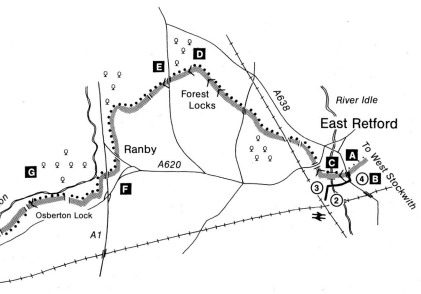

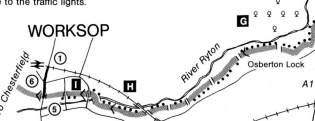

C Retford Basin and Lock

Joining the canal at Carolgate Bridge, the towpath passes opposite the old Retford Basin beyond which is Town Lock. Retford had hopes that wide-boat cargoes would make it up to the town from the Trent and so this far the locks are broad; Town Lock is the first narrow one. It is not known whether or not the Town's 'broad' aspirations were ever fulfilled, there being no record of barges working up this far. By the lock, there are some tasteful modern buildings - one of them a new theatre that faces the wrong way - and above is an old warehouse with the stump of its crane alongside - unusually this is on the towpath side which would have necessitated it swinging out *across* the towpath. Almost immediately the river Idle is crossed on a low aqueduct as the canal swings round and through Kings Park sandwiched between both. The park and the next lock, with the octagonal spire of the 14th century St. Michael's Church behind, see the canal clear of the town and out into the countryside to the northern fringes of Babworth Forest.

D The Forest Locks

It is hard to imagine that the open undulating landscape beyond Babworth Forest and Lady Bridge - where there are quite dramatic rope grooves - is part of a larger and more famous forest, Sherwood. When the four Forest Locks were built they penetrated the northern extremities of this once great forest; today the 'greenwood' has all but gone, given over to pastures and people. There is more evidence of the former than the latter, the first canalside building for four miles being the recently renovated lock cottage and stables at the third lock, where there is also a pocket of woodland with the inflated name of 'Barnby Fox Covert'.

E The Great North Road

The straight road that crosses the canal at Barnby Wharf Bridge was a Roman route that in turn became the Great North Road. Some 200 years ago - before the invention of the juggernaut - the good citizens of Retford got it diverted to go through their town which, with the coming of the canal and two railways - the Great Northern and the Great Central - brought prosperity. About a mile north of here at Barnby Moor is an old Posting House now known as "Ye Olde Bell Hotel", where stagecoaches and their much shaken passengers stopped off awhile; two such travellers were Queen Victoria and her mother.

F Ranby

The slow and seductive pace above the last of the Forest Locks is intruded upon by a scarcely perceptible hum. The hum becomes a drone and then, as the canal sweeps southwards through a wooded cutting, it is joined by the unmistakable resonance of the A1. During the 1914/18 War, there was a large army barracks here but all save one lone cottage has gone. One of the cottages on the towpath side closer to Ranby was once a malthouse - look for the doorway on the first floor. The cut twists and turns round Ranby and exchanges the rowdy A1 for the more tranquil course of the river Ryton across fields to the north by Osberton Mill.

G Osberton Hall

The towpath changes sides at the friendly Osberton Lock for no other reason than to placate the Foljambe family, owners of Osberton Hall. Maintaining their privacy and facilitating the unloading of coal and building materials by the canalside stables were both considerations. The small village of Scofton to the north is the estate village of Osberton Hall; today the estate is mainly known for its horse trials held in September. Its respects paid, the towpath returns to the left at Manton Bridge, at the end of a delightfully secluded remnant of Sherwood - almost the last before Worksop.

H Under and Over

A typical Chesterfield brick accommodation bridge is framed in the second arch of the 9 arch railway viaduct, its long span also crossing the ever closer river Ryton. Beyond Kilton Lock the canal flings itself into an S bend as it crosses the Ryton. Both canal and aqueduct are very much in the shadow of the gaunt and graffitied presence of Bracebridge Pumping Station, its steam-driven beam engine fired by coal from Shireoaks Colliery on the other side of Worksop. Behind the pumping station's tall red brick chimney stack, the unmistakable skyline of Worksop beckons.

I Worksop

The final lock is preceded by two distinctly different bridges, both typical of their times but only one of which seems to attract the graffiti artists. Worksop closes in quite suddenly with the unmistakable evidence of erstwhile canalside activity; the most dramatic being the flamboyant Pickford's warehouse that straddles the canal just before the towpath. Sadly, only the boater gets a view from below of the arch and the trapdoors where goods were hoisted up and lowered down to boats. Worksop's second and larger wharf was across the bridge above Town Lock but a car park has replaced the warehouses, maltings and wharves. The canal is navigable for a little less than $1/2$ mile beyond the bridge but there are hopes that this will be extended as far as Rhodesia which, in the canal's heyday, was a busy area with a large brickworks. The town itself is worth exploring, it is neither as unattractive nor as uninteresting as its popular image.

Sustenance

The only canalside pub between Worksop and Retford is "The Chequers" at Ranby, a friendly place with good food. Both towns have a good selection of pubs, restaurants and take-aways; there is, for example, a restaurant by the canal bridge at Retford and a good canalside pub just before the Pickford warehouse at Worksop.

Counter Attractions

• Clumber Park, nr Worksop, Notts. Open daily. Admission charge. Tel: Worksop (0909) 476592. The 3,800 acre estate was created over 200 years ago for the Duke of Newcastle.
• Lound Hall National Mining Museum, Bevercotes, nr Tuxford, Notts. Open Tues-Sat, 10.30am-5.30pm (or dusk); Sun 2pm-5.30pm. No admission charge. Tel: Mansfield (0623) 860728.

Encore

The junction of the river Trent with the Chesterfield Canal and the river Idle offers an excellent and short walk at the 'wide' end of the canal. Starting at the "Packet Inn" at Misterton (on the Retford/Gainsborough bus route no. 483 - tel: Retford (0777) 702952), head up to the navigable river Idle and turn south-east along its bank to West Stockwith to join the Trent. Follow the banks of the Trent south-west to West Stockwith Basin, formerly a trans-shipment basin where goods were loaded to and from barges and keels that could not only ply the Trent, but also head out to the Humber and beyond. Today the basin is host to a large variety of inland and estuarial craft. From the basin, head due west along the canal and back to Misterton. This walk is one of several featured in the superb guide to the Chesterfield Canal published by the local Canal Society.

Information

Tourist Information Centre, Queen's Bridge, Potter Street, Worksop, Notts. Tel: Worksop (0909) 475531.

The peaceful waters of the Wey

Silhouettes at Braunston on the Grand Union Canal

Newbury swing bridge on the Kennet & Avon

Little Hallingbury Mill - a quiet backwater of the River Stort

Walk 10

Coventry Canal
Warwickshire

Alvecote - Polesworth   **4 miles**

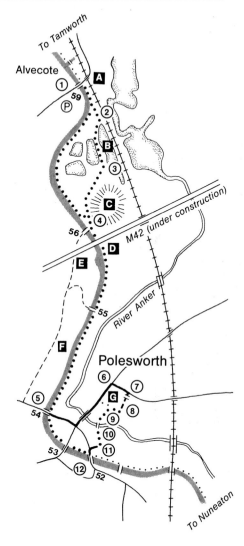

The Walk

This is not a pretty walk but it never lacks interest both waterway and general, and is thus typical of the Coventry Canal throughout its 38 mile course from Coventry to Fradley Junction near Lichfield. In working boat days this route was known as the 'Bottom Road' by the boat people who would use it to reach the North Warwickshire coalfield, albeit reluctantly owing to its shallow waters and recalcitrant narrow-beam locks. Twenty years after the last cargo passed this way, evidence of their trade is not difficult to discern. Additional interest includes ruins of a 12th century priory, a nature trail within former colliery precincts, the oldest inhabited building in Warwickshire, an 18th century river bridge and Polesworth's Abbey.

Start Point

Alvecote Priory picnic site.
OS ref: SK 251043.

Access

Car - Alvecote Priory is on a minor road 3 miles east of Tamworth. Polesworth is served by train (Tel: Rugby (0788) 60116) and bus (Midland Red Mercian Services Tel: Tamworth (0827) 3861) so the walk could be undertaken in reverse if you are arriving by public transport.

Directions

1 Turn right onto road from car park and picnic area, cross canal on bridge and turn immediately right through wooden gate onto nature trail path. Waymarker 1 points the way.
2 Continue on same path bearing left past marker 2. Continue along the path between the pools to waymarker 8.
3 Go through gate and keep to main track at foot of spoil tip.
4 Join towpath adjacent to marker 10 and proceed under M42 for 1 mile to bridge 54.

5 Leave towpath and turn left down Tamworth Road to crossroads, turn left into Bridge Street and go over river, continuing into centre of Polesworth.
6 Turn right into High Street signposted "Polesworth Abbey".
7 Turn right beneath archway to Polesworth Abbey.
8 Turn right by church.
9 Turn left and follow path to footbridge over river.
10 Take left fork in path immediately over footbridge, cross smaller footbridge and head past children's playground. On reaching 3-storey flats, bear right to join main road.
11 Cross road and join canal at bridge 52.
12 Return along towpath to Alvecote Priory.

Points of Interest

A Alvecote
Throughout this walk, one is reminded that in medieval times this corner of north-east Warwickshire must have been of some importance. The Benedictine Priory at Alvecote was founded in 1159, only a ruined archway and dove-cot remain. Alvecote remained a rural community until the opening of the local coalmines in the 19th century. Alvecote Colliery stood immediately to the west of bridge 59. There was also a brickworks in the vicinity linked by narrow-gauge railways to the canal basin now used by a hireboat fleet.

B Miners Path
A red shale path once used by miners to reach the pithead leads between 'flashes' formed by mining subsidence. Over the years the land above the coal seams being worked below ground, subsided and was filled with water during flooding of the river Anker. The area, known as Alvecote Pools, is now a nature reserve. An explanatory leaflet which will add considerably to the enjoyment

of your walk is obtainable from: The Warwickshire Nature Conservation Trust, Northgate, Warwick CV34 4PB.

C Spoil Tip
Emerging from the avenue of trees between the flashes, a huge spoil tip dominates the view. Pooley Hall Colliery, which was situated on the opposite side of the canal, began 'conical' tipping in 1951. At its height the

mound was nearly 200 feet high, though subsequently, spoil was removed for use in roadmaking. An NCB sign warns against climbing the tip, but local people seem to ignore this and certainly there are rewarding views from the top.

D Coventry Canal
Work began on the Coventry Canal in 1768, but it took over 20 years for the route between Coventry and the Trent & Mersey at Fradley to be completed. However, despite difficulties at the outset, the canal contrived to be used commercially right up until the end of long-distance narrowboat carrying in 1970. Indeed it was one of the few canal companies still paying its shareholders a dividend when nationalised in 1947. Bridge 56 once carried a link railway from Pooley Hall Colliery to the main line. Beyond it the new M42 bridge spans the canal.

E Pooley Hall Colliery
The old loading lay-by for Pooley Hall Colliery is easily discernible just beyond the motorway. Brick and concrete ruins remain from the loading shutes. Narrowboats were loaded directly from railway wagons hoisted vertically so as to tip their contents into each boat's hold. Pooley Hall Colliery was opened in 1848. It became the first mine in the country to be equipped with pithead baths under the auspices of the Miners' Welfare Commission. The pit was closed in 1965, narrowboats served it to the end. An evocative account of the loading of a pair of narrowboats at the colliery is contained in "Bread Upon The Waters" by David Blagrove.

F Pooley Hall
Leaving the basin behind, the canal enters a pocket of unspoilt countryside. A monument on the hillside commemorates the men of Pooley Hall Colliery who fell in the Great War. Across the valley, the railway bridges the Anker on a squat 7 arch viaduct of blue brick. This busy, electrified route is the main line between London Euston, the Northwest and Scotland. It was opened in 1847. A spill weir creams off excess canal water down into the Anker whilst on the opposite bank, the 16th century castellated profile of Pooley Hall occupies an elevated position overlooking the canal. Pooley Hall dates from 1509 and was built by Sir Thomas Cokayne who fought for Henry VIII at the Battle of Tournay in France. Subsequent rebuildings have given it a mongrel pedigree. It is said to be the oldest inhabited building in the county.

G Polesworth
In the 18th century Polesworth was famous for its 'hiring fair' held each year at Michaelmas. Records suggest that as many as 3,000 farm labourers would gather here to offer their services to the wealthy landowners of this part of the Midlands. But the discovery of coal in the neighbourhood served to blight Polesworth's rural hinterland. Today new housing spills down the hillside to the little town of Polesworth. For a settlement over-run by mining in the 19th century, there are a surprising number of older buildings of much architectural interest. The 10-arched river bridge dates from 1776; there is a cupola-topped Tudor Grammar School at the junction of Bridge and High Streets; a 15th century gateway remains from the

Sustenance
Polesworth has a number of rather uninspiring pubs and two fish & chip shops. A recent development, however, and open throughout the day is "Foster's Yard", a sort of wine bar where children are welcome - it can be found adjacent to bridge 53.

Counter Attractions
Twycross Zoo - open daily. Located on A444, 4 miles northeast of Polesworth. Tel: Tamworth (0827) 880250.

Encore
Two one-way walks for consideration are:-
1. Coventry Basin to Hawkesbury Junction along the original 1769 section of the canal.

Work stops for the cameraman at the Lees & Atkins boatyard, Polesworth.

Benedictine Abbey; there is a substantial Norman parish church; and the Victorian vicarage occupies the site of an Elizabethan school where the poet Michael Drayton was tutored. Furthermore, on a hillside to the southeast, an obelisk marks the site of a chapel demolished in 1538 during the Reformation. Polesworth was also famous in the canal world for the distinctive painting technique of Lees & Atkins Boatyard which stood to the east of bridge 52.

A detailed guide to this 5½ mile length of waterway is available from Coventry Canal Society, c/o Weighbridge Office, Canal Basin, St. Nicholas Street, Coventry CV1 4BP. A West Midlands bus service operates between the city centre and bridge 4 on the North Oxford Canal ½ mile from Hawkesbury Junction.
2. Nuneaton (Tuttle Hill) to Atherstone. A never less than interesting 5 mile route including the British Waterways section office

and maintenance yard at Hartshill and the upper section of the Atherstone flight of 11 locks. We suggest you start from Atherstone, taking the Midland Red Mercian service (Tel: Nuneaton (0682) 384007) to Tuttle Hill and return on foot.

Information

Tourist Information Centre, Marmion House, Lichfield Street, Tamworth (Tel: Tamworth (0827) 64222).

Walk 11

Cromford Canal

Derbyshire

High Peak Junction

6 miles

The Walk

Since the turn of the century and the collapse of Butterley Tunnel, the Cromford Canal has been out on a limb. We can only bemoan its exclusion from the navigable waters available to today's pleasure boaters, for indisputably, its scenery rivals the Llangollen. Nevertheless, the towpath rambler still has some 5 delectable miles to explore. Two of those miles are part of this circular walk which also takes in one of the old Cromford & High Peak Railway's inclined planes, and a 'green lane' traversing some charming Derbyshire gritstone landscape.

Start Point

Whatstandwell railway station.
OS ref: SK 333542

Access

Train (Local Derby-Matlock service, daily (but of virtually no use on winter Suns) Tel: Derby (0332) 32051.), bus (Trent services - Tel: Derby 372078) or car - car parking at station on A6, 5 miles south of Matlock.

Directions

1 Cross footbridge from platform, cross canal and follow path up to road. Turn left down to canal bridge and join towpath.
2 Proceed northwards along towpath for 2 miles.
3 Cross canal by way of 'low-level' footbridge and continue past pumphouse to swingbridge.
4 Cross swingbridge to railway wharf and follow High Peak Trail up incline under A6.
5 Turn left off trail at 1 mile marker and join 'Intake Lane'.

6 Follow lane to junction with B5035.
7 Turn left downhill for 1/2 mile.
8 Turn left downhill along track between stone walls.
9 Turn sharp right along path parallel to back gardens to reach A6.
10 Cross road and go past barrier down tarmac drive under railway.
11 Beyond railway bear right over river footbridge. Turn left over bridge and remain on path between fences until canal is reached.
12 Turn right back through tunnel and return to Whatstandwell.

Points of Interest

A The Railway

Twenty-five years ago the Manchester 'Blue' Pullman diesel train raced through Whatstandwell on its luxurious way down to St. Pancras. But that famous train and this celebrated 'Midland' route between Manchester and London were victims of 1960s railway rationalisation, the 'Midland Pullman' ceased running in 1966 and the line beyond Matlock was closed in 1968. Today only a single line branch service between Derby and Matlock remains, a revision to the line's modest origins at its opening in 1849. Leaving the old 'down' platform by way of an elegant lattice ironwork footbridge, you immediately cross the Cromford Canal winding its shallow way southwards along the Derwent Valley to Ambergate. After a brief detour into Whatstandwell village you return to the canal and strike northwards along the towpath. Steep wooded banks descend to the canal and the water is strikingly clear.

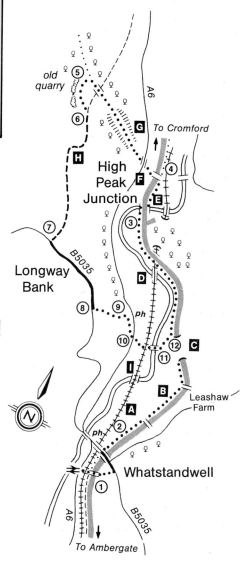

B The Cromford Canal

The canal owes its origin to Richard Arkwright, the cotton mill owner, who required reliable transport for the products of his Cromford mills. The canal was opened in 1794, having been designed by Jessop and Outram. From its Cromford terminus it ran 14½ miles in a south-easterly direction to connect with the Erewash and Nottingham canals at Langley Mill near Ilkeston. The Cromford Canal remained profitable until the coming of the railways. Subsequently, collapse of the 3,000 yards long tunnel at Butterley, near Ambergate, brought an abrupt end to through traffic in 1900. Thenceforward, until abandonment by the LMS railway in their infamous Act of 1944, only a small amount of coal and lead was carried on the isolated northern section of the canal. In 1974 the decaying waterway between Ambergate and Cromford was taken over by Derbyshire County Council who, along with the Cromford Canal Society, have developed it for leisure use.

C Gregory Tunnel

Passing a charming waterside house, the trees on the towpath side open out to offer beautiful views over the river; a distance post notes that it is 2½ miles to Cromford. Presently the portal of Gregory Tunnel looms ahead; 80 yards long with a towpath. After the tunnel the canal becomes ensconced in woodland again. The valley narrows and the banks become higher and more precipitous. The railway, sandwiched by river and canal, is forced to tunnel beneath the canal and the adjoining hillside. The result is a splendid iron troughed aqueduct juxtaposed with the bulky portal of Leawood Tunnel, 315 yards long. Oh, to have been here a century ago when the canal was busy with boats and steam expresses thundered beneath!

D Wigwell Aqueduct

Hardly have you recovered from the excitement of crossing the railway when, passing a ruined cottage at the junction of the former Nightingale Branch to Lea Wood, you reach the 200 yards long, 30 feet high, Wigwell Aqueduct. This handsome stone structure has a main arch with a span of 80 yards and two smaller occupation arches. You can go down through the woods to your left to view the aqueduct from below. A stone inscription celebrates its completion in 1792. A year later Jessop accepted the blame for cracks which began to appear in the structure and the iron strengthening bars inserted to combat this can still be seen.

E Leawood Pumphouse

Adjacent to the aqueduct stands Leawood Pumphouse which was built in 1849 to provide additional water for the canal pumped up from the river Derwent. The Boulton & Watt steam engine has been restored by the Cromford Canal Society and is regularly steamed and open to the public. Another delightful CCS innovation is a horse-drawn passenger boat service between here and the terminus wharf at Cromford - something you could perhaps enjoyably combine with your walk. Details of steamings at the pumphouse and trip boat operating times can be had by telephoning Wirksworth (062 982) 3727.

F Cromford & High Peak Railway

Just past the pumphouse, with its huge 95ft high chimney, stands the old transhipment wharf between the Cromford Canal and the Cromford & High Peak Railway. This astonishing railway was originally conceived as a canal linking the Peak Forest Canal at Whaley Bridge with the Cromford Canal - but there was the small matter of the Peak District in between! Even the railway, opened in 1831, was forced to include 9 inclines in its 33 mile course along which wagons were raised or lowered by a wire rope powered by stationary steam engines. The railway closed in 1967 and its formidable route is now a leisure trail. High Peak Junction retains much of its working ambience. The transhipment shed is now used as a countryside pursuits centre and the old railway workshops are open to the public at weekends and during the school holidays - Tel: Wirksworth 2831.

G Sheep Pastures Incline

Leaving the canal behind, you ascend the spectacular 1 in 8 mile long Sheep Pastures Incline. Old guards vans marooned on a short length of track rekindle the railway atmosphere. Near the foot of the incline the rails were skewed to pass a catchpit for runaway wagons - remains of one such escapee can still be seen. To legs accustomed to gentle towpath gradients the incline comes as something of a shock. But the view over the Derwent valley pays dividends and offers an excuse for 'resting' at frequent intervals.

H Intake Lane

Leaving the incline to complete its ascent to Middleton, you pass through a small abandoned quarry complete with rusty and lichened jib crane. You look back down onto the incline imagining wagons rumbling down into the valley. Intake Lane is a delightful 'green' trackway linking the settlements of Cromford and Longway; perhaps predating the present course of the A6. A short section of walk along the not overtly busy B5035 is soon over, and a path between stone walls takes you down past two curiously shaped stone structures - they are, in fact, old mining shafts - to the A6.

I River Derwent

Derbyshire's premier river, the Derwent, rises on Howden Moors, all of 2,000 ft. up in the Dark Peak, and reaches the river Trent, as its longest tributary, 60 miles to the south near Shardlow. South of Cromford the river pierces a narrow wooded defile; Richard Arkright is reputed to have organised the planting of some 350,000 trees along these banks for posterity - thank you R.A! On the way back along the towpath to Whatstandwell the overriding view is of Crich Stand - a war memorial to the Sherwood Foresters standing above a quarry face along the foot of which runs the track of the National Tramway Museum.

Sustenance

There are just two pubs en route - viz: the Homestead Cottage Inn (Kimberley Ales & food) on the A6 at direction point 9; and the Derwent Hotel (food & accommodation) adjacent to Whatstandwell station. Light refreshments are usually obtainable at Leashaw Farm.

Counter Attractions

● National Tramway Museum - Collection of restored trams running along a mile of track set amidst authentic period street furniture. Open Mar-Oct weekends, daily during high season. Tel: Ambergate (0773 85) 2565. Located 1 mile west of Whatstandwell station.
● Arkwright Mill - Richard Arkwrights original cotton mill of 1771. Tel: Wirksworth 4297 for details of open times etc. Located opposite terminus wharf of Cromford Canal at Cromford.

Encore

More an alternative than an encore really, but if you'd like to see more of the towpath at the expense of the surrounding scenery, simply use the train between Cromford and Ambergate walking the 5 miles of towpath back.

Information

Tourist Information Centre, The Wardwick, Derby. Tel: Derby (0332) 31111.

Walk 12

Erewash Canal

Nottinghamshire

Ilkeston - Sandiacre   9 miles

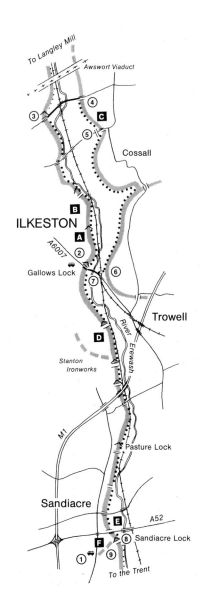

The Walk

This is a walk of surprises. It begins with the Erewash Canal in a residential setting and ends with the same canal in a more industrial mood . . . and in between is the unnavigable and quite beautiful Nottingham Canal. The two waterways, rivals in their time, share different contours along the Erewash Valley. Their chosen routes were an important factor in the survival of one and the decline of the other. In the days of commercial carrying a canal's scenic qualities did not rate highly and thus the Nottingham lost out and, though parts are probably navigable, it is likely to remain exclusively a walker's domain.

Start Point

"The Bridge Inn", Longmore Road, Sandiacre, Nottingham. OS ref: SK 478354.

Access

Bus and car. Sandiacre is on two regular bus routes: Trent's (Tel: Nottingham (0602) 418007) no. 102 Nottingham/Derby route and Barton's (Tel: Nottingham (0602) 254881) Sawley/Ilkeston route. There is convenient parking off the main road (B6002) by turning first right, Springfield Avenue, (going south from the "Bridge Inn") and then first right again, Sandringham Road, parking between the road bridge and the children's play park.

Directions

1 Catch a bus (Barton's no. 15) to Ilkeston, alighting at the "Gallows Inn", just beyond the canal bridge.
2 Join the canal by the lock and head north, remaining on the towpath for 2 miles.
3 Turn right off the canal at the second major road bridge and head east for 1/2 mile.
4 Turn right onto the Nottingham Canal at the 'Canal Footpath' sign.
5 Leave the towpath via the steps on the right, just before the redundant aqueduct,

and cross the road on the adjacent bridge, rejoining the towpath via the steps on the left.
6 Leave the towpath via the gap in the hedge just before the first of the canalside houses and gardens on the right and follow the path downhill, over the railway and up to the main road (A6007).
7 Turn right on to the A6007, cross it and join the towpath opposite the "Gallows Inn", heading south for the 3 1/2 miles to Sandiacre Lock.
8 Cross the bridge at the tail of the lock and proceed along the front of the lockside buildings, turning left up the truncated arm of the Derby Canal.
9 Proceed up along the side of the 'dead end' bridge and follow the bed of the Derby Canal up under the B6002 to the Sandringham Road.

Points of Interest

A Erewash Canal
The short Erewash Canal was the first of five canals to feed the towns of the East Midlands with coal from the Derbyshire and Nottinghamshire collieries. In 1779 it was completed from the river Trent to Langley Basin after only 20 months of work. The collieries, ironworks, foundries and brickworks that in those days lined its banks, ensured its prosperity, despite the arrival of nearby competitors. Indeed three of these, the Cromford (see Walk 11), the Nutbrook and the Derby positively increased the Erewash's tolls; the Nottingham, however, was more of a direct rival. The canal company handled the advent of the railways badly; it refused to reduce tolls to compete more advantageously and by the time it saw the logic of this it was too late. The Erewash became part of the Grand Union Canal Company in 1932 but things did not improve; the Cromford and the Nottingham were abandoned and all but 1/2 mile of the Nutbrook fell into decay. The

privately owned Derby survived longer but was eventually abandoned in 1964.

B Ilkeston

Despite the surrounding decay and dereliction, the Erewash Canal survived the transition from working to recreational usage and for the boater and walker alike offers a blend of rural, industrial and residential backdrops. Walking north from Gallows Lock around the eastern outskirts of Ilkeston, the latter two predominate. The industry is mainly light and modern, the housing a typically cluttered conurbation. A short snatch of 'greenery' is dominated by a landscaped spoil heap; there are allotments too, complete with their almost obligatory tumbledown sheds and outhouses. Remnants of an older canalside activity remain too but are fast disappearing, unlike the tidy canalside community just before we leave the Erewash at Barker's Lock.

C The Nottingham Canal

The walk from canal to canal, via a railway and river, is dominated to the north by the disused iron trestle Awsworth Viaduct - one of only two such structures standing - that originally carried the Great Northern Railway. Before joining the Nottingham Canal take a look back towards the Erewash; this river valley is more steeply sloped to the east and it is along this higher contour that the Nottingham Canal Company cut their $14^1/2$ mile line from the Cromford Canal at Langley Mill to the Trent - little wonder the working boatmen called it the 'top cut'. It was not a successful venture, particularly its northern end where trade ceased earlier than it did in and around Nottingham, where there were several short branches. That said, it is this end that today has so much to offer the walker. Unlike its lower neighbour, the Nottingham Canal wanders along the valley in a delightfully rural mood. Parts are in water, parts are culverted under obstructions, but nowhere is it anything other than a seductive experience. An old milepost, minus its number plate, tells us that we are '- miles from the Trent', while $^1/2$ mile away down in the valley the Erewash sparkles along its parallel course and a few houses watch from the privacy of the valley ridge. There were no locks in this section but there are the remains of an aqueduct and narrows that probably once supported movable accommodation bridges. The Robinett's Cut that leaves one corner of a dramatic hairpin bend acted both as a water feeder and a carrier of coal from a local colliery.

D The Nutbrook Canal

Back on the Erewash, heading south now, the last outpost of Ilkeston is soon forgotten for, just beyond the next lock, the redundant remains of the once proud Stanton Ironworks tell a sad tale. A pipe jutting arrogantly out of the offside bank is all that remains of another canal, the short Nutbrook. It was completed in 1795 between the Erewash at Stanton and Shipley Wharf, $4^1/2$ miles to the north, its 13 broad locks rising parallel to and west of the Erewash. Mining subsidence took its toll and by 1895 it had fallen into disuse; it was ultimately acquired by the Ironworks and the first $^1/2$ mile kept open until 1962 when it was infilled. 20th century reality rudely interrupts such reflections of past canalside activity in the form of the relentless north-south concrete carriageways of the M1.

E Sandiacre

The drone of the M1 in the background is hardly, it might seem, the setting for a lock with the rural connotations of Pasture Lock. But it is well named because, though there are railway sidings on the left, the water meadows on the offside and Sandiacre Church standing atop the rocky outcrop of Stoney Clouds, 'the last of the Pennines', are endearing interludes. Trees, tall elegant chimneys and pleasant canalside gardens precede the span of the A52 seeking out its junction with the M1 before the cut swings round to Sandiacre Lock and its junction with the Derby Canal. The restored lockside cottage and tollhouse here not only make this an especially picturesque setting but also evoke images of what has been, in living memory, a busy meeting place. The toll house on the junction side of the lockside cottage was used by the Derby Canal until 1832 when they built their own lockhouse on the far side of the canal by the bridge, the truncated end of what is left of the canal.

F The Derby Canal

Walking up to the main road along the bed of the Derby Canal, it is clear that this short section once boasted two of the canal's nine mainline locks between Sandiacre and Swarkestone on the Trent & Mersey Canal. The last commercial traffic on the Erewash was to Derby, but the Derby Canal Company (still a private company) in a fit of pique at not being nationalised with the rest of the network, refused to allow a pair of boats, Derby-bound with coal, to leave Sandiacre. The boats were chained in the lock while the matter was adjourned to Westminster where the company's action was upheld when it was discovered that the 'statutory right of all persons to navigate' clause was accidentally omitted from the original Act. The canal itself survived until 1964 when it was finally abandoned. Returning to the bridge under the B6002, it is difficult to visualise the line the Derby Canal took thereafter.

Counter Attractions

● Nottingham Castle Museum, off Castle Road, Nottingham. Open daily Apr-Sept, 10am-5.45pm (4.45pm Sun); Oct-Mar, 10am-dusk, (Sun 1.30-4.30pm). No admission charge. Tel: Nottingham (0602) 281333. Built on the site of William the Conqueror's castle - the only remains above ground being the gate-house originally built in 1252. It has been destroyed and rebuilt several times. Caves beneath can be visited by appointment. Present buildings date from 1674 and house the City's Museum & Art Gallery.
● D. H. Lawrence Museum, 8A Victoria Street, Eastwood, nr Nottingham. Open Mon, Tues, Thur, Fri & Sun 1.30pm-4pm; Wed 9am-noon; Sat 9.30am-4pm. Admission charge. Tel: Langley Mill (07737) 66611. 8A Victoria Street is the birth-place of the controversial novelist D. H. Lawrence; the house is given over to exhibitions relating to his life and works.

Sustenance

There are several hostelries on and close to the Erewash Canal, though not surprisingly, none on the derelict Nottingham Canal. Ilkeston has plenty of sitdown and take-away houses. Should it take your fancy, you could easily find the 'back door' to the M1's Trowell Services.

Encore

Part of the Nottingham Canal still remains active in these days of pleasure cruising - the $2^1/2$ mile length from the Beeston Cut at Lenton to the River Trent in the centre of Nottingham. This is a particularly interesting length of canal both architecturally and historically. It includes the old Fellows, Morton & Clayton Basin and Warehouse, the latter appropriately enough a canal museum these days. An excellent guide to the whole area is produced by Nottingham City Council, North Church Street, Nottingham. There is no shortage of bus services linking the city centre with both ends of the walk, details from Nottingham (0602) 418007.

Information

Tourist Information Centre, Ilkeston Library, Market Place, Ilkeston, Derbyshire. Tel: Ilkeston (0602) 301104.

Walk 13
Gloucester & Sharpness Canal
Gloucestershire

Sharpness   **5 miles**

The Walk
Few parts of today's inland waterway network terminate at quayside walls with towering cranes loading and unloading broad-beamed sea-going ships; still fewer are the canals where you might glimpse such craft heading inland. One of the exceptions is the Gloucester & Sharpness Canal. This walk is about what might have been, a fascinating encounter with a unique corner of the waterways world.

Start Point
The car park of the "Severn Bridge and Railway" inn.
OS ref: SO 677027.

Access
Bus and car. Getting to Sharpness by public transport is not easy. There is a reasonable daily (Mon-Fri) Circle Line service (C54) from Berkeley to Hinton Turn, Sharpness (next to the "Severn Bridge and Railway") and a good connecting service at Berkeley with the Gloucester-Bristol service X20. Tel: Gloucester (0425) 21444 ext. 490 for C54 details; Stroud (045 36) 3421 for X20 details.

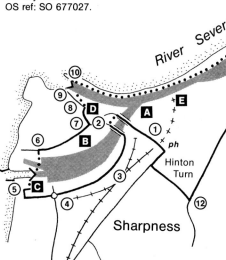

Directions
1 Proceed down the hill from the "Severn Bridge and Railway" and across the 'high' bridge.
2 Take the path to the left that leads down to the 'low' bridge level and cross back over the canal.
3 Follow this road round to the right behind the loading sheds to the roundabout.
4 Proceed straight across the roundabout towards and alongside the new housing as far as the 'sea' wall.

5 Proceed back 'inland' alongside the 'entrance' lock and the Ship Lock and cross this via the top gates and head for the road on the other side.
6 Turn right onto the road and follow this along behind the silo.
7 Turn left at the 'tyre' junction.
8 Take the third of three converging lanes on the right, signposted to Sharpness Marine.
9 Enter the Marina car-park and turn down the lane on the right.
10 Turn left at the bottom and proceed over the gates of the 'old' lock and turn right onto the towpath, remaining on this as far as the 2nd swing-bridge at Purton.
11 Cross Purton Upper Bridge, turn right then first left, signposted to Hinton and Brookend.
12 Turn right in about 1½ miles, the next T-junction is Hinton Turn, the bus terminus; the "Severn Bridge and Railway" is just around the corner to the right.

Points of Interest
A The Gloucester & Sharpness Canal
Standing on the 'high' bridge looking north, the Gloucester & Sharpness Canal is dwarfed by the very reason for its existence, the vast and unpredictable Severn Estuary. The Severn was recognised as an important commercial artery back in the reign of the first Elizabeth but tides and shifting shoals had no respect for the commercial aspirations of Gloucester: smaller vessels could navigate most of the time but larger craft could only do so at spring tides. The idea of a ship canal was first mooted in the 1790s and the Gloucester & Berkeley Canal Company set up - 'Berkeley' because the original sea outlet was to be Berkeley Pill about two miles south of Sharpness. The rest is history: the 16 mile canal was completed in 1827, at that time the broadest (86ft. 6in.) and deepest (18ft.) in the world. How ironic it is that Britain should have created such a waterway and at the same time spawned the narrowest network in the world! As a direct result of the canal's success, improvement works, including dredging and the construction of locks and weirs, were carried out on the upper Severn to facilitate trade with Worcester and Stourport. Sadly, commercial traffic has all but ceased on the canal, killed off in part by the adjacent M5 and the ubiquitous lorry.

B Sharpness Docks
But for the docks Sharpness would be a depressing place; but for the canal it would still be no more than a rocky cliff jutting arrogantly out into the Severn Estuary. The periphery of weary housing is instantly

Carrying grain to Tewkesbury - a barge passes through Purton on the Gloucester & Sharpness Canal.

bridge was never repaired and six years later it was dismantled (the girders were sold to Chile) leaving only the tower that supported the swinging section across the canal and the eastern abutment. Still out in mid-channel, and visible at low tide, lie the remains of "Arkendale H", "Wastdale H" and the span that ended an era. Perhaps the greatest damage done that night was to the closely knit communities of Berkeley and Lydney whose one link was so dramatically severed.

F A Waterways Graveyard
The simple milepost that indicates that you are a mere mile from Sharpness coincides with the end of a pleasant, if unexpected, tree-lined stretch. On the offside are the old and overgrown Marshfield timber ponds where timber was stored afloat until 1928, only to be replaced by a subtle blend of reeds and disused craft. On the foreshore behind a thin line of trees is a more dramatic sight, an endless graveyard of everything from Severn trows to concrete barges. Rib cages rise up from the sand, proud bows beckon in vain, unmarked graves share the pain of this emotional place and its forlorn beauty.

G Purton
The tiny village of Purton is dissected by the canal - if that is indeed possible, for two bridges, two pubs and two reservoirs are almost all there is. The bridge-keeper is based at the second of the swing-bridges. His home is a Regency-style single-storey lodge with fluted Doric columns, a touch of style repeated at most of the canal's bridges. There used to be a cattle ford across the river nearby; local folk-lore recalls how the drover would have to choose his time almost to the minute to ensure a safe crossing to the Welsh coast. The green backdrop 'over there' is the Forest of Dean where Drake and Raleigh selected oaks for the construction of England's sailing fleet. Seemingly one of the Armada's priorities, had it been victorious, was the destruction of this rich and potentially dangerous resource. The walk back over the hill to Sharpness offers occasional glimpses of the canal . . . what a visual impact on the surrounding countryside those coasters must have made.

forgettable, that first glimpse from the high bridge of tall cranes, warehouses and ships with foreign names is what Sharpness is all about. The dock area as it is now dates from 1874 when the original sea locks were replaced to accommodate vessels of up to 1000 tons. Those quay walls have played host to clippers and trows, seen the age of steam come and go and watched ships grow and traffic fluctuate. But what of today? In recent years traffic has, unlike other West coast ports, increased several-fold and there are plans for further development and investment to accommodate more ocean-going ships of up to 5000 tons.

C Sharpness Lock and the Severn Estuary
Until recently Allied Mill's grain barges were locking out of Sharpness regularly en route from Healing's Mill at Tewksbury to Avonmouth. The traffic continues sporadically but usually only as far as Sharpness where imported wheat is collected from the quayside silo. For most inland waterways craft the sea lock is the end of the line. However, an increasing number of intrepid boaters, attracted by Bristol, Bath and the restored western end of the Kennet & Avon Canal, have made the 17 mile dash to the mouth of the Avon. A walk to the end of the entrance lock will put the enormity of the task in perspective. On a clear day the breathtaking span of the Severn Bridge, the M4, can be seen on the skyline . . . and in

between 12 miles of uncertain water and the second largest tidal range in the world. Not a trip to be undertaken lightly in a flat-bottomed boat!

D Sharpness' Marina
After the docks Sharpness' marina is like stepping into another world, albeit a familiar one. Tall masts and flat bottoms rub gunwales along the arm that was, before 1874, the route to the original sea locks - one of which remains almost as it was. It is possible to walk a short distance seawards along the northern pier but a sign soon leaps up to inform you that you are about to cross into forbidden territory. Walking along the towpath to the main line of the canal, trying to work out how many times the old lock would fit into its larger neighbour, don't miss the beached barges that can be seen across the retaining wall to the left.

E The Severn and Wye Railway
If you cast your mind back to the inn sign at the start of the walk you will recall the railway bridge depicted. The stone tower and arched abutment that stand, custodians of the canal, just north of Sharpness are all that remains of the railway link across the Severn. The end came on a foggy night in October 1960 when two tanker barges missed the entrance to Sharpness, continued upstream and, locked together, collided with and demolished part of the bridge with the loss of five lives. The

Sustenance

The choice is simple: The "Severn Bridge and Railway" at Sharpness or one of Purton's pubs, the "Berkeley Hunt" by the lower bridge and the "Berkeley Arms" 150 yds. down towards the river from the same bridge.

Counter Attractions

● Berkeley Castle, Berkeley, nr. Dursley, Glos. Open May-Aug, Tues-Sat, 11am-5pm; Sun 2pm-5pm. Apr-Sept, Tues & Sat, 2pm-5pm. Oct, Sun, 2pm-4.30pm Admission charge. Tel: Dursley (0453) 810332. State apartments, the massive Norman keep, dungeon, great hall and kitchen and the room where Edward II was brutally murdered in 1327 are the Castle's main attractions. Grounds include an Elizabethan terraced garden and an ancient bowling alley.
● Slimbridge Wildfowl Trust, Slimbridge, Glos. Open daily (ex. Dec 24-25) 9.30am-5pm (or dusk if earlier). Admission charge. Tel: Cambridge (045 389) 333. The largest and most varied collection of wildfowl in the world with over 2300 birds of some 180 different species, some of which, like the largest flocks of flamingoes in captivity, are very rare.

Encore

Walking the Gloucester & Sharpness' towpath is hampered at one end by lack of public transport and at the other by the lack of a towpath into Gloucester. But, resourceful to the end, it is possible to explore the area between Framilode and Frampton-on-Severn provided that (if you're relying on public transport) you do it during the school holidays on a Tuesday or a Friday, come from Stroud and wear a funny hat! Details of service 11 are available on Stroud (04536) 3421. This walk not only includes the Gloucester & Sharpness but also allows time for extensive exploration of the Stroudwater Canal on both sides of Saul Junction.

Information

Tourist Information Centre, Council Offices, High Street, Stroud. Tel: Stroud (045 36) 4252.

3 Turn left at the T-junction.
4 Join the riverside walk on the right just before the bridge.
5 Join the towpath at the next bridge (by crossing it), continuing on this for the 4^1/$_2$ miles to Guildford.
6 Leave the towpath (which has changed sides) at the bridge above Mill Mead Lock by turning left and crossing the river.
7 Turn right and proceed along the edge of the car park to rejoin the riverside walk.
8 Turn left immediately beyond the 2nd bridge and proceed up the slope (not the steps) to where it joins the road.
9 Follow the signs thereafter to the station via the underpass.

Walk 14

Godalming Navigation

Surrey

Godalming - Guildford   5 miles

The Walk

The valley of the Wey has a unique charm; it is touched by the influence and affluence of Surrey and yet maintains its individuality. Nowhere is this better illustrated than on the towpath between Godalming and Guildford where the Surrey countryside is in places a spectacular backdrop to a subtle blend of rural tranquillity and sporadic suburbia, natural river and man-made cut.

Start Point

Guildford Railway Station.
OS ref: SU 991496.

Access

Bus, train or car. Guildford has rail links with all points of the compass, London, Portsmouth, Reading and Tonbridge.

Timetable details available from Guildford (0483) 579878. Bus and coach connections too are excellent; Tel: Guildford (0483) 575226. The station boasts a large car park.

Directions

1 Catch a train to Godalming.
2 Leave the station and proceed down the road opposite to the T-junction.

Points of Interest

A The Godalming Navigation
Britain's rivers have been used for navigation since Roman times, but it was not until the 16th and 17th centuries that the full commercial potential of these natural arteries was tapped by the new and aspiring entrepreneurial class, the 'middling sort'. By 1653 the river Wey, equipped with 12 turf-sided pound locks (ie a chamber enclosed within two sets of gates), was navigable from the Thames to Guildford. Such locks were not new but even Mother Thames was, at the time, not as advanced. It was a further century and a bit before the navigation was extended by 4 $\frac{1}{2}$ miles and 4 locks to create the Godalming Navigation.

B Godalming
Boarden Bridge is the limit of navigation on the river though in fact only the smallest craft will get beyond Town Bridge. The riverside walk begins unexpectedly with a cloistered memorial to the wireless operator on the ill-fated "Titanic", a son of Godalming. Godalming is an erstwhile wool town with a host of interesting and historic buildings all of which are pinpointed on an excellent wall-map at the 16th century Crown Court. If you've got time for nothing else, the renovated Hatch Mill and its associated terrace of mill cottages is certainly worth the

short detour - it's only a few yards south of the station.

C The National Trust
A sign on the towpath just below Town Bridge affirms that from here the Godalming Navigation is National Trust property. As trade on both navigations declined, the proprietor of the Wey Navigation, the late Harry Stevens, presented it to the Trust in 1964; four years later the Commissioners of the Godalming Navigation did likewise. With the growth of the pleasure industry the Trust has modernised the waterway and seemingly has had more success with this unusual sideline than with its other charge, the Southern Stratford Canal (see Walk 38).

D Catteshall Lock
The navigation soon takes its leave of Godalming. Its last outpost is the old wharf, on the bend where the river sweeps round to the left towards Cattershall Lock. All the locks on the navigation follow a similar pattern, a straight artificial lock-cut by-passing a meandering loop of the river. Here at Cattershall the river goes off on its circuitous course to the east and reappears below the lock none the worse for the experience. Downstream of Cattershall the 5-arched Trowers Bridge heralds a change of mood with the river wandering between

engaging scrubland and water meadows backed by a narrow wooded escarpment.

E The Wey & Arun Canal
Below Unstead Lock, its cut protected by an old war-time pill-box, the navigation enters a delightfully unspoilt spinney, its sylvan tentacles leaning over the water. Brick abutments stand as lone reminders that the London, Brighton & South Coast Railway from Horsham to Guildford once crossed here. Opened in 1865, the line was one of many that passed away in the 1960s from an overdose of Beeching's powders. Another route-that-was is just around the corner where, at 'Gun's Mouth', the Wey & Arun Canal branched off to the south-east en route to Littlehampton, establishing, via the Thames, an inland waterway link between London and the south coast. As its name suggests, the waterway linked two rivers, both of them already navigable, but it was the 'bit in the middle', the Wey & Arun Junction Canal, that completed the through route in 1816. Although finally abandoned in 1871 - ironically in part due to the now-closed railway mentioned above - the canal is not forgotten and there are stalwart efforts afoot to restore it. The junction's nickname, 'Gun's Mouth', is believed to stem from a wharf here from which explosives were trans-shipped to Woolwich Arsenal.

F St. Catherine's Lock and Chapel
The next lock, St. Catherine's is in the middle of nowhere . . curious the number of places that seem to end up there? But this 'nowhere' is dominated by the ruined 14th century St. Catherine's Chapel high on the hill behind. The main London-Portsmouth railway pierces the hill but not before what was originally the Reading, Guildford and Reigate Railway crosses the river - the adjacent embankment, clearly built to carry a spur south, never had rails. Beyond nowhere is 'somewhere', an amazing horseshoe bend which winds round St. Catherine's hill, its orange-red sandstone slope just crying out to be scaled. The old Pilgrim's Way (the North Downs Way as it is here too) from Winchester to Canterbury crosses via a modern footbridge, the original ferry having been deemed obsolete . . . and much less fun too! Two interesting diversions present themselves here. The steep path up to the left leads initially to the ruins of St. Catherine's Chapel and superb views, and

Walking by the Wey.

the path to the right, across the bridge, will, via the A281, bring you to the quaint 18th century Shalford Mill, a water-mill on the river Tillingbourne.

G Guildford

A house-topped chalk ridge and the 12th century Castle's keep are the first unwelcome signs that the walk's end is in sight. It is clear that for Guildford the Wey is a linear amenity and one which, if the number of boats for hire at the Guildford Boat House is anything to go by, its citizens seem to relish. Mill Mead Lock and its environs, including the Yvonne Arnaud Theatre, Spangles Restaurant and the brick 18th century Town Mill, are as pleasant a riverside setting as you'll find anywhere. There are numerous attractions in the city but a short diversion off from the car park (see direction 7) which was once Hays Wharf, reveals three interesting plaques. On the grass three statuettes depict an Alice in Wonderland theme (Lewis Carroll was born in Guildford) while the new Hays Wharf building remembers its dead, and finally next to St. Nicholas' Church is told the strange story of Dr. John Moussell who fell, broke his arm . . . and died!

H Guildford Wharf

Back by the river the waterside walk goes under the curved iron span of Town Bridge. Between this and a modern concrete offering is the site of the junction of the Wey and Godalming Navigations, Guildford Wharf, which is dominated by an 18th century crane. Despite its modern backdrop this, the only surviving treadmill crane in Britain, retains its dignity, though in such surroundings it is not easy to imagine the 10-man team required to turn the 18ft diameter wheel (inside the building) to lift 10 tons.

Sustenance

It goes almost without saying that in both Godalming and Guildford there is no shortage of places to eat and drink. In Godalming the "King's Arms Royal" not only serves a good pint but is also an interesting building. En route there is the "Ram", a cider house about $^1\!/_4$ mile east of Cattershall Lock. "The Britannia", by the car park in Guildford, is both homely and handy while the Richoux Restaurant - Guildford (0483) 502996 - comes highly recommended (. . . a chap called Ronay) for both quality and price.

Counter Attractions

● Clandon Park, West Clandon, nr Guildford, Surrey. Open daily (ex Mon & Fri) Apr-mid Oct, 2pm-6pm. Admission charge. Tel:

Guildford (0483) 222482. A classical early 18th century rectangular mansion, its roof hidden behind a balustrade. The original gardens were formal but during the 1770s they were redesigned by Capability Brown. The house contains fine furniture, pictures and porcelain.
● Winkworth Arboretum, Heath Road, Godalming, Surrey. Open daily. No admission charge. Over 95 acres containing a lake and rare trees and shrubs.

Encore

Public transport presents difficulties when it comes to exploring other parts of the Wey. That said, the London-Woking line provides

access to the river at Weybridge, returning via the Basingstoke Canal and West Byfleet, around $4^1\!/_2$ miles in all. At Weybridge the river is bracing itself for its final fling before joining the Thames, while further south it climbs out of suburbia through some delightful countryside towards Byfleet. The place where the new M25 and the railway cross is the entrance to the Basingstoke Canal, the first mile of which is being restored and includes a fascinating cluster of residential boats.

Information

Tourist Information Centre, The Civic Hall, Guildford, Surrey. Tel: Guildford (0483) 575857.

Walk 15

Grand Union Canal
Middlesex

Hayes - Brentford   7½ miles

The Walk

To a greater or lesser extent all the featured walks have a nostalgic quality as we reflect on what was and put these linear walkways into their historical perspective. Here on the Grand Union, between Bull's Bridge and Brentford, history is just around the corner, an ever-present reminder that within living memory working boats plied these waters to and from the Thames and the world beyond.

Start Point

Kew Bridge Railway Station.
OS ref: TQ 189782.

Access

Bus, train and car. Being London there are a number of (pricey) car parking facilities in the Kew area. Bus and rail connections are excellent; all enquiries to 01 928 5100 (Waterloo) and 01 222 1234 (London Transport). There are a number of ways of getting to Hayes from Kew, some are more direct than that detailed below but involve a change en route.

Directions

1 Catch a bus (90B) to Hayes. The 90B takes rather a circuitous but interesting route to Hayes via Richmond, Twickenham, Feltham and Heathrow.
2 Alight at the stop just beyond the canal bridge, join the towpath and head east for $6^1\!/_2$ miles until the bridge just beyond the Brentford locks.
3 Turn left onto the main road, High Street.
4 Turn right off High Street just before the "Six Bells", at The Ham.
5 Turn right off The Ham just before Halls Autos, join the canalside walk and cross the canal via the footbridge.
6 Leave the towpath just beyond Thames Locks and cross Dock Road to continue alongside the flats on the far side to view the confluence of canal and river.
7 Return to Dock Road and turn right towards Brentford High Street.
8 Turn right onto the High Street. Kew Bridge Station is about a mile away on the left.

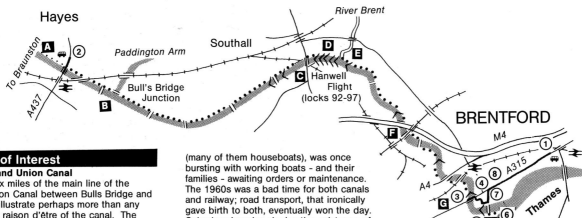

Points of Interest

A The Grand Union Canal

The last six miles of the main line of the Grand Union Canal between Bulls Bridge and Brentford illustrate perhaps more than any others the raison d'être of the canal. The 'Grand Junction', as it originally was, was the key that unlocked the Midlands to London and vice versa. Like some giant family tree the main line between Brentford and Braunston begat many branches: the Northampton Arm, the Aylesbury Arm, the Wendover Arm, the river Chess at Rickmansworth, the Slough Arm and the Paddington Arm, while the Leicester Section, the Erewash Canal, the Regent's Canal and the Hertford Union became kinsfolk. But for 20 years from 1800 Brentford remained the sole outlet to the Thames, the canal becoming a vibrant commercial artery to and from the heartlands of England. It was not until 1820 when the Regent's Canal joined the Paddington Arm to the Thames at Limehouse that the canal had a seaward terminus.

B Bull's Bridge

Hayes is a typical satellite of London, an erstwhile village community that has been raped by the sprawling metropolis. Heading east a distinctive aroma hangs in the air; as they haven't yet invented decaffeinated meat, it can't be the Walls complex on the left . . . the answer is beyond the railway in the form of the Nestle's factory on the offside. At Bull's Bridge the Paddington Arm goes off northwards - by the time it joins the Regent's Canal at Little Venice its directional sense has returned - while below the junction are sad reminders of a time not long gone. What is now the BWB yard was once the nerve centre of the Grand Union Canal Carrying Company's (later BWB's) narrow boat fleet. The adjacent lay-by, now occupied by all manner of strange and not-so-strange craft

(many of them houseboats), was once bursting with working boats - and their families - awaiting orders or maintenance. The 1960s was a bad time for both canals and railway; road transport, that ironically gave birth to both, eventually won the day. Suburban housing denies the existence of the old Hanwell Military Depot loop on the offside but the towpath crosses over the entrance of the only remaining working 'dock' on this part of the canal. Pause awhile here at Adelaide Dock and you will witness a busy scene as boats old and new, narrow and wide, are repaired and refurbished.

C 'Three Bridges'

A straight mile through Norwood Green ends at Norwood Top Lock, for boaters the end - or beginning - of a 6 mile lock-free pound. The short arm above the lock is Maypole Dock, a private cut made in 1912 to serve the Monsted margarine works, now another Walls meat factory. The second Norwood lock is followed by Windmill Bridge, the famous 'Three Bridges', where the road crosses the canal crossing the railway. It is said that there is a fortune to be made by the photographer who can capture a train (preferably belching smoke) a boat (preferably working), a bus (preferably a double decker) and a plane (preferably Concorde) all intersecting the same vertical line, one on top of the other. A tall order perhaps as the road is not a bus route, nor is it often that the remains of the Western Region's Brentford Branch see a train . . . Concorde might be the best bet!

D The Hanwell Flight

A gentle curve of the cut affords the first views of Brentford - notably the gasometer - and encapsulates the tidy 6 lock Hanwell Flight, flanked on the one side by a long wall and the austere bulk of St. Bernard's (Mental) Hospital and punctuated by more friendly lock cottages on the other. At intervals along

the wall are small red 'doors', scarcely large enough to assist the escape of anyone mad enough to want to walk the canal, but just right to facilitate a fireman's hose in its search for water from the canal. Lock 94 was nicknamed 'Asylum Lock' for just above was the entrance, now bricked up, to a short arm into the hospital that allowed for coal deliveries. The bend between this and the next lock is sharper than the rest, which caused more than a few horses to end up in the cut - their undignified exit was made the easier by the little flight of gently sloping steps.

E The River Brent

Below the Hanwell Locks the river Brent joins the canal from the north. The Brent is in fact navigable for about $1/2$ mile northwards and its banks are part of a walk that crosses the canal here and continues on to Osterley Park. From below Hanwell to the Thames the canal is in effect a canalised river, the locks being accompanied by weirs as on other similar navigations. As such, the only water problem that this end of the canal suffered from was *too much!* In 1903, for example, it was closed for several weeks due to exceptionally high rainfall levels. For a while the navigation meanders through the tattiness of corrugated iron and concrete, an unkempt industrial wilderness. But thankfully this is a mere hiccup and instead the increasing presence of the M4 to the west diverts the eye.

Waiting for loading orders at the Bull's Bridge lay-by in the early 1960s.

F Bridges Old and New

Osterley Lock has lost its lock cottage and acquired a new weir. As weirs go it is quite unusual, its toothed design has an aesthetic quality, which is more than can be said for the span of the M4 which leaps across below the lock. The rattling Piccadilly Line does likewise a little further on and then sanity returns in the form of a simple and graceful cast-iron turnover bridge. Gallows Bridge bears the legend 'Grand Union Canal Co. 1820' despite the fact that the Grand 'Union' was the Grand 'Junction' until 1929; closer inspection reveals an almost obscured 'Junction' beneath the 'Union'. The bridge was built by the Horseley Iron & Coal Co. of Tipton in Birmingham and is believed to be the oldest surviving example of the company's famous canal bridges.

G Brentford

The pace quickens and the short bursts of real river and real trees give way to the backdrop of a working waterway around Brentford. But like Bull's Bridge the working has all but ceased. The towpath plunges into the cavernous expanse of a covered dock and opposite, framed in the dock's entrance, are the trans-shipment wharves and ware-houses of Brentford Depot where lighters and narrow boats traded cargoes. With the demise of the narrow boat fleets much of the lighterage traffic went too; empty lighters stand expectant but resigned to the fact that most of the traffic these days makes use of a more immediate artery not too far away. Round the bend to the right are the Brentford Gauging Locks where traffic coming off the Thames was 'gauged' for tolls. Over to the east behind the sheds is the Canal Boatman's Institute through which, right until the end of the carrying era, the souls of the boat people were ministered to.

H Thames Locks

That last glance back at the Brentford Locks can evoke a twinge of frustration. Tidy and expectant they sit, their oversize protective fenders capable of brushing off lighter after lighter, but these days only likely to come into contact with pleasure craft off the Royal River. The route back to the canal from the High Street bridge solves a non-waterways mystery - where do all dead and dying London taxi cabs go for resuscitation? The answer is that they head for The Ham where several diligent taxi doctors put them to rights and turn them lose on the unsuspecting public . . now, not many people know that . . .! The Thames Locks (duplicated and electrified as recently as 1962) are the gateway to the tidal river Thames. Not unusually for the confluence of two rivers, the setting appears a bit of a muddle with backwaters and docks a plenty, but it all soon sorts itself out and the marriage is made at the spot, 'Brent-ford', where Julius Caesar supposedly crossed the Thames in 54BC. The housing development on the right spreads itself across the site of the old Great Western Railways Brentford Dock; like much else in London's dockland the area has succumbed to progress. Across on the northern side of the river another, more landscaped, walkway takes a lower and less dramatic route to Mother Thames . . . and above it all the planes head for Heathrow with monotonous regularity, the pilots ever faithful to their instructions: "Turn right at the Grand Union".

Sustenance

And much of it there is too! There are more than a few canalside pubs, some of which, like the "Grand Junction Arms", have strong canal connections. Hayes and Brentford offer everything from Indian take-aways to Wimpy bars, while "The Fox" (at the bottom of Hanwell Locks) is renowned for its lunchtime menu. Finally at Brentford there's a real waterways pub, the "Brewery Tap" in Catherine Wheel Road (an extension of The Ham).

Counter Attractions

London's on the doorstep but so is:
● Syon House & Gardens, Brentford, Middx. Open Easter-end Sept. Sun-Thur, noon-5pm; gardens open daily all year 10am-6pm. Admission charge. Tel: 01 560 0881/2. Seat of the Duke of Northumberland noted for its fine Sir Robert Adam interior and period furniture - reputedly his finest. Gardens include a butterfly house and Heritage Collection of British Motor Cars.
● National Music Museum, 368 High Street, Brentford, Middx. Open Apr-Oct, weekends.

Admission charge. Tel: 01 560 8108. Started life as a church and became the British Piano Museum; contains an exceptional collection of mechanical and unusual musical instruments, en route back to Kew.

Encore

In terms of its lack of activity, the Grand Union's other access to the Thames at Limehouse, via the Regent's Canal and the Paddington Arm, is just as depressing. But the 8 mile walk from Little Venice to Limehouse round Regent's Park, through Camden Town and Islington, Bethnal Green

and Mile End, is as exciting as it is interesting. This is truly London's canal, a ribbon of water which spawned a vigorous canalside commerce that at the same time kept itself to itself; an almost secret by-way wending its way to Limehouse and the vast watery wasteland of idle cranes and empty wharves. The nearest tube stations are at Warwick Road (Little Venice) and Shadwell (Limehouse).

Information

London Visitor & Convention Bureau, Telephone Information Service 01 730 3488.

Walk 16

Grand Union Canal

Buckinghamshire & Hertfordshire

Marsworth   5½ miles

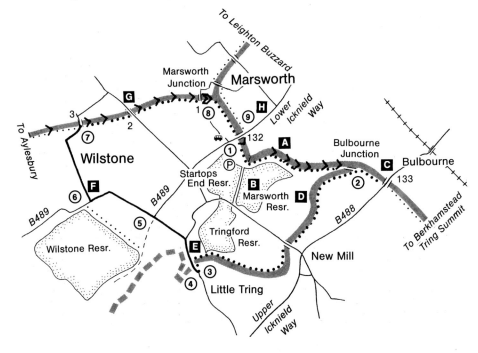

The Walk

This is not a walk of breathtaking scenic beauty - though it does have its moments - it is more about water and the difficulties of maintaining navigable levels on heavily locked canals. There is certain pleasure to be gained from returning to a starting point by a different route. This walk, with its various ups and downs, might well leave you wondering how it is that, after climbing seven locks at the beginning, you have to climb a further eight to get back to the start?

Start Point

Tring Reservoirs Car Park.
OS ref: SP 919141.

Access

Bus and car. United Counties' Aylesbury-Luton (2-hourly) service No. 61 goes through Marsworth, stopping close to the "White Lion". Timetable enquiries from Aylesbury (0296) 84919.

Directions

1 Proceed to the canal bridge (No. 132) on the B489 and turn right onto the towpath and continue until the next bridge (No. 133).
2 Retrace the route back to the Wendover Arm and turn left.
3 Cross the end of the stop lock at Little Tring and follow the towpath up to the road bridge.
4 Turn right onto the road and follow this downhill to where it joins the B489.
5 Turn left onto the B489 and follow this downhill and round to the left.
6 Turn right off the B489 to and through Wilstone.
7 Join the Aylesbury Arm's towpath at the canal bridge (No. 3) follow this for 1¼ miles.
8 Remain on the towpath as the Arm joins the Grand Union's main line and proceed to the next bridge (No. 132).
9 Leave the towpath at the bridge - the reservoir's car park is just across the road.

Points of Interest

A The Grand Union Canal
The route chosen by the original Grand Junction Canal Company between Brentford and Braunston included more than a few formidable natural obstacles. Unusually these necessitated *two* summit levels, one of which, the climb over the Chilterns, itself meant the construction of a long and deep cutting at Tring. The summit level required feeding and it was the area between Marsworth and Tring, north and east of the Tring summit, that was

Bushell's boatyard on the Wendover Arm in the 1920s.

chosen for the reservoirs. There was a further draw on these after 1815 with the opening of the Aylesbury Arm from Marsworth Junction or, as the working boatmen called it, 'Maffers'.

B The Reservoirs

Startops End and Marsworth, two of the four reservoirs that dominate this area, run alongside the west bank of the canal from lock 39 almost to Bulbourne Junction. The reservoirs, now a nature reserve, offer an interesting diversion from the locks wending their way up the summit. In the car park there is a large map of the area and its designated trails which also gives details of the many rare plants and animals that are indigenous to the area . . . if you're peckish you might look out for the *glis glis,* the edible dormouse! On the other hand you might like to compromise and take the higher path alongside the reservoirs instead of the towpath; they run parallel and, as the canal climbs, soon become as one. A highly informative booklet on the wildlife of the area is available from the Nature Conservancy Council, 20 Belgrave Street, London SW1. It is difficult to say whether the reservoirs enhance the locks or if it's the other way round; what is certain is that together they are a delightful duo - all of it man-made yet totally at one with its environment.

C Bulbourne

Back on the towpath the reservoirs are replaced by a narrow water channel to the right. It is only when crossing the towpath footbridge above the top lock and its adjacent dry dock that you realise that this is the Wendover Arm. Bulbourne Junction gets its name from the village slightly further south where the splendidly refurbished 19th century Bulbourne Works of the Grand Junction Canal Company are sited. Today the manufacture of wooden lock-gates continues here, albeit under slightly different management. Opposite is the "Grand Junction Arms" which went through a phase of being the "Lock and Quay" as part of a 'modernisation' scheme by an unenlightened brewery before the boaters' lobby persuaded them to think again.

D The Wendover Arm

The $6\frac{1}{2}$ mile Wendover Arm was conceived as a feeder for the canal's summit level, initially drawing its water from wells in Wendover and other sources in the Weston Turville and Halton area. Today the arm is navigable for a mere $1\frac{1}{4}$ miles as far as Little Tring. It is a pleasant walk with the locks of the main line an early companion over on the right. The mild burst of civilisation at the first bridge is the outskirts of New Mill where the imposing Heygates flour mill dominates all

else. Between it and the bridge (where the towpath changes sides) there was once a boatbuilding yard, Bushell Brothers. The completion in 1934 of a wide-locked route almost to Birmingham inspired the building of wide-beamed craft and one of two built for the Grand Union, "Progress", started life here. But wide-boats were not a success; the canal's profile was rarely wide enough to allow two such craft to pass nor could they pass each other or a narrow boat in a tunnel. When Bushells eventually closed most of the traffic on the Wendover Arm ceased too.

E Little Tring

The wooded screen to the north hides a third reservoir, Tringford, which gives its name to the red-brick pumping station at the end of the navigable stretch of the arm. When the original feeders around Wendover proved totally inadequate, a reservoir was built first at Wilstone in 1802 (see below) then Marsworth (1806), Tringford (1816) and Startops End (1817); the pumping station provided the means by which water, mainly from Wilstone and Tringford, fed the summit level via the Wendover Arm. The stop lock nearby was built to overcome water loss on the arm due to a porous ground base but failed to alleviate the problem and it was abandoned in 1904. An abandonment of a different kind occurred in 1970 when, with the demise of the regular Midlands-South long-distance traffic, a number of erstwhile working boats were dumped here. All the boats ultimately survived and are 'back in service' in various capacities.

F Wilstone
The last 100yds. of the arm from the pumping station to Little Tring Bridge are derelict, though there are hopes that restoration through to Wendover can be achieved one day. The walk downhill affords views over the largest of the summit reservoirs and the first to be built, Wilstone. This too is a nature reserve - and a giant swimming pool - that can be reached via the track up to the left from the junction with the B489. Wilstone village is a quiet, friendly cluster; the local "Half Moon" declares its allegiance to an Aylesbury brewery, which is not surprising with the Aylesbury Arm literally round the corner.

G The Aylesbury Arm
Before joining the towpath stand on the bridge awhile and survey the scene: to the east the canal gradually falls away through lonely open farmland, to the west it curves gently up the north-western slopes of the Chilterns to join the main line of the Grand Union at Marsworth. The construction of the arm was delayed initially due to foreseeable water supply problems but, spurred on by a project that would have linked it, via the Thame Valley and the Thames, with the Wilts & Berks Canal near Abingdon, work went

ahead on the $6\frac{1}{2}$ miles and 16 locks and it opened in 1815. To minimise the demand for water the locks were built narrow and eight of these, the Marsworth flight, lift the canal up to the junction. It is a pretty flight punctuated with a lock-side cottage and even one odd chamber bearing the date 1894, though perhaps its best-known feature is the 2-lock staircase right at the top.

H The Icknield Way
Back on the main line the 2-arched bridge (No. 132) that comes into view ahead is no architectural quirk. In the 1830s, in order to speed up traffic and save water, the locks between Marsworth and Stoke Bruerne were duplicated by the construction of narrow chambers alongside. Most of these have now completely disappeared though at some locks it is still possible to find evidence of their existence - such as bridges with a second arch, the original entrance to the narrow lock. The road above takes the line of one of the major prehistoric routes of Britain, the Lower Icknield Way - the bridge at Bulbourne (No. 133) is known as Upper Icknield Way Bridge. The Way ran from near Brancaster, at the north-eastern corner of the Wash, at first southwards across Norfolk (the homeland of the Icenii), Suffolk and Cambridgeshire and then south-west along the northern edge of the Chilterns to the Thames Valley and on to Salisbury Plain. It was a route that the Romans exploited and one along which the Angles and Saxons established their settlements.

Sustenance
There are three good hostelries en route all of which serve good food: The "White Lion" (Marstons, Combes and Ruddles), the "Grand

Union Junction Arms" (Benskins) and the "Half Moon" (ABC). For a wider choice of food Tring is a little over a mile from the bridge at New Mill.

Counter Attractions
● Pitstone Windmill, Pitstone Green, nr Ivinghoe, Herts. Open Sun & Bank Hol., May-end Sept, 2.30pm-6pm. With timbers dating back as far as 1627, Pitstone post mill is the earliest windmill still standing. Nearby on Beacon Hill is an Iron Age hill fort.
● Zoological Museum, Akeman Street, Tring, Herts. Open Mon-Sat 10am-5pm, Sun 2pm-5pm. Admission free. Tel: Tring (044 282) 4181 ext 41. Founded on a bequest by the Rothschild family, the museum contains a large collection of rare moths, butterflies, crustacea and insects and is the world's premier reference source on fleas! The museum became affiliated to the British Museum in 1938.

Encore
The featured walk highlights the water problems of the summit level; a figure-of-8 walk further north from Wolverton puts the problems of crossing a river valley into perspective. The route, Wolverton-Cosgrove Lock-the derelict Stratford & Buckingham Canal-Old Stratford-the Great Ouse riverside walk-Wolverton, is some 8 miles long; it crosses the Great Ouse on Cosgrove Aqueduct and later goes under it alongside the riverside walk. Wolverton is served by excellent rail and bus connections.

Information
Tourist Information Centre, County Hall, Walton Street, Aylesbury, Bucks. Tel: Aylesbury (0296) 5000.

Walk 17

○

Grand Union/Oxford Canals
Northamptonshire

Braunston
7½ miles

The Walk

Braunston is the Valhalla of the working narrowboat and the archetypal canalside community of the Midland waterways system. Here the Grand Union on its way from London to Birmingham, meets with the Oxford Canal linking Coventry with Oxford and the River Thames, making Braunston a pivotal point for waterway traffic between north and south. This walk sets out to discover the obvious, and not so obvious, attractions of this famous canal centre. There are a number of 'kissing-gates' to be negotiated at the beginning and end of the walk so it would be wise to ensure that you are accompanied by a suitable companion.

Start Point

Braunston Village Green.
OS ref: SP 543663.

Access

Bus (Geoff Amos Coaches) to and from Rugby-Daventry Mon-Sat. Tel: Byfield (0327) 60522 or car - Braunston is on the A45, 17 miles west of Northampton. Kerbside parking is available along the High Street.

Directions

1 Proceed westwards along High Street.
2. Bear left through kissing-gate opposite church and cross field to main road.
3 Cross canal bridge 91 and go down on to the towpath. Proceeding to junction.
4 Bear left under bridge 93, cross bridge 95 and proceed to bridge 98.
5 Immediately under bridge 98, turn right and go up bank on to lane. Follow lane to left for a few hundred yards to view old route of Oxford Canal still in water.
6 Return to main canal, cross bridge 98 and follow lane as it bridges trackbed of old railway.
7 At crossroads, bear right past Wolfhampcote Hall following lane past church and across River Leam back to A45.
8 Join towpath again at bridge 91, this time turning right and continue along the towpath to the top of the flight.
9 Cross bridge 5 adjacent to top lock and turn left along lane passing "Admiral Nelson" pub.
10 Where road turns sharp right, go through

kissing-gate following path straight across field to next kissing-gate.
11 Take right hand path uphill through two more kissing-gates to return to the village green.

Points of Interest

A Braunston

Braunston sits demurely upon a ridge 400 feet up on the northern slopes of the Northamptonshire Uplands. Enclosed fields, still bearing the pattern of ridge and furrow, conjure ghosts from a medieval past. Walking along its High Street from The Green to the tall spired church, one encounters a mixture of stone and brickwork buildings, including a sail-less and now residential windmill and a 17th century manor house. At the foot of a long hill the A45 crosses the canal. This was the Chester road, turnpiked in 1720. The present route of the road dates from 1822 as part of Telford's Holyhead Road improvements. Earlier travellers were faced with a precipitous and twisting descent from Daventry known as an accident blackspot in coaching days.

B Braunston Junction

Spanned by twin-Horseley Ironworks bridges, this is Braunston's second waterway junction and dates from 1834. Prior to that the Oxford Canal, opened in 1778, and its meeting place with the Grand Junction Canal of 1769, lay to the east of bridge 91. The new route, carried upon an embankment and short aqueduct over the River Leam, was part of a series of new cuts made in the 1830s between Hawkesbury and Napton which shortened the Oxford Canal by some 15 miles between these two points. Beside the embankment are 'puddle beds' from which the clay used to line the canal bed was excavated. Between Braunston and Napton, the Oxford Canal shared this route from 1929 with the Grand Union Canal linking London with Birmingham. During the 1930s, the canal was dredged and concrete pilings inserted to strengthen the banks, and bridges were re-built to take wider craft which never materialised. An interesting phenomenon pertaining to this 'joint' section is that boats travelling southwards from the Midlands by way of the Grand Union or Oxford Canal and the River Thames would pass each other in opposite directions.

C Wolfhampcote

Just past bridge 97 the original route of the Oxford Canal lay at right angles to the present line: to the south its course is still in

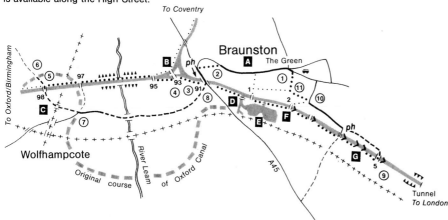

water. Nearby, the former Great Central Railway line from London Marylebone to the north once crossed the canal. Opened at the turn of the century, this was the last great main line of the Railway Age and ironically, it was the first major route to close as a result of the Beeching plan in 1966. The small wayside station of Braunston and Willoughby lay to the north across a massive, now demolished, viaduct over the Leam Valley. Another ghost line passes Wolfhampcote to the south, this was the London & North Western Railway's Weedon-Leamington branch opened in 1895. Wolfhampcote itself has earlier ghosts for it is a 'lost village', swept away during the enclosures of the 16th century. Only the old Hall and Church remain. The latter unloved, saved by the "Friends of Friendless Churches"; the key is available from the adjacent cottage should you wish to see its austere interior. An unfenced road leads across the Leam, a tributary of the Avon, back to Braunston past uneven ground where the good citizens of Wolfhampcote once had their houses.

D Braunston Wharf

Now a marina, the old wharf, approached down an arm spanned by another Horseley Ironworks bridge, was once part of the original Oxford Canal route which passed beneath the main road to continue its winding way to Wolfhampcote. But after the opening of the new route, Fellows, Morton & Clayton opened a depot here, replacing one originally operated by Pickfords, and this became the terminus for a daily steamboat service to and from London. In 1923, this arm was focus point of the strike by FMC boatmen campaigning for better conditions while faced with a reduction in wages. Matters came to a head when FMC management tried to have some of the 50 plus strike bound boats unloaded. Foiled by a blockade of boats, the company again tried to unload a couple of days later under the supervision of a detachment of Northamptonshire police. On this occasion, two boats were emptied, their cargoes continuing to Birmingham by lorry under police escort. Over 300 boatmen with their wives and children were involved in the dispute and it is difficult to associate this now peaceful arm with the angry scenes of 60 years ago. An

Brave smiles at Braunston during the Boat Strike in 1923.

adjacent dry dock belonged to the Nurser family whose high standard of boatbuilding and painting did much to burnish Braunston's reputation as a centre of narrowboating. During the Second World War the yard was taken over by Samuel Barlow, the coal carriers. In the 1960s, up until the end of commercial carrying on the Grand Union in 1970, the pristine pairs of Blue Line Boats also operated out of here.

E Reservoirs

Now connected to the canal and used as off-channel moorings, the reservoirs were provided by the Grand Junction Company in 1805 so that water coming down the locks could be returned to the summit by means of a beam pumping engine. To ensure that the Oxford Canal Company were not recipients of the downward flow, all but 6" of each lock was emptied by side paddles which drained the contents via a culvert to the reservoirs. The present tall-chimneyed engine house dates from 1895, the initials GJC and date being set into the brickwork. Nowadays, inevitably, the water is pumped electrically.

F Bottom Lock

If Braunston itself lies at the core of the Midland's canal system, then it is at Bottom Lock that the very heart of that world beats strongest. All around, the mellow brick of the South Midlands harmonises with the pre-dominant reds and greens of the narrowboat liveries. Cargoes may have long gone, but the tenacious spirit of the canals lives on here, amidst boatyards little changed from the heyday of Willow Wren and S. E. Barlow. Even a brassy new supermarket of a chandlery pumps fresh trade into the lively scene. The chamber itself is framed by a covered dry dock and a handsome row of canal cottages.

G Braunston Locks & Tunnel

Six locks carry the canal up some 40 feet to the western portal of Braunston Tunnel. By lock 3 is the "Admiral Nelson", a famous waterside hostelry where you can still learn the art of 'Northampton Skittles'. It was in the bar here that Leslie Morton, manager of the Willow Wren fleet, regularly held court during the twilight years of narrowboat carrying. Unfortunately, the towpath through to the tunnel is largely impassable. At over 2,000 yards it is a sizeable bore. According to legend, gypsies used to ambush the children leading the boat horses over the top whilst their parents 'legged' through below.

Sustenance

Braunston is well equipped with pubs and shops, though, surprisingly, there are no pleasant tearooms. If you are making up a picnic then don't fail to make for the village bakery. There are no facilities at Wolfhampcote.

Counter Attractions

Althorp Hall - 6 miles north-west of Northampton off A428 near East Haddon. Open all year round: Tue, Wed, Thur, Sat & Sun afternoons. Admission charge. Now famous family home of the Princess of Wales.

Encore

The northern section of the Oxford Canal between Braunston and Hawkesbury on the outskirts of Coventry, is marred by many sections of poorly maintained towpath; a sad state of affairs, for this is an often lovely canal. However, if you are prepared to juggle with local buses, an interesting walk can be made between Hillmorton and Newbold. For this it would be best to make Rugby your start point. Catch a bus out to Hillmorton (Midland Red South, Tel: Rugby (0788) 76090 for details), walk northwards to Newbold and return to Rugby by Midland Red again. Things to see include Hillmorton's flight of 3 duplicated locks and the attractive maintenance yard, the remains of old arms dating from the 'straightening' of the canal, minor aqueducts spanning the rivers Avon and Swift and, by following a path through the churchyard at Newbold, the abandoned portal of the original Newbold Tunnel.

Information

Tourist Information Centre, Rugby Library, Rugby. Tel: Rugby (0788) 71813.

Walk 18 ☒

Grand Union (Leicester Section)

Leicestershire

Foxton - Kibworth   8 miles

The Walk

Contemplated from the viewpoint of the pleasure boating era, the 'Leicester Section' of the Grand Union Canal generally carries such epithets as: remote, winding, forgotten. Yet, it had the potential to be a heavily used commercial waterway if its original concept as a broad beam link between London and the East Midlands had ever come to fruition. For reasons touched on below, such developments never accrued and the canal was abandoned to a long diminuendo of falling trade, despite the brave but brief heyday of the astonishing Foxton Inclined Plane; highlight of this gentle exploration of the mellow Shires.

Start Point

Kibworth Beauchamp.
OS ref: SP 683938.

Access

Bus (Midland Fox offer a daily service connecting with Leicester and Market Harborough. Tel: Leicester (0533) 29161) and car - Kibworth Beauchamp lies just off the A6, 10 miles south-east of Leicester. There is plenty of kerbside parking available adjacent to "The Square".

Directions

1 Catch one of the 'Fox Cub' mini-bus services from "The Square", Kibworth to Foxton, asking the driver to drop you by Foxton Church. The Fox Cubs don't run on Sundays and you should check departure times on Market Harborough (0858) 65319 as the service is infrequent and liable to local revision.
2 Alight at Foxton Church. Go up the hill and turn right on to lane signposted "Foxton Boat Services", proceeding 1/3 mile to the canal.
3 Cross bridge over canal arm and turn left along 'Lift Trail'.
4 After crossing top lock, turn right down the flight to junction.

5 Cross roving bridge 62 and proceed northwards on towpath for 4 miles to Saddington Tunnel.

6 Saddington Tunnel has no towpath so follow the horsepath across the top of the hill. The path is clearly defined, running between high hedgerows and crossing a minor road.

7 Regain towpath (which has changed sides) and proceed 1½ miles to bridge 75.

8 Leave towpath through gate and turn right over bridge along minor road for 1 mile.

9 Immediately beyond junction of minor roads, cross fence into field on right, proceeding to stile by houses at the far side of the field.

10 Go through alley between houses and proceed down Hall Close to the A6, turning right along pavement.

11 Turn right down alley, cross Hillcrest Avenue and continue down path over railway.

12 Follow School Road to High Street and turn left back to "The Square".

Points of Interest

A Foxton's Waterways

Foxton is so famous for its locks and inclined plane that its situation at a junction of independently promoted canals is often overlooked. In fact, Foxton wasn't included on the inland waterways map until 1809 with the final push southwards to Market Harborough of the Leicestershire & Northamptonshire Union Canal. This penurious company had been founded in 1793 with an ambitious proposal to link Leicester with Northampton, but the project was under-capitalised and progress fell short at Debdale (of which more anon). Foxton became a canal junction in 1814 with the arrival of the 'Old Grand Union Canal's' route from the Grand Junction Canal at Norton which gave the East Midlands a direct link with London for the first time. Both canals were absorbed into the Grand Junction in 1894, the latter becoming what we now know as the Grand Union in 1929.

B Inclined Plane

For reasons best known to themselves the 'Old Grand Union Company' built the 23 mile Norton Junction-Foxton route to a 7 feet 'narrow gauge', thus restricting through traffic between the wide beam Leicestershire & Northamptonshire Union and Grand Junction canals to narrow gauge craft. By the turn of the 19th century, the route's prime users, Fellows, Morton & Clayton, were agitating for improvements to the bottle-neck staircase flights at Foxton and Watford. In a brave

response, the route's new owners, the Grand Junction Canal, proposed a boat lift, or more properly, inclined plane, to bypass both flights. The Foxton inclined Plane was constructed first and opened in 1900. It consisted of two counterbalanced caissons mounted on sets of wheels running upon ex-railway lines laid on a 1 in 4 slope. Haulage ropes, connected to winding drums driven by a steam engine, provided the impetus by which boats were carried from the summit level at 412 feet to the old Leicestershire & Northamptonshire Union route 75 feet below. Each tank could accommodate a pair of narrowboats or a wide beam barge. Unhappily, this ambitious scheme was not rewarded by an upsurge in traffic. The

scheme for a similar structure at Watford was put aside. It was soon found to be uneconomic to maintain the inclined plane and keep the engine in steam when faced with the sporadic pattern of boat movements. So Foxton Inclined Plane was closed in November 1910. The machinery was maintained throughout the First World War

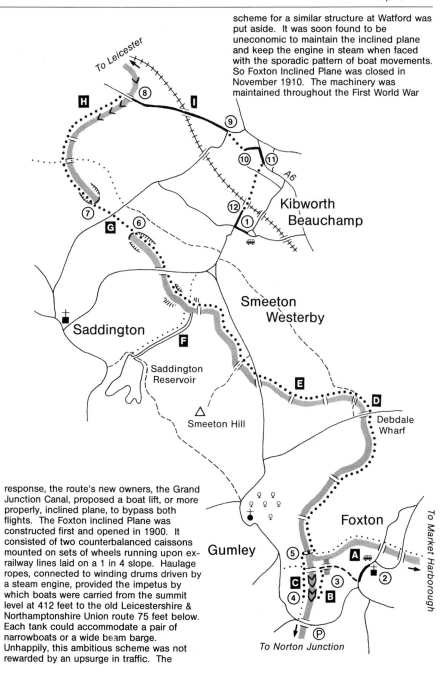

but never used and eventually the structure was dismantled in the 1920s. For nearly 60 years, nature was allowed to reclaim the raw remains of the slope, but in 1980 a trust was formed with the intention of rebuilding the inclined plane. Volunteers have painstakingly cleared the site to reveal much of industrial archaeological interest. They are currently reconstructing the old boilerhouse as a museum. As a second stage, they intend to re-water the upper approach arm. Then finally will come the ambitious reconstruction attempt.

C Foxton Locks

Even without the poignant juxtaposition of the disused inclined plane, Foxton Locks would be a famous waterway feature; rarely is such an abrupt canal gradient encountered. The 10 chambers are grouped in 2 staircases of 5, an arrangement which only served to exacerbate delays to working boats. Indeed, queues can still occur here during the cruising season when delays of up to 4 hours are not unknown. Again, in the 1930s, the newly formed Grand Union Canal Company considered widening the locks here and at Watford to put the East Midlands on the 'wide beam' map. But, unlike the mainline to Birmingham, the plan was never formulated and trade continued to diminish, departing the route altogether by 1956, apart from a brief revival by the local Leicester firm of Seymour Roseblade who, in 1963, carried timber from Wisbech to Leicester via the River Nene and Grand Union Canal.

D Debdale Wharf

The canal to Leicester heads due north from Foxton with the village of Gumley on a shallow rise to the west. Passing a low cutting, bordered by trees, it reaches Debdale Wharf. Here, bereft of capital, construction southwards of the Leicestershire & North-amptonshire Union Canal was halted for a dozen years from 1797. A subtle clue to this hiatus can be found in the peculiar winding hole arrangement; unorthodoxly eating out of the towpath side of the canal. Here stood all the usual appendages of an inland waterway terminus. Horsedrawn wagons threaded their way down deep-rutted lanes with goods from Market Harborough and further afield destined for Leicester and Nottingham. Not surprisingly, there was a well patronised ale-house, now relegated to farm use. Somehow, even the establishment of a hireboat base, albeit largely hidden behind a belt of trees, has failed to expunge all the ghosts from Debdale Wharf.

E Bridges

Twisting eastwards, the canal winds about the gentle slopes of Smeeton Hill (515 ft.); as bucolic a waterway as you are likely to find. The mellow shires extend to their undemonstrative horizons. High steeples and squat towers of distant village churches punctuate the skyline. One anticipates the thunder of the Fernie Hunt materialising over some adjacent brow. An astonishing feature of this canal is the wide variety in style and construction of its over-bridges. It is almost as though this length was used in some madcap competition for itinerant bridge designers of reduced circumstances. Most extravagant of all is bridge 66, which has its twin over the basin at the foot of the inclined plane back at Foxton. As you proceed, red-brick, blue-brick, stone, iron and concrete are all in evidence.

F Saddington Reservoir

At a particularly tortuous section of canal, the narrow feeder channel from Saddington Reservoir makes an unobtrusive entrance. The reservoir was a contemporary of the canal and was built to supply the summit with water. A footpath, reached through the adjoining aqueduct, runs between Mowsley Brook and the feeder to the banks of the reservoir where sailing takes place. The canal curves round upon a high embankment which burst in 1865 following an accumulation of heavy rains in the reservoir. A boatman, moored for the night, became aware of his boats being drawn towards a huge breach but managed to secure his craft and raise the alarm. The floodwater reached Kibworth somewhat more rapidly than you will!

G Saddington Tunnel

More trouble befell the canal in 1917 when bridge 72 collapsed during a snowstorm; the reconstructed bridge is of stone with a skew blue-brick under-arch. An insubstantial cutting leads to the southern blue-brick portal of Saddington Tunnel, 882 yds. long. As you trudge the narrow-hedged corridor over the top, it is worth considering something of the eventful history of the tunnel. During construction it was found to be misaligned and in later years was twice rebuilt; as witnessed by dates inscribed on the southern portal. During the 1920s, an FMC steamer sank inside the tunnel after colliding with a submerged pile. Its cargo of chemicals was entirely lost. The northern portal is of red brick!

H Kibworth Locks

Passing the largely industrial village of Fleckney, the canal turns eastwards again and begins to descend into the valley of the River Sence. No trace remains on the opposite bank from the towpath, south of bridge 74, of an erstwhile boathouse belonging to one Percy Preston, where small pleasure boats could be hired for recreation. At the top lock, the keeper's house dates from 1923, replacing an earlier building which predated the canal. The wide beam lock chamber is a taunting reminder of the mixed-gauge which prevented the route from realising its full traffic potential. A handsome GJC cast iron mile post quotes 13 miles to Leicester. The third chamber down is known as Taylor's Lock, after the family who owned the now boarded up farmhouse which presides gloomily over the lock. In better days, as a sideline, the farmer brewed ale for the boatmen and this was known as the "Navigation Inn".

I The Railway

When we researched this walk, the railway was undergoing change and another traditional scene was being swept away as a group of semaphor signals were usurped by new multiple aspect colour lights. One imagines that even the Midland Railway signal box will have been demolished before many of you follow in our footsteps. The line itself continues to flourish though, as South Yorkshire's and the East Midlands' link with London St. Pancras, and where once the 'Crimson Ramblers' ran, and later the 'Jubilees', now inter-city 125s streak sonorously by, doing a 'ton' with ease. And Kibworth, when finally you reach it, through housing estates and down alley-ways, is a pleasantly busy little place, fittingly friendly for this particular journey's end.

Sustenance

"Bridge 61" at Foxton Junction is a freehouse offering bar meals; outside there is a garden and inside old photographs of the canal decorate the bar. Kibworth has a fish & chip bar and numerous shops and pubs.

Counter Attractions

Victorian Butchers, Gumley - $\frac{1}{2}$ mile west of Foxton. Open Mon-Fri, 12.30-5.00pm, Sun & Bank Hols. 11.30-dusk. Admission by donation. Fascinating little village museum.

Encore

This walk could be extended by 5 miles to include the Market Harborough arm, scene of the Inland Waterway Association's first National Boat Rally in 1950; a regular Midland Fox bus service operates between Kibworth and Market Harborough. A more sporadic service links Market Harborough with Husbands Bosworth, a village on the A427, between which and Foxton, the canal flows through some particularly attractive countryside; so careful consideration of bus timetables could produce an appealing 10 mile walk between Husbands Bosworth and Market Harborough, complementing that featured here. To the north of Leicester, the Soar navigation is generally regarded as an integral part of the 'Leicester Line', but it is currently subject to considerable engineering works as the Severn Trent Water Authority grapple with the river's propensity for sudden violent flooding. Only southwards from

Cossington Lock, adjacent to the village of Rothley on the A6, towards Leicester is the river likely to remain unaltered in the foreseeable future. This 6 mile section, though not always exactly picturesque, is used in part by the only regular narrowboat commercial traffic remaining in the whole country. A small fleet of narrowboats carry sand and gravel in the vicinity of Thurmast and, if you are at all interested in traditional working craft, this walk is worthwhile for that reason alone. A frequent Midland Red bus service links Leicester with Rothley and the towpath is in good condition throughout.

Information

Tourist Information Centre, 12 Bishop Street, Leicester. Tel: Leicester (0533) 556699.

Walk 19

Huddersfield Narrow Canal
Yorkshire

Diggle - Greenfield   3 miles

The Walk

Any walk in Yorkshire is a delight and this walk of a little less than three miles, is no exception. Feet will not suffer, but eyes will need to be alert as the story of this, the third and shortest of the trans-Pennine routes, unfolds. As with its western neighbour, the Rochdale Canal (see Walk 33), the restoration work continues; it is, therefore, a walk that will change over the years as gradually the boater too begins to share in its delights. The villages along the Valley of the Tame are largely creations of the Industrial Revolution; the coming of the canal was thus for this valley the beginning of the transformation.

Start Point

Greenfield Station.
OS ref: SD 992047.

Access

Bus, train and car. Greenfield Station is on the Manchester-Huddersfield-Leeds line and has a regular service; it is also on a direct

bus route from Oldham and Manchester. Rail enquiries from 061-832 8353; bus details from 061-226 8181.

Directions

1 Catch a bus to Diggle (service 431) from the A670 above Greenfield Station.
2 Alight at the terminus and view the Old Wharf area.
3 Retrace the bus route across the bridge, viewing the railway tunnels en route, and follow the road round to the left.
4 Turn left off the road by the telephone box towards the mouth of Standedge Tunnel and join the right hand path along the canal (the towpath is on the other side).
5 Pass under the canal to the towpath just before lock 30W.
6 Leave the path at Woolroad, crossing this diagonally to where the canal reappears by the canopied warehouse, rejoin the towpath (it is culverted under Brownhill Bridge).
7 Stop at Brownhill Visitor Centre.

8 Rejoin the towpath, remaining on it (except where it is clear a road has to be crossed or it changes sides) as far as the A635.
9 Leave the towpath and walk up the hill to the station (the road bears sharp left and then sharper right).

Points of Interest

A The Huddersfield Narrow Canal

On a map the logic of the Huddersfield Narrow Canal is inescapable: a direct 20 mile link between Sir John Ramsden's Canal at Huddersfield and the Ashton Canal at Dukinfield. But the reality is less simple, for the canal aggressively pierces the uncompromising Pennine terrain by two long ladders of narrow locks, 74 in all, that climb from east and west to the highest canal summit in England, 645 feet above sea level. Work began on the canal in 1794 and took some 17 years to complete, due largely to that summit level which consisted almost in its entirety of the 5,477 yard Standedge Tunnel, Britain's longest canal tunnel.

B Standedge Tunnel

The story of the Huddersfield Narrow and that of Standedge Tunnel go hand in hand. Difficulties of construction and the related problem of finance coupled with a succession of contractors resulted in delays and even talks of abandonment until, on 4th April, 1811, a 10,000 strong crowd assembled at the Diggle end of the official opening. The euphoria of that day did not pay a dividend to the canal's shareholders for a further 13 years for, like the other trans-Pennine canals, the bulk of the traffic tended not to be across the summit level and the Rochdale (its nearest competitor) had the distinct advantage of broad, full-length locks and no 3 mile subterranean 'adventure'. Nothing, however, can detract from the remarkable engineering feat exemplified in the completion of such a tunnel. There was no towpath and boats had to be 'legged' through, not an easy task because of the irregular form of the tunnel which was largely cut through rock, being lined only where this gave way to unstable shale. Horses were led over the top via Boat Lane which leads up past the side of "The Diggle Hotel", directly opposite the bus terminus. The last working boat is said to have passed through Standedge in 1921; it was officially closed in 1944 though until 1967 charter trips were allowed inside - access now is limited to maintenance work.

C The Railway Tunnels

The area around the bus terminus is

alongside the original line of the canal to and from Standedge before the coming of the railway and its tunnels. Two sections of this original course can still be seen: the first is at the edge of the track leading to the terminus where a long stone wall marks the original wharves and basins; the second is behind the walls of the old aqueduct and the upstream side of Diggle Brook. Three railway tunnels were cut through the Standedge watershed, two single line bores in 1849 and 1871 and a double line bore in 1894. It was during the construction of the first of these to the east of the canal for the Huddersfield & Manchester Railway that the cut was diverted to run more to the west (the original tunnel entrance was close to the present mouths of the railway tunnels). The 1871 tunnel for the then LNWR was to the east of the first and, therefore, did not affect the canal, but the double bore was to the west and had to be brought across the (already) diverted line of the canal on an S-shaped curve. This involved extending the canal tunnel by 221 yards - thus the date of 1893 on a southern portal.

D Diggle
Standing back from the tunnels' portals it is easy to imagine the busy scene here, particularly with steam trains belching their way in and out of the hillside, their noisy passing echoing forth from the canal tunnel. Diggle once had a busy station which was

elevated to infamy in 1823 when a double-headed express from Leeds shot out of Standedge and straight into the back of a stationary goods train at the station; four people died in the accident. Down below to the right stood Diggle Mill which once boasted Britain's second largest waterwheel. The 64ft. 8in. waterwheel incorporated 192 buckets each with a capacity of 37 gallons, but just why such a gigantic supplier of power was required is unclear. The mill was owned and operated by one William Broadbent, who, being blind, never actually saw this incredible provider of his livelihood. Heading south-west from Standedge, the canal almost immediately crosses Diggle Brook before swinging to the right where its old line is rejoined above the first of the locks, 32W, down to Dukinfield.

E Dobcross Loomworks
Like many of the walk's 13 locks, 32W's chamber has been partially infilled and concreted, but the 9 lock flight down to Woolroad has its own uniqueness in that seemingly the locks had single gates top and bottom and it was worked from the offside. The landscaped recreational area to the left of the next lock started life as a blot on the landscape, being a former tunnel spoilheap - cross-passages to the canal tunnel facilitated excavation of the railway tunnels. The unusual, but by no means out of place, gothic-style clock tower to the west is the office building of what was originally Dobcross Loomworks - now used for the manufacture of pallets. It is an impressive complex and typifies that Victorian compromise between utility and elegance. A direct branch line to the works from Diggle Station crossed the canal here but is now disused.

F Woolroad
There is a beauty in the wildness of this Yorkshire landscape - even the locks in their various guises assert themselves in this rugged tapestry. The milepost at lock 26W indicates that it is 12 miles to Huddersfield, while across the valley the old Woolroad (A670) heads down the valley. It was along this road that goods were taken between the Tame and the Colne valleys in the 11 years from the canal's completion thus far and the opening of Standedge Tunnel. "The Navigation Inn" and its attendant weavers' cottages look across the canal to where, below lock 25W, there was once a boat repair yard and dry dock. Across Woolroad - under which the canal is piped - is a transshipment warehouse and wharf, the sole surviving building, with its cantilevered roof belying the bustling activity that was its birthright.

G 'Old Sag'
The canal is culverted again before Brownhill Bridge but reappears to enhance a different scene. On the left is the Brownhill Visitor Centre, ahead lies the restored Lime Kiln Lock (23W), built into an aqueduct crossing the Tame and, dominating it all, the multi-arched Saddleworth Viaduct. The Brownhill Centre is a must for a break and therein is a mine of information and ever-changing exhibitions. The restored lock is one of two between Diggle and Greenfield and is largely due to the persistence of the Huddersfield Canal Society who operate a trip boat, named "The Benjamin Outram" after the canal's engineer, along this stretch. The lock sits

To Huddersfield
Standedge Tunnels
C Boat Lane
④
Diggle **B** ③
D ㉕②
Lock 32W
A
A670 ⑤
Lock 30W
E
Lock 28W
Dobcross
Lock 24W
F ⑥
⑦
G Saddleworth
Viaduct
⑧
Lock 22W
Uppermill
River
Lock 21W **H** Tame
A670
Lock 20W
Greenfield ① **I**
⑨
To Dukinfield

Over and under - Lime Kiln Lock on the Huddersfield Narrow Canal.

along 'Old Sag', a short stone aqueduct over the Tame that is known for the 'dip' in its arch - best appreciated by scrambling down the bank between lock and viaduct. The viaduct itself is a truly magnificent structure. It was erected in the late 1840s and, in addition to being on the radius, contains a number of skew arches - one of which spans the canal. For a time, railings were erected along the edge following an incident on Christmas Eve in 1866, when a man stepped off the train which had overshot Saddleworth Station, and fell to his death.

H Uppermill
The excitement over, the canal now enters a more secluded and increasingly wooded stretch before the restored Dungebooth Lock and Uppermill. Across to the east, Buckley New Mill straddles the wandering Tame before it swings alongside the canal, its weir crossed by stepping stones. Uppermill is just around the corner and under Cloggers Knoll Bridge which, like many on the canal, is without a towpath - it changes sides here anyway. In the 19th century some bridges at Stalybridge were provided with towpaths after local residents complained about the obstruction caused by towropes. There are two wharves at Uppermill alongside what is now the car park for the museum; one, Albert Wharf, dealt in coal while Victoria Wharf served Victoria Mill, a cotton spinning mill that stood where the car park now is - the museum being its former gassing room. All in all it is a superb setting and invites further exploration.

I Greenfield
The right bank remains wooded as the unrestored lock 21W and Oldham Road necessitate crossing a road where the towpath reverts back to the left; here too the 13 mile marker is secreted below the wall. The valley sides become steeper and the Tame comes in closer and runs parallel to the canal. Another weir expands the river over the goit that took water down to Frenches Mill (on the left after the next lock) - the first fulling mill in Saddleworth and later a dyeworks. Tastefully renovated cottages alongside lock 20W still bear the grooves on their corner stones from many years of rubbing towropes. Another group of cottages is viewable from the Chew Valley Road Bridge where we leave the canal. These are across

on the offside behind what was a coal wharf although it started life as workshops, pub and stables, the latter being the tall isolated building furthest away.

Sustenance

"The Diggle Hotel" right at the beginning of the walk sells real ale and does good food - what more could you ask? But there are other hostelries en route and "The Navigation Inn" on Woolroad can be recommended particularly for its food. Uppermill too has much on offer including several take-aways.

Counter Attractions

● Saddleworth Museum, Uppermill, nr Oldham, Manchester. Open Sat-Sun 2pm-5pm, Mon-Tues, Thurs-Fri 1.15pm-5pm, Wed 10am-5pm. Admission charge. Tel: Saddleworth (044 77) 4093. A clothier's cottage, working woollen mill gallery, Victorian rooms, vintage cars, bikes and art exhibitions on display in this former woollen mill.
● Tunnel End Canal & Countryside Centre, Waters Road, Marsden, Yorkshire. Open Easter-end Sept, Tues-Sun, 11am-5pm; Oct-Easter Tues-Fri, 11am-4pm (Sat and Sun 4.30pm). No admission charge. Tel: Huddersfield (0484) 846062. Set in a striking location by the Standedge Tunnels, two converted cottages house an interpretative centre of canal history; there are also features on the natural history of Marsden Moor.

Encore

Having explored the southern end of Standedge Tunnel, it would seem logical to want to have a look at the Marsden end. It can be approached from Diggle by walking the 3 miles via Boat Lane or from Marsden Station; alternatively the $3^{1}/_{2}$ mile walk along Colne Valley from Slaithwaith to Marsden not only takes in the tunnel but also some of the most dramatic of Pennine scenery. (A permanent exhibition on the canal and its environment is featured at the Tunnel End Centre). The 365 bus service links Huddersfield and Oldham via Slaithwaith and Marsden while the 350/1/2 services terminate at Marsden. Tel: Huddersfield (0484) 26313.

Information

Tourist Information Centre, 84 Union Street, Oldham, Greater Manchester. Tel: 061-678 4654.

Walk 20

Kennet & Avon Canal

Berkshire

Aldermaston - Newbury   9 miles

The Walk

Over the next few years this walk, perhaps more than any other in this book, will change almost monthly as the locks and the 'fixed' bridges are gradually restored and access to Newbury from the Thames is again a reality. At present it starts and finishes with restored locks between which almost every stage of dereliction and reclamation can be seen. But it is not only about locks and bridges, for delightfully natural river stretches and the picture-postcard setting of waterside Newbury assure a varied walk alongside what Tom Rolt described as a navigation that, "might have been deliberately laid out to create the maximum difficulty for the navigator".

Start Point

Newbury Railway Station.
OS ref: SU 472667.

Access

Bus, train and car. Newbury is on the main London-Plymouth line and also has good bus connections. Rail timetable information is available on Reading (0734) 595911, bus details from Newbury (0635) 40743. Newbury Station has a good car park.

Directions

1 Catch a train to Aldermaston.
2 Cross the station footbridge and proceed to the main road via the car park and turn left.
3 Join the towpath by turning right, having crossed the lift bridge, and remain on it for $8^{1}/_{2}$ miles until Newbury Bridge.
4 Leave the towpath at Newbury Bridge, cross the main road and proceed down the pathway opposite which goes round to the left and joins the towpath again.
5 Proceed along the towpath to West Mills Swing Bridge and cross it.
6 Turn left off the swing bridge and return to

the main road along the south side of the river.
7 Cross the main road into Wharf Street and then turn right almost immediately and follow the road signs back to the station.

Points of Interest

A The Kennet Navigation

Since the 13th century the river Kennet had been navigable from its junction with the Thames for about a mile, but it was not until the early 18th century that Parliament approved a plan to create an $18^{1}/_{2}$ mile navigable waterway between Reading and Newbury by cutting $11^{1}/_{2}$ miles of new canal and constructing 20 turf-sided locks. The prospect of such a navigation did not please everyone, especially in the Reading area where in 1720, while work was well under way, an attempt was made to sabotage the works. Particularly displeased were mill owners of the Kennet valley who were dependent on a free flow of water, and Reading barge-men who saw the centre of distribution moving upstream to Newbury. Despite these difficulties the works were completed in 1723. Towards the end of the century the Kennet & Avon Canal project got under way to link the Kennet with the navigable Avon at Bath. As a direct result of this the Kennet & Avon Canal Company bought the navigation in 1812.

B Aldermaston Wharf

For most people Aldermaston means CND and the annual Easter marches. Such means of mass destruction contrast sharply with the peace, almost isolation, of the canal at Aldermaston Wharf. (The village itself and its cluster of olde worlde houses is over a mile away and is easily reached from Froude's Swing Bridge). For years one of the major obstacles to any hope of re-establishing through-navigation was the 'fixed' Aldermaston Bridge; the road crossing is a busy one and so a hydraulically operated

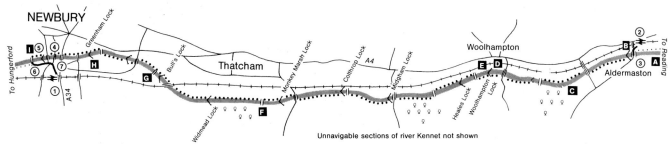

Unnavigable sections of river Kennet not shown

replacement was installed. Rebuilding of the lock was completed in 1985, its scalloped brick chamber deserving of a Design Centre Award. Above the lock a truncated arm branches off towards the railway to the north; this dates from the 1850s when the GWR, by then owners of the navigation, established an interchange point between railway and canal.

C The River Kennet
The generally rural aspect of the lock cut above Aldermaston - known as Salmon's Cut, soon takes on a green overcoat as the river Kennet rejoins the navigation on the left. Indeed the river channel is navigable for about 1/3 mile to Aldermaston Mill, to which barges used to carry corn. Most of the mills that worked the Kennet valley are no more. Those that remain are usually private residences, the exception being Aldermaston which is available for private functions. There is no mistaking the natural meanderings of the Kennet but it is to be a short-lived rendezvous for it is soon off again on its incessant wanderings to the south of Woolhampton.

D The Last Line of Defence?
Just before Woolhampton (Free) Wharf and Lock stands one of many World War II pillboxes that are a feature of the canal throughout Berkshire. The Kennet & Avon was regarded as a natural anti-tank defence line and so pill-boxes were strategically placed alongside its banks to thwart the invading Hun. In some cases, such as at the next lock, Heales, they were erected so close to the lock-gates that the balance beams had to be shortened. Such was the inaccessibility of some of the sites that the materials were carried by water.

E Turf-sided Locks
Paradoxically Midgham Station is at

Woolhampton, the name having been changed by the GWR to avoid confusion with Wolverhampton. Woolhampton Lock is where it should be and undergoing restoration but Heale's Lock, a little over 1/2 mile away, remains one of the few turf-sided locks on the navigation. These were constructed of timber to about 2ft above the lock's lower level and then the turfed sides sloped away at an angle of about 45°; they were also longer and wider than the brick chambers that gradually replaced them. Sadly it seems that these unique locks will all be replaced, though between Reading and Aldermaston the turf-sided lock is still successfully in use.

F The Long Cut
With the Kennet off on its wanderings, the canalised navigation heads through partially wooded, often windswept, countryside. The chimney of Colthrop Paper Mill is an approaching landmark on the skyline. The water meadows to the north recall a proposal that, had it been implemented, would have made this walk impossible. In 1892 a plan to solve London's water needs was mooted - the idea was to construct a gigantic reservoir in the Kennet valley by creating a lake from about a mile east of Newbury to Aldermaston and submerging the villages of Woolhampton and Aldermaston, several mills and parts of the A4, the railway and the canal! A tidy wharfside community precedes Colthrop Lock and a sudden - and extensive - outburst of industry in the form of Colthrop Mill, now part of the Reed Group. Branches of the river weave in and out of the cut before the turf-sided Monkey Marsh Lock and the beginning of a mile-long dead straight Long Cut to another similar lock at Widmead. Open pastures to the south become gradually wooded whilst opposite, the water meadows merge with Thatcham Marshes, once osier beds and now an important ecological site. Like most of the 'swing' bridges from Aldermaston, Long Cut Swing Bridge has spent most of the recent past in the 'fixed'

position - enough to make the inventor of the ball-bearing and architect of the Kennet & Avon Canal, John Rennie, turn in his grave. A little over a mile to the south of the Long Cut is another focus of anti-nuclear protest, the controversial Greenham Common Airfield.

G Bull's Lock
For some time the short burst of river above Widmead Lock has been the limit of navigation from Crofton in the west. But the next lock, Bull's, has an even more important claim to fame, for it was the first - and last - to be restored by volunteer labour. But first the railway crosses the river which in turn is off to the north this time. The whole setting, with canal, river and railway clustered around the first signs of Newbury's industrial outskirts is enhanced by what must be one of the most attractive swing-bridges on the navigation.

H Of Mills and Coat
Despite the modern road bridge above Bull's, all is not lost for one of the navigation's most picturesque settings is just ahead. No, it's not the lock, which, being an unfortunate mix of concrete and steel piling, is on the ugly side of ordinary; but alongside the lock to the north is Ham Mill, a corn mill before its conversion to a private residence, above which the Kennet reappears; it is a delightful setting. Newbury's influence is ever-increasing; Whitehouse Wharf is followed by railway abutments that once carried the Didcot, Newbury and Southampton Railway and Greenham Lock. A backwater of the river to the south leads to Greenham Mill which, as a cloth mill, was involved in 1811 in the so-called 'Newbury Coat' wager. In order to bolster confidence in the local cloth-making industry (in the face of northern competition) Sir John Throckmorton wagered 1000 guineas that he would sit down to dinner at 8pm wearing a coat the wool for which was still on the back of a sheep at 5am. It was at Greenham Mill that the wool was spun; the coat was then made in Newbury and Sir John was putting it on with 40 minutes to spare . . .

unimpressed the cloth trade continued to decline. (An exhibition on the 'Newbury Coat' features in the local museum).

I Waterside Newbury
Between river and canal is Greenham island and its attendant moorings. As the two merge the A34 crosses the navigation; the construction of the bridge in 1965 destroyed most of what was left of the original Kennet Navigation's terminal wharves, its buildings and basins now long gone. Beyond, the towpath opens out to a fine landscaped riverside walk, indeed the next bridge, a 'temporary' war-time construction, gives the walker considerably more headroom than the boater. The attractive single-arched stone and brick balustraded bridge is the gateway to the Kennet & Avon Canal, work on which began from Newbury Wharf in 1794. The bridge predates the extension of the navigation and therefore has no towpath. This caused problems for horse-drawn boats, particularly so as it was forbidden for horses to haul across the street above - see the notice by the lock-keeper's cottage. Working upstream was particularly difficult here and for this purpose a special float used to hang outside the same cottage. With the barge tied up below the lock, the horse would be unhitched and led across to the Reading side of the bridge from where the float (attached to the horse via a long line) would be allowed to drift back under the bridge to the waiting barge. Working downstream was less of a problem as the flow and the momentum would keep the boat going under the bridge. The area around Newbury Lock, flanked by two arteries of the river, is enhanced by the 16th century St. Nicholas Church and an attractive assortment of red-brick cottages: an almost idyllic waterways setting. The lock itself, the first of the Kennet & Avon *Canal,* has unusual ground paddles, unusual that is for the south, for such jack or slide cloughs are a common feature of the Leeds & Liverpool Canal. The walk along to the swing bridge and back along the other side includes a mixture of old restored cottages and new housing that is not out of place - both old and new, some of which stand on the site of the Town Mill, create a picturesque backdrop to this marvellous waterway.

Sustenance

There are pubs aplenty from start to finish, most of which also serve food. If it's good food you want then pop into Moreda's Gourmet (at the entrance to the Kennet Centre on the way back to the station) for

sandwiches with such exotic fillings as spiced beef and sugar baked ham, or alternatively try some hare pie or a mussel and prawn pasty.

Counter Attractions

● Newbury District Museum, Wharf Road, Newbury, Berks. Open during normal shopping hours - EC Wed. No admission charge. Tel: Newbury (0635) 30267. The building itself is a museum piece - built in 1626 as a cloth weaving workshop. Displays trace Newbury's past from prehistoric times to present day. Models illustrate the Battles of Newbury.
● Littlecote House, nr Hungerford, Wilts. Open Apr-Sept, Sat & Sun, 2pm-6pm; also weekdays Jul-Sept, 2pm-5pm. Admission charge. Tel: Hungerford (0488) 82170. Gabled Elizabethan manor house with a splendid great hall displaying great Cromwellian armour amid excellent oak panelling and furniture. In the park next to the Kennet are excavations of a Roman Villa and the fully restored Orpheus mosaic.

Encore

There is little natural water in Wiltshire's chalk downs - the exception is Wilton Water which explains the siting of Crofton Pumping Station and the Kennet & Avon's short 3 mile summit level. A 6½ mile circular walk from Great Bedwyn via Castle Copse, Bedwyn Brail, Wilton Windmill, Wilton Water, Crofton and back along the canal not only puts the water supply problem into perspective but also touches on one of the last obstacles to through navigation, the 6-lock Crofton flight. Crofton Pumping Station houses the oldest working steam engine in the world, a 1812 Boulton & Watt. Details of 'steaming' weekends from Marlborough (0672) 810575. Great Bedwyn Station is on the same line as Newbury and Aldermaston.

Information

Tourist Information Centre, Newbury District Museum, The Wharf, Newbury, Berks. Tel: Newbury (0635) 30267.

Walk 21

Kennet & Avon Canal
Wiltshire/Avon

Bradford on Avon - Bath   **11 miles**

The Walk

This is a walk along part of the restored western end of the Kennet & Avon Canal that combines breathtaking scenery with spectacular engineering. It starts in the old wool town of Bradford-on-Avon and heads west into the Wiltshire countryside to cross the Avon twice, at Avoncliff and Dundas, on two majestic aqueducts; the sylvan Limpley Stoke valley ends at Bathampton, beyond which is the almost secret water-world of Sydney Gardens and finally the serenity of classical Bath . . . and as a bonus there's even a 'house of ill-repute' and a hidden coin cache.

Start Point

Bath Railway Station.
OS ref: ST 753644.

Access

Bus, train and car. Bath has excellent bus and rail connections - only a few hundred yards separate the two stations. Details from Bath (0225) 63075 (rail) and Bath (0225) 64446 (bus); there is a convenient multi-storey car park by the bus station.

Directions

1 Catch a train to Bradford-on-Avon.
2 Leave the station area and turn right at the main road.
3 Keep right at the fork, following the signs to Frome - Bradford Lock Bridge is about 250 yds. further on. View Bradford Lock and Wharf from the bridge.
4 Retrace your steps and turn left by the side of the "Canal Tavern" to join the towpath, remaining on this until Avoncliff Aqueduct.

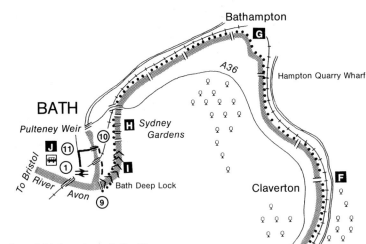

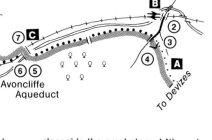

5 Turn sharp right down towards the "Cross Guns" at Avoncliff and then sharp left under the aqueduct.

6 Follow the path up and around to the other side of the aqueduct

7 Cross the aqueduct and continue to Dundas Aqueduct and Wharf.

8 Cross the towpath bridge at the exit from Dundas Wharf and remain on the towpath to Bottom Lock in Bath.

9 Cross the bridge below the lock and proceed northwards along the riverside walk as far as the first road bridge.

10 Climb the steps within the bridge's abutments onto the main road to view Pulteney Weir.

11 Proceed westwards to the traffic lights and turn left - Bath Station is straight ahead, about 300 yds.

Points of Interest

A The Kennet & Avon Canal

Both the rivers Kennet and Avon had been canalised and made navigable early in the 18th century. From Reading - where the Kennet joins the Thames - navigation was possible to Newbury, while over in the west the Avon was navigable from the sea to Bath. The idea of linking the two - and at the same time creating an inland route between London and Bristol - did not get Parliamentary approval until 1794, when work began at Bradford-on-Avon. The canal was finally completed in 1810 when the astonishing Caen Hill flight of locks (see *Encore*) was opened at Devizes. Throughout its history the Kennet & Avon has suffered

from water shortage problems, often through leakage, which has caused more than a few to question the abilities of the canal's surveyor and architect, John Rennie. There can be little doubt that Rennie left a legacy of superb and unique artefacts, such as his aqueducts and bridges, but at the same time dispute surrounded the line he chose south of Marlborough with its short summit level at Crofton. With the coming of the Great Western Railway the Kennet & Avon suffered; not only was its route duplicated but the GWR eventually bought the canal and trade necessarily declined. The Kennet & Avon

soon fell into disrepair, the last through passage being made in 1951. That same year the Kennet & Avon Canal Association was formed to try and stop the rot and later (1962) reconstituted as a charity to actively work for the canal's restoration.

B Bradford-on-Avon

In one sense the canal, by skirting its southern outskirts, by-passes the best of Bradford-on-Avon. The town is a microcosm of Bath, the same yellowed stone rising in 18th century terraces up the steep-sided valley, particularly north of the river. This erstwhile wool town once boasted at least 32 mills specializing in the manufacture of high-grade cloth but its standards were its downfall, for its namesake (and others) in Yorkshire was able to market a cheaper product. Bradford has an abundance of architectural treasures, from the Saxon Church of St. Lawrence to the unique 9-arched bridge over the Avon with the town lock-up, once a chantry chapel, in the middle. Bradford's lock and wharves - one above and one below the lock - and the nearby pubs occupy an attractive setting, though it is a long time since working craft used these facilities. Heading west the canal runs

alongside the great stone 14th century Tithe Barn, one of the finest in Britain and another of this seductive town's treasures. Grips Wood is to the south, its sylvan slopes falling down to the water's edge, while below is Barton Farm Country Park which extends as far as Avoncliff. Back in the days of a working waterway this stretch was particularly prone to land slip; it is all too clear that in places the canal is clinging to the hillside by the slenderest of threads.

continued on page 65

Dramatic lighting gilds Pontcysyllte Aqueduct on the Llangollen Canal

Towards the Brecon Beacons

The Oxford Canal winds through the Cherwell Valley near Tackley

Northern waters · Hebden Bridge Basin on the Rochdale Canal

continued from page 60

C Avoncliff

As the river Avon closes in on the canal opposite Becky Addy Wood a cluster of houses and a pub gather themselves round the first of Rennie's aqueducts, Avoncliff. The canal boldly turns sharp right and strides across the river and railway. The towpath changes sides here but before crossing under, a walk along the eastern side will not be wasted . . . the view up the valley back towards Bradford is nothing short of magnificent. On either side of the river are two flock mills both of which were powered by the adjacent weir, its waters still rattling down to Bath, Bristol and beyond. If you can tear yourself away from the "Cross Guns" in its olde worlde, almost idyllic, setting on the valley wall, it's time to look at both sides of the aqueduct from below, en route to the towpath on the other side. That little sag in the centre arch has always been there, the assorted patchwork of brick hasn't! But neither can take away from the sheer audacity and beauty of such a structure in these surroundings.

D The 'Dry Section'

A contradiction in terms? Not so . . . more than any other part of the canal the two miles between Avoncliff and Limpley Stoke was notorious for its leaks and was constantly being repaired. The problem was eventually solved in 1976-78 when it was totally relined using modern materials; nevertheless one sceptic managed to record a cryptic comment in the concrete along the edge: "I bet it leaks". If you can avert your eyes from scouring the towpath for this message you might well notice that this valley continues its magnificent wooded way towards Bath; superlatives cannot do it justice, repetition of its splendour merely lessens the impact. Evidence of Murhill Wharf still remains on the offside about a mile from Avoncliff; Murhill was one of three small wharves between Bradford and Bathampton served by a tramroad from a quarry close by. Like that at Conkwell (near Dundas) the stone from Murhill Quarry was not of the best quality and its use was thus soon discontinued. As the canal sweeps northwards the picturesque hamlet of Limpley Stoke - a quick walk down the hill from the canal if only to check that the river and railway are still there - reveals a world where time has stopped, a sleepy one-shop-one-pub village . . . but then the pub, the "Hop Pole" *is* 400 years old.

E Dundas Aqueduct and Wharf

The impressive road viaduct over to the west, that momentarily diverts the attention away from Conkwell Wood, carries the A36 over Midford Brook and the disused Somerset Coal Canal-cum-Limpley Stoke to Camerton railway line. Suddenly, just beyond the old lengthsman's cottage, the canal swings sharply left and once again sweeps across the Avon valley on another of Rennie's aqueducts, Dundas.

Though shorter than Avoncliff, the setting is somehow more dramatic, for what unfolds as you cross the aqueduct (and out of Wiltshire into Avon) is a story of canal rivalries in and around the bustling trans-shipment wharf. The recent excavation of the first $^1/_4$ mile of the Somerset Coal Canal (see below) for private moorings has brought to light new evidence about traffic on the canal before company rivalries took a hand. Opened in 1805, the SCC provided an outlet for Somerset's coal via the (then unfinished) Kennet & Avon. It was known that the narrow entrance lock (closed to boats in 1898) by the towpath lift-bridge was originally broad and thus used by the wider craft of the Kennet & Avon, the original basin/wharf having been beyond the stop lock on the SCC close to the lock cottage. And yet for some reason - and one can only assume that there was some dispute between the canal companies - a narrow lock was substituted. Now it appears that the SCC basin was also broad at its southern exit, supporting the theory that wide boats *did* for a time carry stone from Tucking Mill near Midford. Before leaving Dundas Wharf there is one other puzzle to solve: there is a story that a cache of coins was secreted in the fabric of Dundas Aqueduct during its construction but that to date these have never been found . . . now where would *you* hide such treasures in an aqueduct? (Two tracks lead up from Dundas Wharf to the A36 along which regular bus services run to and from Bath - No's. 253 & 264; like Claverton, $1^1/_2$ miles further north, this would be a convenient point at which to 'split' the walk).

F Claverton

Just beyond Dundas Bridge a house can be seen peeping down through the trees, a house that had at one time the doubtful distinction of being a place of 'ill-repute'. Before the A36 joined the river, canal and railway along this valley, the easiest access to the area was via the canal and, so the story goes, boat loads of rowdy and pleasure-seeking gents used to head for Dundas . . . but not to view the aqueduct. Warleigh and

Claverton Woods vie for your attention until Claverton Bridge, below which is Claverton Pumping Station - a must for a short detour. Here two large water-wheels, powered by the river, used to pump water from the Avon up into the canal; it was designed by Rennie to feed the 9 mile pound between Bradford and Bath and is the only such device on Britain's canals. Today it is all done by electricity but the pumping station has been restored and is open to the public on certain weekends - details on Bristol (0272) 712939. Back on the towpath Claverton's outlets, old and new, are just beyond the bridge; here too the canal is less hemmed in by the wooded slopes of the valley and Warleigh Manor is able to assert itself from its hillside setting.

G Bathampton

Holcombe Swing Bridge and its adjacent wharf are at the end of a mile long inclined tramway from Bathampton Quarry - the line of which can easily be followed up to the A36. The swing-bridge was replaced in 1982, one of the last to be built in wood now that more substantial - and less aesthetic - materials are available. John Rennie is often credited with inventing the ball-bearing; whether or not he 'borrowed' the idea is uncertain. What is agreed is that such technology was first used to help bridges 'swing' on the Kennet & Avon. Through three sweeping bends the canal leaves the Limpley Stoke Valley; since Dundas the river, canal, railway and road have clung to the valley wall or filled its floor and now, though they part company, the divorce is only temporary for the goal, Bath, is the same. Bathampton itself is small and displays a friendly face to the canal. A memorial chapel in the Parish Church of St. Nicholas contains the remains of Admiral Philip, the first Governor of New South Wales but, rightly or wrongly, the best-known canal-side feature is "The George", one of those canal places that attracts dozens of people on a warm summer's evening to drink by the 'river'. Rennie's original plan was to construct a 5-lock flight down to the Avon here but that would have entailed expensive engineering works to make the river navigable above Pulteney Weir.

H Sydney Gardens

Scenic and engineering delights have thus far been a feature of this walk and there are more to come as the canal, separated from the railway by a retaining wall, approaches Bath. Already the views across this Georgian city are spectacular but these are temporarily forfeited for a brief sojourn in the secret walled-world of Sydney Gardens, a green

Sylvan scene at Sydney Gardens.

time-trap spanned by two ornate cast-iron bridges, ERECTED ANNO 1800, and guarded by two short tunnels. Above the second of these stands Cleveland House, the original headquarters of the Canal Company, and between the two is a small orifice in the tunnel roof through which messages were passed to boatmen below. The towpath changes sides here and again at the next bridge by Sydney Wharf, still active albeit with a more leisurely trade. Another erstwhile wharf on the offside, just above the locks by the old stone malthouse, was originally the terminus of the packet boat service between Bath and Bradford.

I The Widcombe Flight
The descent to the river is dramatic and awesome. Bath displays itself for all to see, the scene always changing as six locks descend the valley accompanied by long well-kept gardens. A stone chimney on the right is the sole remains of a pumping station that fed water to the top of the locks. The ornate footbridge by lock 10 (Wash House) contrasts sharply with the chasm-like chamber of Bath Deep Lock, at 19ft. 5in. the deepest in the country. This mighty chamber is a recent phenomenon resulting from the amalgamation of two locks, Bridge and Chapel, to facilitate a road improvement scheme; the site of Chapel is beyond the road bridge, where the reason for its name becomes fairly obvious. A new hotel complex borders the side pound above the last lock but in no way competes with the simplicity of Thimble Mill which used to house a coal-powered pumping station that lifted water from the Avon to a basin by the other pump-house near the top of the locks.

J Bath
The navigable water route west of Bottom Lock falls through eight more locks to Bristol and the sea; eastwards it ends in the shadow of Bath Abbey at Pulteney Weir less than $\frac{1}{2}$ mile away. Bath's historic pedigree is not unknown and its secrets are easily untangled by following any one of the hordes of tourists that infest its Georgian terraces and Roman remains. Alternatively, you might try getting there early in the morning and in the privacy of the dawn's eastern light share the reality of this remarkably beautiful city with yourself.

Sustenance

As major tourist centres, both Bath and Bradford-on-Avon are bursting with all manner of hostelry, cafes and restaurants. Pub-wise on the canal there are several to choose from and most do food as well; "The Viaduct" on the A36 at Dundas, though off the cut, was a firm favourite with the working boatman, as was "The Ram" at Widcombe. The cottage just up the hill from the south-eastern end of Avoncliff Aqueduct does excellent afternoon teas.

Counter Attractions

Bath and Bradford are themselves interesting attractions and a visit to Bath's Information Centre will keep you busy.
● The American Museum, Claverton Manor, Bath, Avon. Open daily (ex Mon), Apr-Oct, 2pm-5pm. Admission charge. Tel: Bath (0225) 60503. Domestic life in America from the late 17th century to 19th century is featured in 18 furnished rooms; also galleries of silver, glass, pewter, quilts and sections devoted to the American Indian. Teas with American cookies!
● Monkton Farleigh Mine, Monkton Farleigh, nr Bradford-on-Avon, Wilts. Open every Sat,

Sun & Bank Hol; Easter-Oct, 10.30am-5pm. Admission charge. Tel: Bath (0225) 852400. A World War II secret underground city illuminated by 25000 bulbs. This bewildering bomb-proof 'Temple of Mars' was constructed by the British army in total secrecy but its 80 acre labyrinth of tunnels and storage remain as a fascinating subterranean memorial.

Encore

No visit to the Kennet & Avon is complete without experiencing the dramatic climb up the 29 locks of the Devizes flight, 16 of which have been likened to a dinosaur's vertebrae as, in perfect formation, they climb Caen Hill. Work continues to restore the flight and re-open it to through navigation; in the meantime controversy continues to surround the decision to fit lock gates with scarcely traditional 'kinked' balance beams on what is one of the seven 'wonders' of the canal world. A good Badger Line bus service, the 271/2/3 linking Bath and Devizes, provides access to the flight at both ends.

Information

Tourist Information Centre, Abbey Church Yard, Bath, Avon. Tel: Bath (0225) 62831.

Walk 22

Lancaster Canal

Lancashire

Carnforth - Lancaster   **10 miles**

The Walk

The Lancaster Canal's wide and winding northern section along the coastline of Morecombe Bay is an exhilarating walk. The flurries of housing at Bolton-le-Sands and Hest Bank are punctuated by rich and rolling farmland and an unexpected seascape, and then, as a final flourish, the canal strides across the river Lune on a spectacular stone aqueduct. Here, almost impulsively, we leave the canal and join the Lune to Lancaster for a final appointment with the canal in its urban setting.

Start Point

Lancaster Railway Station.
OS ref: SD 472617.

Access

Bus, train and car. Lancaster has good rail connections with London, Scotland, the Midlands and Yorkshire; Tel: Lancaster (0524) 32333 for details. Similarly Ribble run extensive bus services in the area - Tel: Lancaster (0524) 64228.

Directions

1 Catch a train to Carnforth.
2 Leave the station and turn right into Market Street.
3 Proceed straight across the traffic lights and turn right at the play-park about 250 yds. further on and join the canal towpath, remaining on this until Lune Aqueduct.

4 Proceed down the steps at the eastern end of the aqueduct onto the riverside walk/cycle-way below for a little over a mile.
5 Leave the riverside walk just before the second bridge over the river and follow the path under the road to the left and into Sainsbury's car park.
6 Cross the car park diagonally to the gate into Cable Street and turn right.
7 Take the first turning on the left (Stonewell) off Cable Street.
8 Take the third on the left (more of a fork), Moor Lane; the canal bridge is 250 yds. along Moor Lane.
9 Join the towpath and walk south to bridge 98.
10 Leave the canal and turn right and almost immediately left at the T-junction.
11 Take the 2nd on the right (just before the railway) and remain on this road until the T-junction in about 1/2 mile.
12 Turn left at the T-junction into Meeting House Lane - the station is a short distance up the hill.

Points of Interest

A The Lancaster Canal
Had the original plans of John Rennie, the Lancaster's surveyor, come to fruition, the canal today would probably be a busy part of Britain's connected waterways network. But things didn't go according to plan and a 5 mile gap between the Ribble at Preston and Clayton permanently separated the 'North End' from the 'South End'. The latter, from Clayton to Westhoughton (east of Wigan), became a part of the Leeds & Liverpool Canal while the northern end, originally from Preston to Kendal, was the 'disconnected' Lancaster Canal. The saga had its beginnings back in 1792 when work began on a canal that would link the coalfields of Wigan with the north while lime and manufactured goods could be carried south. For much of its length it would be lock-free and two great aqueducts were planned to span the Lune at Lancaster and the Ribble at Preston - here an earlier survey by Robert Whitworth had advocated locking down to the river, crossing it on the level and locking up again. But it was the failure to cross the Ribble by canal and the construction instead of a 'temporary' tramway across the river on a wooden trestle bridge that finally sealed the Lancaster's fate.
Today, with a little help from the M6, the northern end between Kendal and Tewitfield is walkable but not navigable, though an active Canal Trust is trying to change that and is even exploring the possibility of a so-

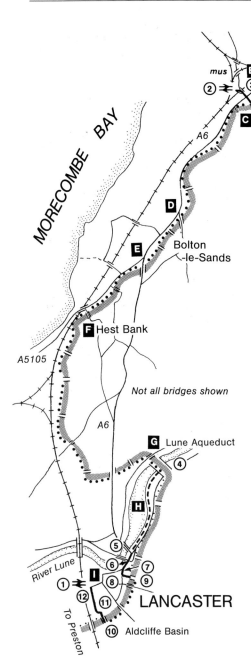

Not all bridges shown

called 'Ribble Link'. What remains are 44 navigable miles which include a short 6-lock branch to the sea at Glasson which, though completed long after the main line, gave the Lancaster Canal a vital link with coastal traffic.

B Carnforth
North-east of Carnforth are the stepped limestone scars of Warton Crag, believed to be a mere 280 million years old; Carnforth itself has a more modest history. It is not an inspiring place and though almost dissected by the canal its leanings are westward towards the railway. The main line through the town became part of the LNWR network but started life as the Lancaster & Carlisle Railway, opened in 1846. In 1867 the Furness & Midland Railway joined with the Furness Railway at Carnforth, thus establishing the town as an important railway junction. Carnforth was, by virtue of its Motive Power Depot, one of the last places in the country to retain steam locomotives. When they finally went out of service in 1968 a private company leased the depot and has since built up a fine collection of locomotives and coaches - see *Counter Attractions*

C Mileposts
Carnforth's wharf is south of the town just as its outskirts are on the wane; nearby is an engraved stone milepost bearing the numbers 8 and 19 . . . mentally alert walkers will soon divine that the total is considerably less than the length of the canal! The explanation is simple, though the reason less so. There are two distinct types of milepost on the canal, those north of Lancaster that indicate distances to and from Lancaster and Kendal and those south of Lancaster which originally displayed mileages to Preston, Garstang and Lancaster on elliptical cast-iron plates fixed to stone slabs. The most likely explanation for the differing styles and concepts seems to be that two different contractors worked north and south of Lancaster.

D Lancaster Canal Craft
South of Carnforth the canal clings to the edge of the contour round the base of a partially wooded hill, the A6 is a constant companion below. By bridge 123 at Bolton-le-Sands there is the "Packet Boat" which derives its name from being one of the staging posts on the Preston-Kendal passenger boat service. The first Scottish-built 'swift' boat, "Water Witch", was operating on the canal by 1833 and reduced the time for the 57 mile trip to less than eight hours; by 1839 a further three such craft had joined the fleet. Travel on these was, by all other standards, comfortable; cabins were heated in winter, refreshments were available and, weather permitting, passengers could avail themselves of seating in the forward well and aft cockpit. By contrast the canal's carrying craft were broad-beamed like those on the Leeds & Liverpool, though the locks enabled them to be longer, 72ft., with a beam of 14ft. 6in. These were built by Allsupp & Sons on the Ribble at Preston and, as there was no navigable link between the shipyard and the canal, were towed round the coast to Glasson Dock and thus onto the canal. Some coastal craft also ventured up onto the canal via Glasson but would have had to substitute horse for wind power.

E Bridges
As the outskirts of Bolton-le-Sands merge with those of Hest Bank, the A6 crosses the canal on a typical, though more ornate than usual, stone bridge. Bridges on the canal are nearly all of stone and were clearly built to last; all bear numbers and most have names which sometimes tell a tale - bridge 125 is Bolton Cinder Ovens Bridge, No. 116 is Rakes Head and No. 112, Folly. The first - and last - swing bridge north of Lancaster is No. 120 (Hatlex Swing Bridge), set amid some attractive and individual canalside housing.

F Hest Bank
The cry of gulls mingles with the whiff of salt in the air as the canal creeps to within $\frac{1}{4}$ mile of the coastline at Morecombe Bay. It is possible to wend your way down from bridge 118 to where, at low tide and with the assistance of an experienced guide, the sands are crossable to Kents Bank on the Cumbrian side of the bay. The original plans for the canal included access to the sea at Glasson (5 miles south of Lancaster) but financial difficulties delayed completion until 1826. While work continued at Glasson, Hest Bank was the obvious location for trans-shipment between coasters and canal boats.

G Lune Aqueduct

As the canal leaves Hest Bank behind and continues to twist and turn round the higher ground to the east, don't turn your back on the view. In the distance, across Morecombe Bay, are the Lakeland hills and the Furness Fells, a vista that momentarily makes you wonder whether you are really on a canal. The unfettered sights, smells and sounds of the countryside exude from the rolling pastures above and below while slowly Lancaster's urban peaks loom larger on the skyline. The extremities of the city begin to touch the canal when suddenly it swings east and north and treats us to another short, sharp snatch of upland pastures, a fitting prelude to the majestic leap of the Lune Aqueduct as it straddles the river. If nothing else John Rennie is known for the strength and style of his major aqueducts, Lune , Dundas and Avoncliff (Walk 21 features the latter two): but Lune was the first and arguably the most impressive. Russian timber for piles, pozzalono (volcanic ash) for mortar from Italy and local stone were skilfully put together from Rennie's drawings like some giant jigsaw. And as a final flourish, the Rennie signature, balustrades sweeping across the aqueduct and round its curved abutments - the doric columns a mere dotting of the 'i'. Having seen it from the canal, the urge to get down below for a different perspective is irresistible.

H The 'Little' North Western

The walk alongside the Lune could not be described as spectacular. Once the aqueduct is out of sight the river widens but the scruffiness of the foreshore hardly does it justice. A time therefore to reflect that, but for a gent named Beeching, you might well be about to get run over by a train! What is now a 6 mile walk and cycle-way between Lancaster and Caton Green started life as the 'little' North Western Railway and a plaque and crane commemorate the line and its demise on the landscaped site of what was once Green Ayre Station. Standing here it is not difficult to imagine how the second road bridge across the river, Greyhound Bridge, once carried the railway en route to Morecombe.

I Lancaster

Lancaster's most famous non-waterway feature is its castle. Its castellated keep overlooks the bustle of modern urban activity; but then even it owes its existence to the strategic importance, since Roman times, of the river - accessible from the sea at high tide, fordable at low tide. Lancaster thus has an important maritime past. At one time it was the 4th largest port trading with the West Indies but after 1800 it declined quickly while its closest rival, Liverpool, expanded. Today the old Customs House on St. Georges Quay houses the Maritime Museum, a permanent record of a time when tall masts and tales of exotic climes embraced the quay walls. The canal and the Industrial Revolution went hand in hand and created a new trade. The new textile mills sought out the canal so that coal-power could be easily tapped and the end-product conveniently dispersed; the remains of some of Lancaster's eight canalside mills still stand, inactive and expectant, by the water. Just before bridge 98 are the Aldcliffe basins and wharves (now a BWB yard), once the headquarters of the canal company, and just beyond is the 2-storey building where the packet boats were maintained; the lower storey accommodated two boats on the water while a further two could be hoisted up to the workshops above.

Sustenance

'Spoilt for choice' just about sums up the eating and drinking facilities in Lancaster and, to a lesser extent, Carnforth. Lancaster's "Castle Cafe" is one of those insignificant little places that does 5-star chips et al while the "Farmers Arms Hotel" by bridge 99 caters well for a totally different market. There's "The Shovel" at Carnforth, a Boddingtons house, but those with an historical bent just won't be able to resist the "Packet Boat" at Bolton-le-Sands.

Counter Attractions

Lancaster itself is worth further and extensive exploration - the Information Centre (see below) has leaflets on everything!

● Steamtown Railway Museum, Warton Road, Carnforth, Lancs. Open daily 9am-5.30pm. Steam operations, 11am-5pm: Sun, Easter-Oct; Sat, June-Sept; daily, July & Aug. Admission charge. Tel: Carnforth (0524) 732100. The museum houses 30 main line and industrial locos inc. "Flying Scotsman", "Sir Nigel Gresley" and "Lord Nelson". It covers 26 acres complete with workshops, turntable, and signal box.

● Leighton Hall, Yealand Conyers, nr Carnforth, Lancs. Open May-Sept, Sun, Bk Hol Mon, Tues, Wed & Thur. Admission charge. Tel: Carnforth (0524) 734474. A neo-Gothic facade superimposed on this classical house (built 1765) stands against a background of wooded hills and peaks of the Lake District in a memorable setting. Eagles and other birds of prey are flown in the park most afternoons.

Encore

Galgate is a bus-ride (Ribble services 140/142) from Lancaster and gives good access to the 2¾ mile Glasson Branch which drops through six locks to the dock on the Lune Estuary. Glasson is still an active port, with such contrasting trade as the container traffic to the Isle of Man and the export of scrap metal to Spain mingling with the leisure market. The walk is through open and windswept terrain but is never lonely as the gulls circle overhead in anticipation of the seascape ahead. Service 139 will return you directly to Lancaster.

Information

Tourist Information Centre, 7 Dalton Square, Lancaster, Lancs. Tel: Lancaster (0524) 32878.

Walk 23

Lee & Stort Navigation
Hertfordshire

Sawbridgeworth - Bishop's Stortford   6 miles

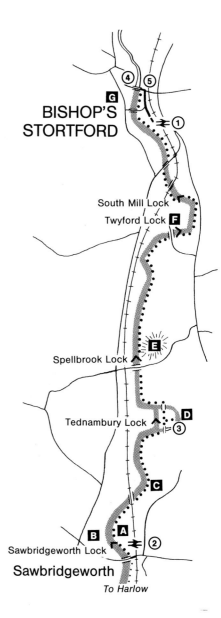

BISHOP'S
STORTFORD

South Mill Lock

Twyford Lock **F**

Spellbrook Lock

Tednambury Lock

Sawbridgeworth Lock

Sawbridgeworth

To Harlow

The Walk

The pace of the river Stort is slow. It weaves its gentle way through the flatlands of Hertfordshire to join the Lee on its more purposeful route to London and the sea. This walk reflects the Stort's wistfulness; no-one leaves this peaceful valley extolling its splendid architectural features or breathless from its scenery . . . it touches instead something inside, a quiet and private place.

Start Point

Bishop's Stortford railway station.
OS ref: TL 492209.

Access

Bus, train or car. Bishop's Stortford is on the main London-Cambridge-King's Lynn line; it also has a good bus connection and a large station car park. Train details from Bishop's Stortford (0279) 53378; bus information on Bishop's Stortford (0279) 52476.

Directions

1 Catch a train to Sawbridgeworth.
2 Turn right out of the station onto the main road (A414) and right again onto the towpath east of the river bridge and remain on the towpath for 2 miles.
3 Turn right at Tednambury Lock across the path to view Little Hallingbury Mill and then retrace steps to continue along the towpath for 3½ miles.
4 Leave the towpath at The Causeway bridge (A1250) and turn right.
5 Take the first right, Dane Street, and follow the signs to the station.

Points of Interest

A The River Stort
The Stort is generally viewed as part of the Lee & Stort Navigation for indeed it is a tributary of the Lee - or Lea, both spellings

being extant. Parts of the latter were navigable in pre-Roman times; the first record of a 'cut' being made to improve the navigation goes back as far as the late 12th century. The first Act to promote navigational works on a British river in 1424 concerned the Lee but it was not until 1571 that the first major attempt was made to improve the navigation between London and Hertford. The same year a pound lock at Waltham Abbey was fitted with mitred gates - believed to be the first in Britain. With such a pedigree the river Stort's rise to navigational status seems somewhat insignificant. Indeed, but for Bishop's Stortford's expanding malting industry and its need to have good access to London's breweries, the Stort might never have been canalised. In the late 18th century the town sold more malt to the metropolis than any other town in Britain so it is not surprising that there was much jubilation - and a near riot - in October 1769 when the town was 'open to the ports of the world'. The navigation is 13¾ miles long and joins the Lee at Feilde's Weir near Hoddesdon; an imaginative scheme to extend the Stort northwards to link with the Cam and the Fenland waterways never materialised.

B Sawbridgeworth
Bishop's Stortford was not the only malting centre on the Stort, barley was brought to Sawbridgeworth from the corn lands to the north to be malted and the area boasted many fine riverside malthouses. The town itself is atop the hill at and around the junction of the A414 and the A11; it is an attractive little cluster with many fine 16th-19th century houses, a place where time seems to have stood still. The overgrown path down to the towpath soon leads to Sawbridgeworth Lock and the remnants of its watermill and its attendant outbuildings have been tastefully converted to charming waterside dwellings.

C The Railway

The allotments on the left roll down to the river as Sawbridgeworth beckons farewell and the railway takes a more direct overhead route to Bishop's Stortford. The first train ran into Bishop's Stortford in 1842 on the Northern & Eastern Counties Railway's broader gauge track. Three years later the Eastern Counties Railway connected the town with Cambridge and beyond, using standard gauge track; the whole length was subsequently converted to the latter under the supervision of George Stephenson.

D Little Hallingbury Mill

The valley opens out and wanders the mile to Tednambury Lock; across the meadows and several bends away the lock's balance beams can be seen, as can a line of moored boats. These are not on the main line of the navigation but on a loop that once 'fed' the impressive Little Hallingbury Mill, the only Stort mill in working order. This splendid brick building, complete with weather-boarding (insurance against rain leakage that might soak the mill's contents), deserves a closer look before continuing north. The last commercial carrying on the Stort came here in 1972 from Atherstone on the Coventry Canal with stone used in repairs to the mill.

E Walbury Camp

The approach to Spellbrook Lock is less open but still as attractive. Like Sawbridge-worth Lock and the next two locks to the north, Twyford and South Mill, (and unlike Tednambury) the natural flow of the river is diverted round the shortest of lock cuts - in complete contrast to the incessant wandering of, for example, the Wey (see Walk 14) and the Kennet (see Walk 20). Above the lock the river skirts the western edge of the Iron Age fortress of Walbury Camp. The lower slopes of the fort exude an almost mystical quality, its primeval secrets as deep as the roots of the trees. Will its banks and ditches ever reveal their knowledge. Will we ever know whether the scourge of the Romans, the queen of the Iceni, Boudicca, was indeed born here? And was it here rather than at a similar site on the Lee at Wheathampstead that the British king, Cassivellaunus, capitulated to Julius Caesar in 54BC?

F Twyford Lock

The green enigmas of Walbury behind, the Stort Valley opens out again and continues its quiet meanderings through the adjacent water meadows - don't be tempted to cut across any of the bends unless you happen to be wearing thigh-length boots! The towpath changes sides at Twyford Lock where the attendant mill buildings have been reclaimed as flats. Thames Water Authority, who are responsible for drainage and flood control on the Lee and Stort, have installed new weirs here and at Spellbrook and South Mill. Despite the rural aspect above Twyford, there is that inexplicable feeling that civilisation is close at hand; the birds are still chattering but there is that unmistakable hum of traffic in the background.

G Bishop's Stortford

The towpath changes sides again at the road bridge north of the railway crossing and for a while becomes the footpath. Bishop's Stortford's entrails are scarcely attractive. The dozens of maltings (what an aromatic haze they must have made over the town) are no more; they have been overcome by a 20th century shabbiness, albeit an ailment for which other towns have managed to find a cure. Shortly before the Causeway crosses, the truncated arm that goes off to the west is all that remains of the channel to the original basin (on which the library now stands) and the old course of the river. A wharfside crane stands forlornly waiting for someone to make it say something to its environment. In fairness to Bishop's Stortford the riverside walk north of The Causeway is set out more attractively. Being the market centre for a large farming community, the town itself thrives despite the demise of the malt industry. Its most famous son was Cecil Rhodes who founded Rhodesia but got the name wrong; the Memorial Museum (see below) features collections relating to his life at home and abroad. For the connoisseur of ales Bishop's Stortford is a haven . . . not only in terms of the variety available but also the many old inns that have survived the 20th century's breweries plague.

Sustenance

At Sawbridgeworth the "King William IV" (McMullans) is a short walk up the hill towards the town - there is a handy bakery almost next door. En route there's the "Three Horseshoes" west of Spellbrook Lock, a fine 15th century building, and "The Tanners" just south of Bishop's Stortford. In the town you will be spoilt for choice but "Angela's Chophouse" at the north-west edge of the town is worth a visit.

Counter Attractions

● Rhodes Memorial Museum, South Street, Bishop's Stortford, Herts. Open daily, Mon-Sat, 10am-4pm (closed 1st two weeks in August). No admission charge. Tel: Bishop's Stortford (0279) 51746. There are 15 Cecil Rhodes-orientated rooms including features on Old Bishop's Stortford, Schooldays and Boyhood, the Kimberley Diamond Mines, Creation of Wealth, the Pioneer Column of the North, the Jameson Raid and the Boer War.
● Scott's Grotto, Scott's Road, Ware, Herts. Open the last Saturday of each month, Apr-Sept, 2pm-4.30pm. Admission charge. Tel: Ware (0920) 4131. An 18th century grotto (now set among modern housing) built in the grounds of Amwell House by John Scott the Quaker poet. Consists of underground passages linking six rooms; made of flint walls covered with ivy, inside the decoration is of shell which covers everything but the floor.

Encore

It has been said that to leave the Lee to join the Stort is like entering another world, a slow and wayward world. You can judge for yourself on a $3\frac{1}{2}$ mile ramble from Broxbourne on the Lee to Roydon on the Stort - another 3 miles will take you on to Harlow New Town. Broxbourne, Roydon and Harlow are all on the Bishop's Stortford-London line.

Information

Tourist Information Centre, Council Offices, The Causeway, Bishop's Stortford, Herts. Tel: Bishop's Stortford (0279) 55261 ext. 251.

Walk 24
Leeds & Liverpool Canal
Yorkshire

Crossflatts - Shipley   **5 miles**

Directions

1 Catch a train to Crossflatts Halt.

2 Leave the Halt and turn right at the main road and take the first right off this, Altar View.

3 Follow this road round and take the next on the right, Sleningford Road.

4 At the end of this road stop to view Bingley 5-Rise just ahead before turning left up the track to the towpath.

5 Turn right onto the towpath and follow this to bridge 208 at Shipley.

6 Walk beyond bridge 208 to view the infilled end of the Bradford Canal on the offside then return to the bridge, cross it and follow the path round the 'dead end' of the Bradford Canal turning right onto the road and under the railway.

7 Turn right at the T-junction, cross this road and head back towards Shipley. The station is on the left, 150yds. down the hill.

The Walk

From both the towpath and the water, flights of locks have a special magic. Lockwise the Leeds & Liverpool Canal is well endowed but one flight has to be seen to be believed, the Bingley 5-Rise, this walk's star attraction! But locks are not all that is on offer; man's ingenuity and his flights of fancy compete with unexpected scenic beauty and the unassuming valley of the river Aire.

Start Point

Shipley Railway Station.
OS ref: SE 150374.

Access

Bus, train or car. There are regular train connections with Shipley from Leeds, Bradford, Ilkley and Keighley; Tel: Leeds (0532) 448133 for details. MetroBus services link with the same towns and also Harrogate and Otley; details from Bradford (0274) 734833. Free car parking is available at the station.

Points of Interest

A Leeds & Liverpool Canal

This walk includes perhaps the best-known feature of the Leeds & Liverpool but the canal has other less dramatic idiosyncracies. The swing-bridges are, for boaters, notoriously heavy and, on some stretches, all too frequent- walkers can thus find themselves in great demand. The paddle gear at locks too varies from one part of the canal to another, often between one lock and another on the same flight. The ground paddles in particular are of three main types, all of which are known locally as 'cloughs' (pronounced 'clows'), the conventional windlass-operated sort, a vertical worm drive often operated by a fixed windlass and, most unusual of all, the wooden lever known as the jack or side clough which is raised through an 80° arc.

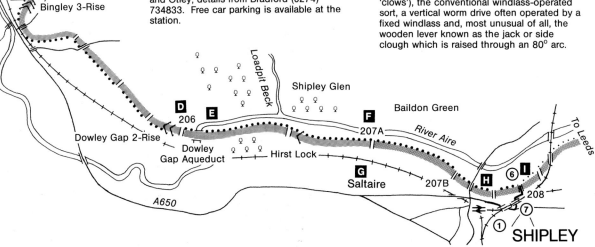

B Bingley 5-Rise
The 13 mile lock-free section between Bingley and Skipton was the first part of the Leeds & Liverpool to be completed. The following year (1774) this was extended westwards to Gargrave and eastwards to Shipley, the latter including the spectacular Bingley Great Lock, a broad staircase of five locks with a combined rise/fall of almost 60ft. over 320ft. The plaque by the lock cottage at the top of what became better known as Bingley 5-Rise acknowledges the skill of its architect while another set in stone on the towpath side commemorates the bi-centenary of its completion. The 5-Rise is an awe-inspiring engineering masterpiece, a monument to the ingenuity of man. It attracts many visitors (gongoozlers to the boating fraternity), the more so when there are boats about and the resident lockkeeper can demonstrate his skill, not only at locking boats up and down but also at flicking their bow ropes under and over the narrow bridges at the tail of each chamber.

C Bingley 3-Rise
Walking down to the next flight, Bingley 3-Rise, more than a few backward glances at the magnificent 5-rise are inevitable; from the top of the 3-Rise itself there is an unusual view of it back across the curve of the canal. The staircase of three is no less spectacular than its more famous neighbour, though the setting is more industrial with the adjacent Damart complex - they of the thermal underwear. The overflow weir alongside the bottom lock actually flows under an extension to the Damart buildings.

D Bridge 206
As Bingley recedes so too does the derelict industrial backdrop. It is replaced, momentarily, by housing on the one side and on the other by undulating fields, punctuated by dry stone walling. A canalside mill, erstwhile workshops and "The Fisherman" precede the 2-Rise at Dowley Gap before bridge 206 takes the towpath across to the left. Dowley Gap Changeline Bridge is what is known elsewhere as a turnover bridge, 'changeline' is merely a term peculiar to the Leeds & Liverpool. It is usual for such bridges to be situated close to aqueducts for where a canal, especially one hugging a particular contour, crosses a river valley the towpath needs to change sides in order to remain on the downhill side of the canal.

Bingley Five Rise on the Leeds & Liverpool.

E The River Aire
Not surprisingly bridge 206 is followed almost immediately by a 7-arched stone aqueduct which carries the canal over the river Aire. (There are steps down from the western end from which it can be viewed). From Bingley the Aire has been a constant, if discreet, companion down in the valley to the south; now, as both canal and railway stride across, the mood changes. Gently wooded slopes on the one hand and the river on the other are kept apart by the canal clinging to the edge of the valley. The working boatmen found this area intimidating, even haunted, and would always ensure that they were beyond it before nightfall. It is 15 miles before the river and canal are as one. When the Leeds & Liverpool finally drops into the Aire & Calder Navigation, the Aire is a far cry from the ebullient stream back at Gargrave (see Walk 25).

F Shipley Glen
North of the river and canal between Hirst Lock and Saltaire are two areas of outstanding natural beauty, Shipley Glen and Baildon Green. Shipley Glen has been rediscovered in recent years and its woodland paths, valley stream and amazing rock formations are a favourite venue for walkers and sightseers alike. In 1895 a cable-hauled tramway was opened near Saltaire, its open cars ran on a double track 386yds. up and down a 1 in 12 incline. Today the tramway still runs thanks to its restoration by the local Bradford Trolleybus Association. Shipley Glen is certainly worth the diversion, there might even be the chance of a spot of boating on the Aire.

G Saltaire
Soon the classical idiosyncracies of Saltaire break into the skyline ahead. The Utopian dream of Sir Titus Salt, a Victorian reformer and entrepreneur, was to create a model textile village, an industrial settlement incorporating excellent housing and working conditions, a high standard of education for the young, security for the not-so-young and leisure facilities for all. Saltaire became the reality and remains today as a monument to a man of vision and is, like Shipley Glen, well worth the detour - right over Saltaire Bridge (No. 207A) by the imposing Italianate (United Reform) church. All the streets are named after members of Titus Salt's family (he had 11 children), the only exception being Lockwood and Mawson Streets which bear the names of the two architects of the scheme. Titus was a man of temperance so Saltaire was conceived 'dry' . . . and so it has remained to this day.

H The Water Bus

As Saltaire's majestic mills recede (even the derelict one seems to retain its dignity), a less attractive vista is not far off. Old, once proud, mills and warehouses have been left to decay while a modern equivalent probably died as it was being conceived. Stalwart little stone cottages and a converted mill are the sole gems in this rag-bag of architecture before reaching the warehousing and loading bays by bridge 207B, built after the closure of the Bradford Canal. On the other side of the bridge is the base of Apollo Canal Carriers who specialize in carrying people and run the water bus, the 'stops' for which no walker can have failed to notice en route. Apollo run this enterprise in conjunction with the West Yorkshire Transport Executive and provide a regular service from Metro-style 'bus' stops between Bingley and Shipley.

I The Bradford Canal

The 3$\frac{1}{2}$ miles and 10 locks of the Bradford Canal are no more, all that remains is the memory and the indentation on the offside just beyond bridge 208, a typical junction bridge. The canal opened in 1774 by which time the main line was completed as far as Skipton, thus facilitating the limestone traffic from the Craven quarries to kilns outside Bradford. A court order closed the canal to traffic in 1867 due to heavy and noxious pollution but it reopened, a more aromatic three miles now, in 1873 and finally closed in 1922.

Sustenance

Shipley is not short of places to eat and drink but as "The Bull" backs onto the canal and is directly opposite the station its Bass and bar food come highly recommended. At Crossflatts there is the "Royal", a Tetleys house, and somewhere in between, in Main Street Bingley, is the "Old Queen's Head" which is famous for its mammoth Yorkshire Pudding!

Counter Attractions

● East Riddleston Hall, Bradford Road, Keighley. Open Apr-May and Sept-Oct. Wed-Sun, 2pm-6pm; Jun-Aug, Wed-Sun, 11am-6pm; Admission Charge. Tel: Keighley (0535) 607075. An early 17th century furnished manor house containing a wealth of oak panelling, country furniture and pewter-ware. The tithe barn in the grounds is considered to be one of the finest examples.

Encore

A 4 mile walk in total contrast to that featured can be found at the Leeds end of the canal between the junction with the Aire & Calder Navigation and Kirkstall Abbey (leaving the canal at either bridge 222 or 221A). The canal at Leeds is more in tune with its city than is found elsewhere and even Kirkstall Power Station, until the 60s fuelled by barge, effuses a grotesque charm. The ruins of the Cistercian Abbey and the attendant museum are equally impressive and the surrounding parkland ideal for a picnic. Kirkstall Station is on the main Harrogate line from Leeds; timetable information is available on Leeds (0532) 448133.

Information

Tourist Information Centre, Central Library, Princess Way, Bradford, West Yorkshire. Tel: Bradford (0274) 753678.

Walk 25

Leeds & Liverpool Canal

Yorkshire

Gargrave   **8 miles**

The Walk

Words to describe this marvellously exhilarating walk do not come easily - all too often superlatives seem contrived. But memorable it is as, from Gargrave, it explores the serpentine meanderings of the Leeds & Liverpool Canal as it approaches its summit level, returning to Gargrave via the Pennine Way - the first and greatest of Britain's long-distance footpaths.

Start Point

Higherland Lock, Gargrave.
OS ref: SD 931544.

Access

Bus, train or car. There are two small car parks off West Street, which leads to the canal by Higherland Lock. Ribble bus services 567, 569, 580 and 581 from Skipton to Settle (and beyond) stop on the A65 at the end of West Street. Details from Lancaster (0524) 64228. The canal is $\frac{1}{2}$ mile downhill from Gargrave Station which is on the Leeds-Lancaster line. There are two useful morning services that stop at Gargrave, Mon-Sat, and one on Sunday. Details from Leeds (0532) 448133.

Directions

1 Join the canal at Higherland Lock and walk westwards.

2 Leave the towpath at Double Arch Bridge (No. 161) at East Marton and head uphill towards the "Cross Keys".

3 Turn right just past the pub and follow the road back over the Canal, keeping on the road as it runs alongside the cut.

4 Leave this road by taking the track to the right signposted 'Pennine Way'. Thereafter follow Pennine Way signs and/or symbols (yellow spots on stones/yellow arrows on gateposts etc.) for about 2 miles.

5 Stop to view the surrounding countryside as the path reaches its highest point - there is a tall post marker that can be seen from some distance off.

6 Continue on the Pennine Way, joining the track (to the farmhouse down on the left) which eventually becomes more substantial before crossing the railway.

7 At the first T-junction turn right and at the next turn left for the bus or car, right for the station ($\frac{1}{4}$ mile up the hill).

8 At the A65 T-junction (travellers by car and bus only) bus users will find themselves back where they started; those seeking out their car only have to cross the road to West Street.

Points of Interest

A Leeds & Liverpool Canal

The Leeds & Liverpool is Britain's longest canal. In over 127 miles its main line rises

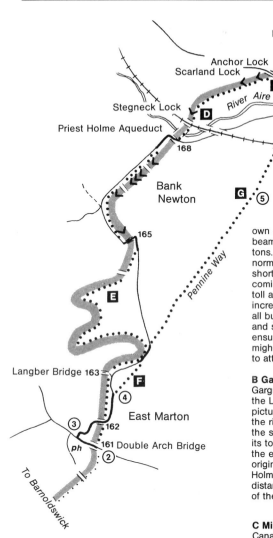

D The Aire Valley

Gargrave's Locks are soon left behind. The last, Stegneck, affords breathtaking views of the Pennine ridge to the north and east. Almost immediately the Leeds-Carlisle railway crosses and then, via Priest Holme Aqueduct, the canal in turn crosses and finally leaves behind the valley of the Aire. Almost immediately beyond the aqueduct, at Priest Holme Changeline Bridge, the towpath changes sides and becomes a tarmac road for a short distance. (A more detailed look at 'changeline' bridges on the Leeds & Liverpool can be found on Walk 24). It is interesting to note that the canal's early promoters reckoned that they were the first to hit upon the potential of the Aire valley - despite evidence of trade as far back as the Bronze Age: "It must be acceptable to the public to be informed that a person with great industry and application has discovered an opening between the mountains of Yorkshire and Lancashire, which is the most eligible, if not the only one, nature has formed for this particular work".

E Contours and Canals

The 6-lock Bank Newton flight is an attractive interlude. A hire-base has taken over the former carpenter's yard, an ideal starting point for a holiday and surely the envy of other operators. Above the locks the towpath changes sides once more and again briefly makes use of the road for a short distance. The amazing twists and turns that now follow almost pale the infamous winding Wormleighton on the Southern Oxford into insignificance. If there are boats on the move it is easier to pinpoint the line of the canal which is only a short distance as the crow flies across the fields; another focal point, a radio mast, first appears to the south and then seemingly changes location time after time. Gently rolling pastures cascade down to and from the cut, their woolly inhabitants casting an occasional weary eye at the intrepid walker and sometimes coming up onto the towpath to chew things over. The last, and most acute, bend boasts two stout posts which once supported rollers that, in horse-drawn days, kept the tow-lines from cutting across behind the towpath and pulling the boat sideways.

This part of the Leeds & Liverpool was surveyed and cut at a time when canal technology was in its infancy, when changes in the lie of the land were overcome by locks, tunnels and aqueducts or, as here, by taking the long way round and keeping to the contour. Between Leeds and Bank Newton the valley of the Aire provides a natural path for the canal.

own distinctive craft, the 'short-boat', a wide-beam vessel with a capacity of around 45 tons. Though through traffic was never the norm, local traffic flourished despite water shortage problems on the summit. The coming of the railways not unnaturally took its toll and what carrying survived became increasingly localised until, in the early 60s, it all but ceased. However, the magnificence and strength of the canal's structures ensured their survival and today it remains a mighty linear monument that curiously seems to attract more walkers than boaters.

B Gargrave

Gargrave is the most northerly settlement on the Leeds & Liverpool. It is a small, picturesque hamlet mostly clustered between the river Aire and the canal. The church, on the southern outskirts, is largely Victorian but its tower - an ever-present landmark towards the end of the walk - has 16th century origins. The first of Gargrave's six locks, Holme Bridge, ends the 17 mile pound from distant Bingley; Higherland Lock is the third of the flight.

C Mileposts

Canal Companies were required by law to erect mileposts as a basis for calculating toll charges. Styles and materials used varied between companies and some even provided 1/2 mile and 1/4 mile markers as well. The Leeds & Liverpool's 3-sided mileposts are quite distinctive, each, like the one between Higherland and Anchor Locks, bearing the mileage to both Leeds and Liverpool. There are also 1/2 mile markers between Anchor and Scarland Locks and by Langber Bridge (No. 163).

and falls through 91 broad locks linking the Aire & Calder Navigation at Leeds with the river Mersey (via Stanley Dock) at Liverpool. Its two main branches, the Rufford Branch, the link with the tidal river Douglas at Tarleton, and the Leigh Branch, the link with the Bridgewater Canal, gave on the one hand, access to coastal traffic via the Ribble estuary, and on the other the rest of the inland waterways network. The dimensions of the canal's locks, 62ft. x 14ft., gave rise to its

F The Pennine Way

A secluded wooded cutting heralds the end of the canal's contortions, the rock through which the cut was made protruding from both the canal's edges and the towpath. The unusual double-arched bridge at East Marton, created when the road level was raised, marks the start of the Pennine Way section back to Gargrave. The Pennine Way has its conceptual origins back in 1935 when the idea of a continuous footpath from the Derbyshire Peaks to the Scottish Border was first mooted. 'Trespassers will be Prosecuted' was the united voice of the opposition. Undaunted, local ramblers' committees surveyed the proposed route in 1939 and ten years later the newly formed National Parks Commission adopted it with minor variations. But it was not until 1968 that the completion of the Pennine Way in England was celebrated and it was a further 12 years before the Scottish leg finally established the 250 mile footpath. The Way passes through some of the roughest and most remote

Steam days on the Leeds & Liverpool.

country in Britain and seduces the senses with sights and sounds that have remained unchanged down the years.

G The View

Over stile and stream, up hill and down dale, the Pennine Way leads us (almost) straight back to Gargrave . . . a time to reflect on what canal engineers might have had to do had *they* taken the direct route! From the highest point on the Way the view is truly spectacular. The Pennine backbone extends dramatically north and south, while down in the valley a little to the west the railway spans the canal and river at Priest Holme. The beckoning tower of Gargrave's church is down there too, a goal for the end of a splendid walk.

Sustenance

Gargrave has three pubs, all of which offer good food. Two, the "Anchor" and the "Mason's Arms" are at either end of the walk. The "Cross Keys" (Theakstons, Free House and food) at East Marton offers a convenient half-way break. In addition there is a good fish and chip shop in Gargrave and several small cafes and restaurants.

Counter Attractions

● Skipton Castle, Skipton, Yorkshire. Open daily ex Good Friday and Christmas Day from 10am; Sundays 2pm. Admission charge. A rare example of a fully-roofed mediaeval castle with an enchanting Tudor courtyard. The castle was in the thick of the Wars of the Roses and the Civil War.
● Bancroft Mill Engine, Gillians Lane, Barnoldswick. Open Tues, Thur, Sat & Sun (Easter-Oct), 2pm-4pm. Admission Charge. Tel: Colne (0282) 865500 ext. 440, ask for Mrs. Smith. A massive steam-operated mill engine which once powered upwards of 1000 looms. The museum is normally open for static display though the engine is 'in steam' on certain dates.

Encore

A short 2½ mile walk along the Leeds & Liverpool in Burnley shows another side to the canal's character. Between Colne Road Bridge (No. 131) and Gannow Tunnel the canal encircles the town for nearly a mile, 60ft high on the famous Burnley Embankment. Between here and the tunnel is the so-called Weaver's Triangle area where the canalside industrial heritage of the 19th century has been preserved and restored; the original Toll House is now a museum and the information centre for the area. Burnley's two stations, Central and Barracks, are conveniently placed at either end of the walk.

Information

Tourist Information Centre, High Street Car Park, Skipton, North Yorkshire. Tel: Skipton (0756) 2809.

Walk 26

Leeds & Liverpool Canal (Rufford Branch)

Lancashire

Burscough Bridge - Rufford   4½ miles

The Walk

This walk explores a seldom visited part of the inland waterways network and to many will be a revelation in its confirmation that between Liverpool and Wigan there is something of scenic and historical value. Much of the terrain has a low country feel to it - take away the locks and you could be on a Dutch canal - and where else will you find such a compact and attractive canalside community as that at Burscough Junction?

Start Point

Rufford Railway Station.
OS ref: SD 466156.

Access

Bus, train and car. Rufford Station is on the main Liverpool-Preston line; timetable details from Liverpool (051 709) 9696. There is also an hourly Ribble bus service, No. 761, from Preston to Liverpool that goes through Rufford. There is a car park at the Station.

Directions

1 Catch a train to Burscough Junction Station.
2 Turn right at the T-junction outside the station.
3 Turn right at the main road.
4 Join the canal towpath at the far side of the bridge over it.
5 Cross the bridge at the junction with the Rufford Branch and turn left onto its towpath for 3½ miles.
6 Leave the canal towpath at Chapel Bridge (No. 3) and turn right and cross the railway line to the river bridge beyond to view the Douglas.
7 Retrace steps to the station on the left.

Points of Interest

A The Main Line
In October 1774 a 21-gun salute celebrated the opening of the 35 miles of the Leeds & Liverpool Canal between Liverpool and Wigan. For the most part this was virgin canal but the last three miles, from Gathurst to Wigan, initially made use of an earlier navigation, the river Douglas. The Douglas had been made navigable from Wigan to Tarleton (where it becomes tidal) and the Ribble Estuary as early as 1742 thus providing an important coastal outlet for coal from the Wigan area. In 1772 the Leeds & Liverpool Canal Company purchased a majority share in the Douglas Navigation, not only as it was a potential competitor but also to gain access to its water supply. Unlike the remainder of the Leeds & Liverpool, the locks on this section were built long enough (72ft.) to take the coastal flats that once plied the waters of the Douglas. By 1880 the Gathurst to Wigan section was completed as canal and the following year the man-made alternative to the lower Douglas, the Lower Douglas Navigation - now known as the Rufford Branch - was complete.

B Burscough Bridge
The built-up area around the station and the junction of the main line and the Rufford Branch is known as Burscough Bridge, though the 'Bridge' bit is often dropped. Within a square mile two major roads, two railway lines and two canal routes cross or join but it was the latter that first brought prosperity to the village. The canalside buildings tell of better times; but it was not just goods that were carried for, as soon as the canal opened, packet boats were carrying people in eight hours between Liverpool and Wigan, Burscough being one of the staging posts. The traffic continued until the late 1840s, by which time competition from a more direct rail link, opened in 1845, had taken its toll. The Preston-Liverpool line crosses the main line here (and later the Rufford Branch near Rufford) and then, just

as civilisation is thinning out the broad stone curves of Junction Bridge lure the unsuspecting into another world.

C Burscough Junction

The scene from the bridge is quite unexpected. The attractive cluster of buildings surrounding the first two locks is built of solid stone block, weathered almost black. On the left is the almost oval crater of a dry-dock capable of accommodating two 'short boats'. Above the first lock is a narrow swing bridge and on the right the stone façade of well-kept lockside cottages. In behind these is the "Ship", known locally as the 'Blood Tub', a nickname from the time when an enterprising landlady who used to make black pudding 'paid' locals a mug of ale for each bucket of blood (pig's usually) brought in. At the other side of Burscough there is another canal-side pub that boasts the nickname 'Smelly Nelly's' . . . the explanation - and the location - are best left unrecorded. Beyond the locks and the first fixed bridge the landscape opens out to a gently sloping and fertile farmland, hardly a tree, hardly a high point in sight. From the towpath the junction bridge can be seen to bear the date 1816 - not the year the branch opened (1781) but when the Leeds & Liverpool finally fulfilled its goal of linking the cities of Leeds and Liverpool.

D The Rufford Branch

The need for locks at all in such terrain seems at first puzzling but between Burscough and Rufford there are seven in all, seven steps that gently drop the canal towards the Douglas valley. Two railways cross the canal, the Wigan-Southport and the Liverpool-Preston lines, but in between is a quiet, almost secret, world where the warm fields and the reedy canal let life drift by - even the typically northern boldness of the locks is subdued here.

E Rufford and beyond

At the last lock, Rufford, the steeple of the small Victorian church in the background heralds a return to civilization. Rufford is an attractive village dominated for many by Rufford Old Hall (see below); access is from the main street (over the bridge to the left) and is certainly worth the diversion if only to enjoy the abundance of rhododendrons in the grounds. On the other side of the bridge is a pub, the "New Fermor Arms"; until recently a much older inn of the same name - without the 'new' - occupied this site and was known for its pronounced tilt . . . did it fall or was it pushed . . .? The river Douglas

is now quite close and from White Bridge it can be seen flowing north within the confines of an embankment. This was constructed when flat lands were reclaimed from the huge lake that once flooded the area where, according to legend, that hand rose up from the waters to catch Excalibur, King Arthur's trusty sword. At Sollom, two miles north of Rufford, the river and canal change places - the 'canal' becomes the original route of the river and the river now has its own 'new' cut - until the tidal lock at Tarleton which explains the lack of a towpath beyond Sollom.

Sustenance

There are several pubs in and around Burscough but the "Ship" at the junction definitely deserves a visit. At Rufford the "New Fermor Arms" offers food and home-brewed ale.

Counter Attractions

● Rufford Old Hall, Rufford, Lancs. Open daily Apr-Oct (ex Fri), 2pm-6pm. Admission charge. Tel: Rufford (0704) 821254. A medieval timber-framed hall with Jacobean extensions, a fine example of the richly ornamented 'black and white' buildings of the north-west. Until 1936 it was the home of the Hesketh family. The Hall also houses the Rufford Village Museum - the history of rural Lancashire from the Stone Age to the mid-19th century.

• The Wildfowl Trust, Martin Mere, nr Burscough, Lancs. Open daily Mar-end Oct, 9.30am-5.30pm; Nov-Mar 9.30am-dusk. Admission charge. Tel: Burscough (0704) 895181. An amazing collection of wildfowl - some of them quite rare - can be viewed in their natural habitat of the marsh and mere from strategically placed hides; binoculars may be hired.

Encore

There can be no better way of ending a visit to Lancashire than exploring the waterways in and around Wigan. For years at the receiving end of Music Hall jokes about 'Wigan Pier', the town has boldly embraced its canal,

creating one of the most imaginative and aesthetic urban canal walks anywhere - Wigan has had the last laugh! A 3^1/$_2$ mile walk combining the Wigan Pier/Trencherfield Mill area and 25-lock flight is as interesting as it is satisfying. There is a regular bus service from the top of the flight that returns to the town centre - Tel: Manchester (061 226) 8181. Wigan has excellent rail connections with all points of the compass.

Information

Tourist Information Centre, Cambridge Arcade, Southport, Merseyside. Tel: Southport (0704) 33133/40404.

Walk 27

☒

Llangollen Canal

Clwyd

Froncysyllte - Chirk   7 miles

The Walk

Thousands boat the Llangollen Canal every year but comparatively few walk its towpath. This is sad, because the boaters, faced with shallow water and an excess of traffic, stand to miss much of the canals more esoteric attractions. Inevitably Pontcysyllte Aqueduct chooses itself to feature in any Llangollen Canal itinerary, but we have a sneaking admiration for the hardly less spectacular aqueduct at Chirk too, so a route including both was a prerequisite. This whole section of canal from Chirk right through to Llangollen itself is currently part of an ambitious rolling programme of improvements being carried out by the British Waterways Board.

Start Point

Chirk - OS ref: SJ 291378.

Access

Train (local Shrewsbury-Chester service bi-hourly, Mon-Sat, Tel: Shrewsbury (0743) 64041,) bus (Crosville service D2 Oswestry-Chester, hourly, Mon-Sat, Tel: Chester (0244) 381515), or car - Chirk is on the A5, 7 miles

southwest of Llangollen; car parking is available off the main road in the centre of Chirk.

Directions

1 Catch a Bryn Meyln bus from the stop opposite the "Hand Hotel" (Mon-Sat service) Tel: Llangollen (0978) 860701 for details and book to Froncysyllte.
2 Alight from bus at Froncysyllte and walk down B5434 signposted "Trevor" 1 mile. After ^{1}/$_2$ mile this bridges the River Dee offering dramatic views of Pontcysyllte Aqueduct to the east. Cross the river and follow the road up to Trevor.
3 Cross bridge 31 spanning the Llangollen arm and continue to road junction turning right into New Road. Cross bridge 29 and turn right down on to the towpath.
4 Proceed over aqueduct and continue along towpath for approximately 3 miles to Chirk tunnel, note that the towpath through the cutting approaching Chirk Tunnel can often be very muddy.
5 Proceed on towpath through Chirk Tunnel. The towpath surface through the tunnel tends to be rather pitted and a pocket torch would

be of great use. However, there is a towpath rail throughout. If you prefer, follow the road running parallel to the railway across the top, rejoining the towpath at the southern end of the tunnel.
6 Cross the aqueduct and continue on the towpath to bridge 21.
7 Turn left off the towpath down a steep road to the A5. Cross the river bridge, then immediately turn left into the field signposted "Public Footpath" which should be followed along the river bank passing beneath the aqueduct and viaduct.
8 Turn right and follow B4500 uphill back to Chirk.

Points of Interest

A Pontcysyllte Aqueduct

It bears remembering that outside the world of canals, few people are even aware of the existence of this monumental piece of engineering, let alone have the ability to get their teeth around its knotty consonants. Pronounced Pont-ker-sulth-tee, the bare facts are that it is over 1,000 ft. long and 120 ft. high above the River Dee and consists of an iron trough supported by 19 stone piers. If you are something of a lateral thinker, you may wonder why such a monumental structure was contemplated at a point where the canal was apparently barely short of its terminus. The fact is, the canal was intended to be a direct route between Chester and Shrewsbury, linking the two great trading estuaries of the Mersey and the Severn. At Trevor the main line would have continued up and over the ridge to Wrexham. The branch coming in from Llangollen was and is still, merely a feeder supply channel to the main line. The aqueduct was opened in 1805, the original mortar of local lime and oxblood remains to this day!

B Trevor

The through route to Chester and the Mersey thwarted, Trevor eventually became the site of extensive canal-rail interchange basins. Moreover, there were numerous industries in the area, not least the iron foundry at Plas Kynaston where the trough for the aqueduct had been cast. Opposite the feeder junction, a sizeable boatyard developed for both building and repair of craft. Nowadays, a busy hire-base ensures there is seldom a lack of boating activity here, apart from in Winter. By mid-week when all the pleasure boats from the English end of the Llangollen Canal have reached their point of return, there is usually a glut of craft, which is one reason why the old trans-shipment basins

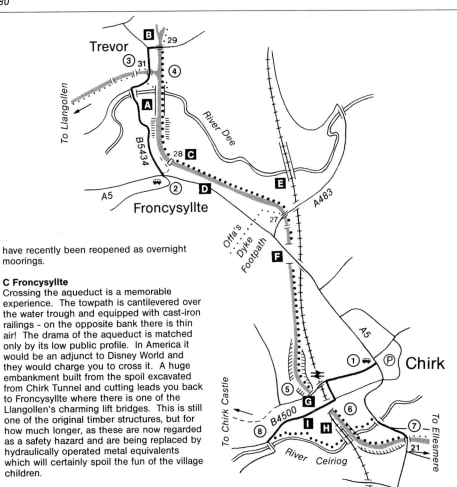

G Chirk Tunnel
A lengthy, wooded and invariably damp cutting leads to the northern portal of Chirk Tunnel steeped in perpetual twilight. Having examined your resistance to vertigo, we now put you through a test in claustrophobia, for the 459 yard long tunnel is naturally of impenetrable darkness inside. Nevertheless it is a remarkable and rewarding experience to walk through the tunnel which, as canal bores go, is remarkably dry.

H Chirk Aqueduct and Viaduct
Emerging from the tunnel a short broad pool leads to the aqueduct which, were it not overshadowed by that at Pontcysyllte, would be the highlight of any towpath walk. Here Telford experimented with an iron trough in a more traditional masonry structure before fully allowing his imagination to fly at Pontcysyllte. The result is a 10 arch, 70 feet high hybrid which spanned the Ceiriog and the border for 40 years before the loftier railway viaduct was built alongside. The juxtaposition is almost but not quite unique. The story goes that in Victorian times a small girl fell off the aqueduct but was saved from certain death by her starched petticoats acting as a parachute!

I Ceiriog Valley
Telford's Holyhead Road crosses the River Ceiriog on a short bridge dated 1793 - interesting to think that this pre-dates his aqueduct by some eight years. It is a charming walk along the river bank beneath the two graceful bridges. Another, more modest, stone bridge carries a minor road over the river at a point where you begin the climb up the B4500 back to the centre of Chirk. An unusual light railway once followed the same route. The narrow-gauge Glyn Valley Tramway was opened in 1872 to bring minerals down from the quarries at the far end of the valley. It also carried passengers in quaint box-like 4-wheel carriages. There was an interchange basin with the canal at the north end of Chirk Cutting. Tragically, the line closed in 1935, had it survived it would have been a splendid tourist attraction today.

Sustenance
Both Chirk and Froncysyllte have fish & chip shops. "The Aqueduct Inn" at Froncysyllte does Border Ales and bar snacks and has a wonderful view over the approaches to the aqueduct from its elevated position on the A5. Beside Trevor Basin "The Telford" does coffees, lunches and teas; it's a free house and children are welcome. "The Bridge Inn" (Banks's & bar food) nestles at the foot of the

have recently been reopened as overnight moorings.

C Froncysyllte
Crossing the aqueduct is a memorable experience. The towpath is cantilevered over the water trough and equipped with cast-iron railings - on the opposite bank there is thin air! The drama of the aqueduct is matched only by its low public profile. In America it would be an adjunct to Disney World and they would charge you to cross it. A huge embankment built from the spoil excavated from Chirk Tunnel and cutting leads you back to Froncysyllte where there is one of the Llangollen's charming lift bridges. This is still one of the original timber structures, but for how much longer, as these are now regarded as a safety hazard and are being replaced by hydraulically operated metal equivalents which will certainly spoil the fun of the village children.

D Old Quarry
Just to the east of 'Fron', remains of the former Pen-Y-Graig limestone quarries are evident alongside the canal. The actual quarry faces lay uphill to the west and the stone was brought down by a series of tramways and inclines on horsedrawn wagons. The tops of the 6 lime kilns were at road level with the bottom exits beside the canal. Leaving the old kilns behind, the canal rides on a high woodland shelf above the Dee Valley.

E Railway Viaduct
The Newbridge railway viaduct is 500 yards long and stands 150 feet above the Dee. Built in 1848, it carries the former GWR Shrewsbury-Chester line on, coincidentally, 19 arches. Today the route is largely used by local trains although there remains one early morning through train to Euston, and quite regularly steam specials also come this way.

F Whitehurst Tunnel
Turning sharply south away from the River Dee, and left behind by the Offa's Dyke Footpath which has kept company with the towpath since Trevor, the canal passes through the short tunnel at Whitehurst. Beyond the tunnel, crossed by the A5, canal and railway run together through mellow countryside towards Chirk.

Horsedrawn narrowboat on Chirk Aqueduct in the 1930s.

canal at Chirk Bank. "The Hand Hotel" in the centre of Chirk includes an informal buttery.

Counter Attractions

● Chirk Castle - 14th century border stronghold belonging to National Trust. Complex opening times so telephone Chirk (0691) 777701 for up to date details.
● Canal Exhibition Centre, Llangollen - the canal age effectively portrayed by models, mock-ups and audio-visual material; plus horsedrawn trips along the Llangollen Canal to Horseshoe Falls. Open daily Easter-end Sept. Tel: Llangollen (0978) 860702.
● Lots of other attractions open to public in the area - see tourist information.

Encore

Up to date details of the state of the towpath along the whole 42 miles of the Llangollen Canal from Hurleston Junction, near Nantwich, to Horseshoe Falls above Llangollen can be found in "Pearson's Canal Companion to the Llangollen & Shropshire Union Canals", price £2.75. Parallel public transport is predictably sparse in the remote countryside traversed by this lovely canal, but the railway stations at Nantwich, Wrenbury and Whitchurch make linear walks at the English end of the canal easy. Shropshire's own lakeland around Ellesmere is dissected by the canal and attractive walks can be devised in that vicinity. The dramatic feeder westwards from Trevor to Llangollen itself defies superlatives for its scenery but has been breached twice in recent years and at the time of writing has not yet re-opened. When it does, the Bryn Meyln Motor service again offers the chance of a one-way walk between Llangollen and Froncysyllte.

Information

Tourist Information Centre, Town Hall, Parade Street, Llangollen, Clywd. Tel: Llangollen (0978) 860828.

Walk 28
Macclesfield Canal
Cheshire
Bollington   **3 miles**

○

The Walk

Macclesfield Borough Council - go to the top of the class! This walk is a textbook example of how a local authority could, and should make the most of the canal towpaths and abandoned railways under their jurisdiction. MBC, as part of an ambitious county-wide plan to refurbish the whole of the Cheshire Ring circuit of towpaths, have improved a 15 mile section of Macclesfield Canal towpath within their area by resurfacing and the provision of seating and historical information points. Concurrent with the revitalisation of the towpath, MBC have transformed the parallel former Macclesfield, Bollington & Marple railway line from a decaying eyesore into a footpath, bridleway and cycleway known as the Middlewood Way. This short circular walk samples both developments. If you are as impressed as we were, then you can easily extend the circuit northwards to Marple or southwards to Macclesfield.

Start Point

Adlington Road car park, Bollington.
OS ref: SJ 931782.

Access

Bus (Crosville services from Macclesfield and Stockport, half-hourly Mon-Sat, hourly Sun. Tel: Macclesfield (0625) 28855) or car.

Directions

1 Adlington Road car park (toilets and information boards) lies at the foot of the former Bollington railway viaduct. Take the path from the car park which leads up to the north end of the viaduct and turn southwards across the viaduct and along the Middlewood Way. Note that if you're arriving by bus then there are steps up to the south end of the viaduct adjacent to the bus stop.
2 Cross the road and follow the cobbled lane up through the old goods yard. Heavy lorries use this as a parking area - take care!

3 Turn left and follow the path through Tinkers Clough Wood to join the canal at bridge 28.
4 Head north along the towpath for 1$\frac{1}{2}$ miles to bridge 25.
5 Climb the steps to the roadway. Turn left down to the railway bridge and follow the Middlewood Way back to the car park.

Points of Interest

A Macclesfield, Bollington & Marple Railway

It is an unusual experience to cross a railway viaduct on foot. You can peep over the parapet into Bollington's backyards, a view familiar to commuters who used this busy line until it closed amidst controversy in 1970. The line opened in 1869 and was later part of the famous Great Central Railway Company. The passenger trains were steam hauled until 1957 when diesel multiple units took over; services ran through to Manchester London Road (later renamed Piccadilly). Coal from the Poynton collieries further up the line was carried to Bollington's mills, a traffic stolen from the canal.

B The Macclesfield Canal

Between the old railway goods yard and the canal the route of the walk lies through Tinkers Clough Wood; the term clough is a peculiarly 'Pennine' word meaning ravine or gorge. At the foot of the deep descent a wooden causeway runs charmingly across a little stream. An equally steep climb leads up to the canal running at 500ft. above sea level. The Macclesfield Canal was completed in 1831 to the designs of Thomas Telford; though Thomas Brown was engineer in charge of the site work. The 'cut & fill' technique of digging out cuttings through high ground and using the resultant spoil to cross valleys by embankments was used. Connecting with the Peak Forest Canal to the north and Trent & Mersey to the south, it

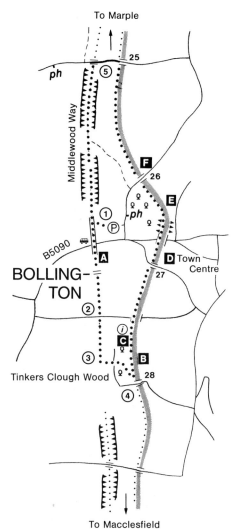

linked Manchester and the Potteries by a route much shorter and easier to navigate than the long haul round by the Trent & Mersey and Bridgewater canals.

C Adelphi Mill

One of a pair of overtly conspicuous mills which command the landscape of Bollington, Adelphi Mill dates from 1856. It began life as a cotton mill but after the last war turned to man-made materials, finally closing in the Seventies. The old gatehouse, reached by steps down from the towpath, is now a visitor and information centre.

D Bollington
The now spick and span little mill town of Bollington nestles in the confined valley of the river Dean. The canal overcomes this obstacle by way of an impressive embankment and a short stone aqueduct 60ft. high. Wide views are to be had from the towpath. To the south-east Kerridge Hill is topped by a curious monument known as 'White Nancy', thought to commemorate the Battle of Waterloo. The cotton mills came to Bollington late in the 18th century. Originally their machinery was powered by streams pouring off the surrounding hills, but later steam took precedence. When the mills closed down the town became a residential retreat, the stone built terracing which clings to the hillsides providing homes for people who commute to Stockport and Manchester to earn their living. Bollington is now a conservation area, fresh and pretty since the grime of busier years has been erased from its sturdy stone buildings.

E Clarence Mill
At the far end of the embankment stands Clarence Mill, dating from 1840. It belonged to a Martin Swidells whose two sons later built the Adelphi Mill. An interpretative board on the towpath side details some of the mill's operations and illustrates the important role played by the canal in the transportation of incoming raw materials and finished goods.

F Skew Bridge
Beyond the mill the canal suddenly emerges into open country with stone-walled fields climbing eastwards to the summit of Nab Head, 935ft. high. Bridge 26 is stone built on a 'skew'; that is diagonally across the waterway to avoid the road having to be realigned. Extra skill was required of the stonemason who would have to design each stone of the arch individually. The Macclesfield Canal is generally blessed with extremely handsome bridges, and it's worth contrasting their design with those on the adjoining old railway where brick has been introduced to the arches. Your return along the Middlewood Way is down in a cutting for most of the way. Although the 13 arch viaduct at Bollington was the railway's only major engineering work, virtually half of the 11 route miles lay in cuttings with the rest on embankments.

Sustenance
Bollington boasts no less than 19 pubs, but particularly handy to the walk are "The Vale", a free house adjacent to the car park, and "The Windmill", another free house $^1/_4$ mile west of bridge 25; both provide food.

Counter Attractions
Macclesfield Heritage Centre & Paradise Mill - Twin museums in the centre of Macclesfield. Open Tue-Sun. Tel: Macclesfield (0625) 618228.

Encore
The Macclesfield Canal and the Middlewood Way keep close company northwards from Macclesfield all the way to Marple, a distance of 11 miles. Thus a number of circular walks can be undertaken to explore the whole route. "Cheshire Ring Canal Walk No. 1", an informative booklet produced by Cheshire County Council, covers the whole of the towpath on this section.

Information
Tourist Information Centre, Town Hall, Market Place, Macclesfield. Tel: (0625) 21955.

Walk 29 ☐
Monmouthsire & Brecon Canal
Powys
Llangynidr - Brecon   11 miles

The Walk
Few canals are located almost entirely within the boundaries of a National Park; the exception is the Brecon & Abergavenny in South Wales. This is, therefore, a walk of breathtaking beauty starting at the locks at Llangynidr and ending in the market town of Brecon. And in between, the canal wends its way through sylvan glades around the ever-present backdrop of the purple-green slopes of the Brecon Beacons and, down in the valley, the bubbling enthusiasm of the river Usk. It is thus no idle overstatement to label, as did Tom Rolt, this waterway "the most beautiful length of canal in Britain".

Start Point
Brecon Square, Brecon. OS ref: SO 046284.

Access
Bus and car. Local and express National Welsh Bus Services connect Brecon with Abergavenny, Merthyr, Cardiff, Newport and Hereford; details from Cwmbran (063 33) 72581/5118. Brecon has several large pay & display car parks.

Directions
1 Catch a no. 42 bus from Brecon Square to Llangynidr. (Alternative services approach Llangynidr from different directions; the A40 (Bwlch) route involves a longer walk into the village but is the only one in operation on Sundays).
2a Alight at the school in Llangynidr and turn north into Forge Lane and walk down towards and across the canal bridge to view the river Usk bridge.
2b Alight at Llangynidr Turn on the A40 and turn south off the main road towards Llangynidr to the bridge over the Usk.
3 Join the canal at bridge 131 and continue north-west along the towpath for 10$^1/_2$ miles to Brecon.
4 Proceed a short way along Canal Road from the 'dead end' terminus at Brecon and turn right into Rich Way.
5 Turn left to Watton Mount, the town centre is a few hundred yards ahead.

Points of Interest
A What's in a name?
This walk is along the Brecon and Abergavenny Canal yet the title refers to it as the Monmouthshire & Brecon; all rather confusing . . . or is it? Originally there were two distinct canals, the Brecknock & Abergavenny, completed in 1812 between

Brecon and Pontypool, and the Monmouthshire opened in 1796 between Newport and Pontypool. In 1865 the two canal companies amalgamated in a last ditch stand to thwart the rival railways . . . but to no avail and bit by bit the Monmouthshire Canal was closed, but the line to Brecon remained open, although as a water channel rather than a cruising route. However, the amenity potential of the waterways did not go unnoticed and in 1970 navigation was again possible between Pontymoile and Brecon - with some craft being able to travel even further south. The walker, of course, does not suffer the same constraints and much of the line to Newport is traceable and hopefully might yet be reclaimed.

B The Usk Valley
The bus ride from Brecon will have already left its mark, for this is no ordinary terrain and the walk back to Brecon no commonplace stroll. From whichever side of the valley you approach Llangynidr, the splendid bridge over the Usk is the goal. The Usk valley forms a northern boundary of the South Wales massif; by cutting the canal above the river on the southern slopes of this valley, the canal company hoped that it could tap, by means of connecting tramroads, the output of the industries at the heads of South Wales' valleys. Tramroads and their related wharves thus became a feature of the waterway, notably so at Talybont, Llangattock, Gilwern, Golivon and Llanfoist; in addition, two further tramroads at Brecon and Llanfoist fed the canal from the northern valleys. Where the valley floor widens, river and canal keep their distance, where it narrows there are spectacular views down the wooded valley wall to the sparkling waters of the Usk.

C Llangynidr Locks
The Llangynidr Locks are neither narrow nor wide, neither short nor long; compared with the rest of the inland network the 9'6" x 65' chambers are totally unique. Unique too is the setting; 5 locks lift the canal 48 feet through exceptionally beautiful countryside, the wooded hillside to the south being set against the undulating line of the Brecon Beacons. Above lock 64 the canal swings round to the right to cross the River Crawnon. The stone curved aqueduct is visible across the bend with the waters beneath stumbling past pretty stone cottages. Round the bend, the remaining locks climb in quick succession against a bosky backdrop. The building by lock 65 was once a toll office where, in 1933, the last toll was paid on the canal - ironically, the railway that killed off the

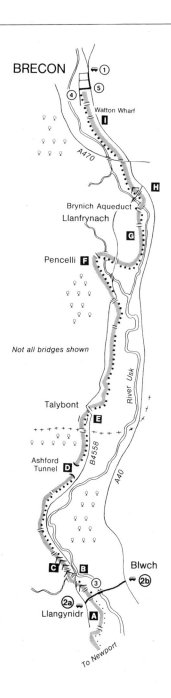

traffic has itself gone, subjugated by road transport. The canal, meanwhile, wanders timelessly on. Above the same lock is the old wharf area; behind the main workshop (now a BWB base) is a single lime-kiln which burnt lime for mortar for building purposes. The 1805 ft. peak of Tor-y-Foel looms up in the south, a silent sentinel for the three remaining locks secreted in a woody glade. The short distance between the top two explains the width of the canal here, and the side pond beyond the towpath that ensure the level doesn't drop with each locking. By the top lock (no. 68) a half-mile post ($33\frac{1}{2}$ miles to Newport) is the best preserved on the canal: equally well preserved are the stone cottages by the next bridge. Its name, Workhouse Bridge, gives more than a clue to their original function.

D Ashford Tunnel
Views up, down, across and beyond, spectacular and sombre, unassuming and unsurpassed, but above all breathtaking . . . and to think that such sensory abstractions were the furthest thing from the mind of the canal's engineer. The valley begins to open out and, a shallow brackeny cutting later, the canal enters the short Ashford Tunnel - the towpath goes over the top and is easily followed but what is a puzzle is the need for a tunnel at all. It is cut through relatively soft marls and there is no hill worth the description; so wouldn't a cutting have sufficed and been easier to construct?

E Talybont
Many of the canal's stone bridges look as if they might conceivably fall into the cut one day. Graiglas Bridge did and its abutments now support a less aesthetic steel girder replacement just before Talybont Wharf and its disused lime-kilns, the terminus of the Bryn Oer tramroad. Benjamin Hall, who gave his name to Big Ben, initiated the tramroad to connect with the Rhymney ironworks. Its course can still be followed up the hill by leaving the canal at bridge 143 and then crossing back over the disused line of the Brecon & Merthyr Railway - itself walkable in both directions. There is no record of Talybont having a church or being a parish; it is likely, therefore, that it is solely a product of the canal and the railway. Two of the village's pubs back on to the canal before it crosses the fast flowing Caerfanell on another stone aqueduct. Here too is a symbolic monument to restoration of the canal, an electrically-operated lift bridge, the opening of which in 1970 reunited the two ends of the canal. Perhaps more than any other this is a

place to linger awhile, and explore this ruggedly picturesque hamlet which even has a handsome red sandstone former station.

F Pencilli

Beyond Talybont the scene changes as the canal breaks out of a short cutting and wanders through a more pastoral setting punctuated with wooden lift bridges. The Usk swings in closer and there are excellent views from the exceptionally wide towpath down through the lightly wooded valley as it weaves its tortuous way north-west. There is not a lot to Pencilli and it is certainly hard to imagine the tight cluster of buildings as the head of a medieval lordship - a large farmhouse to the left with the grand name of 'Pencilli Castle' occupies the site of the original castle, the seat of Norman authority. North of Pencilli the canal, fiercely hugging its contour, swings away from the Usk across flat marshy land towards the ancient parish of Lanfrynach on the Nant Menascin. The canal crosses its brook on yet another short stone aqueduct close to a tall erstwhile mill with its own short arm, now disused.

G The Usk and the Beacons

River and canal reunite by bridge 160 and what follows is the icing on the cake. Below, the Usk tumbles its ancient way seaward. Its wide waters, hemmed in by overhanging trees, chatter to pebble and stone. The temptation to scramble down the bank, to weave in and out of the overhanging trees, to listen to the music of this beautiful valley, is hard to resist. But there is more to come, for no sooner does the river swing slightly to the north than the view south-east across to the Beacons compensates for the temporary loss. Cribyn, Pen-y-Fan and Cron Du reach skyward, their hard grit caps protecting a myriad of textures and hues.

H Brynich Aqueduct

The towpath changes sides at bridge 162 just after the canal swings sharply right to cross the Usk. Some aqueducts pass almost unnoticed while others stamp their authority on their environment. Like some magic carpet they make the improbable possible and fly boldly across their valley. Brynich is such an aqueduct. Its statistics do not make the record books, but its warm stone and shallow arches are an extraordinary blend of strength and grace, of audacity and energy. With the Usk now to the west, the canal works up through the last of its locks, Brynich, whose picturesque setting is overshadowed by the aqueduct and the river below.

I Brecon

Brecon is close and the canal, hemmed in by the main road on one side and the river on the other, settles for a less spectacular but not unattractive finale. There are several mile posts to look out for and a row of lime-kilns on the lane parallel to the canal before Watton Bridge. This has a double arch; the one on the right was originally to facilitate the Hay tramroad that came down to the wharf here. The basins and wharves that were once the canal's busy terminus are long gone. Instead, an uninspired 'dead end', into which water from the Usk is fed by a culvert, is what modern man has to offer - still the infilled basins have been put to excellent use as a car park! Brecon itself is an important market town serving a large agricultural community. It has long had strategic importance due to its position at the confluence of the Usk and the Honddu and consequently has featured in more than its fair share of 'scraps' down the ages. But if history isn't your forte then the town's river frontage and the old stone bridge across the Usk will compensate for the ignominy of that car park.

Sustenance

There is, not unnaturally, an excellent choice of hostelry at Brecon. "Sarah Siddons", for example, does a wide range of good food and en route there is more than one occasion when the temptation to adjourn from the towpath is great - particularly so at Talybont. Crusty's Coffee Shop at Brecon exudes inviting smells while Luciano's Italian restaurant has more universal appeal.

Counter Attractions

● Brecknock Museum, Captains Walk, Brecon, Powys. Open all year, Mon-Sat, 10am-5pm. No admission charge. Tel: Brecon (0874) 4121. Exhibits of local life, farming, archaeology and natural history; preserved Assize Court Room.
● Tretower Court and Castle, Tretower, nr Crickhowell, Powys. Open from 9.30am, Mon-Sat, 2pm Sun. Admission charge. Tel: Bwlch (0874) 730279. 13th century circular keep within remains of Norman structure and one of the finest surviving medieval houses in Wales, mainly 15th century.
● The Brecon Beacons National Park offers a vast range of outdoor activities; leaflets on almost everything are available from the National Park Information Centre, Watton Mount, Brecon, Powys. Tel: Brecon (0874) 4437.

Encore

A shorter and contrasting walk on the canal can be found near Abergavenny. Abergavenny itself is not on the canal to which it gives its name, but is close enough to make use of the X46 bus service (Tel: Cwmbran (063 33) 72531) to Llanfoist for the 3 1/2 mile walk north-west to Gilwern to catch the same bus back. The walk includes three wharves - Llanfoist, Govilon and Gilwern - that were fed by major tramroads; the setting of the latter is especially memorable. Abergavenny has direct rail links with Crewe and Newport.

Information

Tourist Information Centre, Watton Mount, Brecon, Powys. Tel: Brecon (0847) 4473.

Walk 30
⊠

Montgomery Canal
Powys

Llanymynech - Welshpool   11 miles

The Walk

Border regions invariably have a difficult to define, almost fey quality about them incurred, one assumes, by the ebb and flow of political, social and economic tides across the sands of the centuries. The upper Severn valley is no exception. Offa built his dyke hereabouts, and a thousand years later a band of barely more sophisticated navvies cut an unlikely canal across a marshy plain broken by limestone and granite outcrops. This Montgomery Canal, as it has come to be known, runs for 35 miles across these border Marches and is one of the loveliest of the presently unnavigable canals which have aspirations of being restored for boating use. Indeed, part of the fascination of this walk is the opportunity to compare unnavigable and navigable lengths and to decide for oneself just what is to be gained and lost by awakening this sleeping princess of the inland waterway system.

Start Point

Welshpool High Street.
OS ref: SJ 223076.

Access

Train (Shrewsbury - Mid Wales services. Tel: Shrewsbury (0743) 64041); bus (Crosville services. Tel: Oswestry (0691) 2402) and car - Welshpool is on A458 20 miles west of Shrewsbury; the town centre boasts several 'pay & display' car parks with toilet facilities.

Directions

1 Catch Crosville service D71 (Approx bi-hourly Mon-Sat, not Sun; tel no. above) from stop on High Street, Welshpool to Llanymynech (pronounced Lan-a-man-uck). Note that this bus also stops at Burgedin (6), Arddlin (7½) and Four Crosses (9) should you wish to shorten the walk to the mileages quoted in brackets.
2 Alight at Llanymynech and proceed to

canal at bridge 92.
3 Follow towpath westwards for 11 miles back to Welshpool.

Points of Interest

A Llanymynech

The border between England and Wales actually runs along the rather austere main street of Llanymynech. It divides the bars in the "Lion Hotel" so that when Montgomeryshire was 'dry', its patrons simply passed into the next room to expedite their Sunday drinking. The bold outcrop of Llanymynech Hill, rising to 650ft, dominates the view north. Its limestone quarries were the goal of the Llanymynech branch of the Ellesmere Canal, opened in 1797, which forms the 'English' section of the Montgomery Canal. Later, in the 'Railway Age', several lines met at Llanymynech for the same reason; notably the idiosyncratic Shropshire & Montgomeryshire Railway which also had an eye to the recreational potential of their route from Shrewsbury, advertising excursions to the unlikely golf links on top of the hill. The walk commences, coincidentally with the end of a dry section, and Llanymynech is soon left astern as the now Welsh waterway heads in a south-westerly direction towards its crossing of the river Vyrnwy.

B Flattened Bridge

Bridge 93 is one of several flattened bridges on the Montgomery Canal which present a major obstacle to restoration for boaters. Ownership of the bridges passed, with official abandonment of the canal by the LMS railway in 1944, to the local highway authorities who have often found it more economical to divert their roads across the bed of the canal rather than incur costly maintenance. Shortly beyond the bridge itself, now isolated from the road it was built to carry, an aqueduct

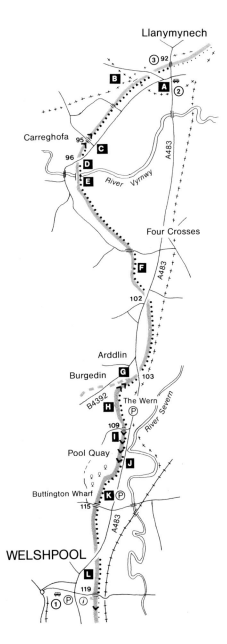

spans the trackbed of a dismantled railway.
It's interesting to note the course of two
backwaters off the canal which would have
been part of a temporary diversion whilst the
aqueduct was constructed beneath the canal.

C Carreghofa
The two locks at Carreghofa have been
restored by the Shropshire Union Canal
Society. An interpretative board describes
the former importance of this 'junction' which
marked the western end of the Ellesmere
Canal and the eastern beginning of the
Montgomeryshire Canal. The lock chambers,
side pond, wharfinger's office and lock-
keeper's house present an attractive scene
best appreciated, we feel, from the foot of the
lower lock with Llanymynech Hill filling the
horizon.

D Bridge 96
If this section of towpath seems more busy
than usual with walkers it could be because
this is also the route of the Offa's Dyke long
distance footpath. Part of a series of land
arches built to cope with floods from the river
Vyrnwy lead to bridge 96; perhaps the most
controversial of the flattened bridges, for it
was demolished as recently as 1980 at a time

when commitment to full restoration of the
canal was growing. But transport today is
dominated by the road lobby and appeals by
such august bodies as the Prince of Wales
Committee were ignored by Powys Highways
Department, so that when the canal is
eventually re-opened to boats a costly about
turn in policy will be required here.

E Vyrnwy Aqueduct
The Vyrnwy, or Newbridge aqueduct is one of
the highlights of this walk. When it was built
in 1796 to the design of the canal's engineer
John Dadford it cost a mere £4,500. Dadford
followed the more conservative approach of
building heavy walls of stone and brick lined
with a clay puddle bed, eschewing the
pioneering use of iron favoured by Telford at
Pontcysyllte. This reactionary attitude
subsequently proved problematical and
extensive repairs were undertaken in 1823
when the tie bars - which can be seen to this
day - were inserted to stabilise the structure.
Again, as recently as 1971, the aqueduct was
repaired and it will doubtless continue to
span the broad waters of the Afon Vyrnwy in
centuries to come. Incidentally, stirring as it
is to lean upon its parapet, a greater
appreciation of the structure can be had from

*Where do we go from here? The infamous
flattened road bridge 96 on the Montgomery
Canal.*

the adjoining road bridge best reached from
bridge 96.

F Maerdy
South of the Vyrnwy interest subsides
somewhat as the canal heads for the Severn
Valley. Clues to a busier past can be gleaned
as various former wharves are passed.
Evidence of current activity is offered by
British Waterways Board 'temporary' offices at
flattened bridge 102. When navigation
returns, the 2 mile section between Maerdy
and Burgedin will need to be lowered some 8
feet to expedite passage beneath the A483,
so it is planned to take out Burgedin top lock
and rebuild it at Maerdy!

G Burgedin
From Burgedin a 2$\frac{1}{2}$ mile arm led to
Guilsfield. Now almost entirely derelict, its
course can be enjoyed from the bus on the
way out along the B4392. The Monty has
now reached its base, or 'sump level', an

oddity amongst canals which more normally reach a central summit section fed with water.

H The Wern

A dramatic change comes over the canal at The Wern for here, at the time of writing, commences a 5 mile navigable section to the outskirts of Welshpool. A colony of little GRP cruisers are resident on this picturesque length, trailable boats can use the slipway, and the Heulwen-Sunshine - a purpose built narrow boat for the handicapped- operates between Buttington and The Wern. Another of the Montgomery Waterway Restoration Trust's excellent interpretative boards absolves us from providing more information here about The Wern, and there are picnic tables and a car park too.

I Breidden Hills

The canal turns briefly eastwards to confront the Breidden Hills, 1324 ft. at their highest. A restored milepost quotes 18 miles to Newton and 17 to Welsh Frankton, so this is virtually the halfway point. Bank Lock is the first of four which come in quick succession, raising the canal by some 35 feet.

J Pool Quay

Pool Quay Lock is a gem. The lock-keeper's house is cream washed, the lock machinery - including the distinctive Montgomery segmented paddle gear - picked out in black and white, and there's a delightful chamberside garden inhabited by a wide variety of ducks. Down across the road a bend in the river Severn marks the former head of navigation. Unwittingly, perhaps, the advent of the canal brought about the demise of navigation on these upper reaches of the river. Reclamation of the marshland, made possible by improved communications, resulted in a reduction of water levels in the river.

K Buttington Wharf

For a couple of miles to Buttington, the canal runs between the meandering Severn and the dramatically wooded slopes of Yr Allt, sounding far more romantic in Welsh for 'The Hill'. There are two lift bridges. The first, 112, adjacent to the site of Strata Marcella Abbey, a Cistercian monastery which fell foul of the Reformation in 1536. Buttington Wharf has car parking facilities, picnic tables and another interpretative board. Neatly restored lime kilns recall that the Montgomery's main traffic was limestone which, brought here by boat from Llanymynech, along with coal from pits in the Chirk area, would be burnt to produce lime, a commodity in much demand

to neutralise the acidic soils of the farmland around Welshpool.

L Welshpool

Again the A483 cuts remorselessly across the bed of the canal, as it heads into the important Powys market town of Welshpool. In the canal's commercial heyday numerous wharves and warehouses lined its passage through the town. A cast iron aqueduct, reminiscent of Telford's on the Birmingham & Liverpool Junction, spans the Lledan Brook and an adjoining overbridge was formerly the route of the narrow gauge Welshpool & Llanfair Railway. Near the centre of the town stands the basin wharf and warehouse which is now open as an exhibition of the canal and its history; a fitting end to your perambulation of the Montgomery Canal.

Sustenance

Llanymynech has three pubs, two fish & chip shops and a post office stores. Arddlin has a

pub and a general store with tea rooms attached.

Counter Attractions

● Welshpool & Llanfair Light Railway. Weekends Easter - October and daily in high season. Tel: Welshpool (0938) 810441.
● Powis Castle. Restored medieval castle set in beautiful parkland. Tel: Welshpool 4336.

Encore

One doesn't have to look too far to seek out alternative walks along the Montgomery Canal. A splendid series of leaflets, available from the Montgomery Canal Project, 2 Canal Yard, Welshpool, Powys SY21 7AQ. Tel: Welshpool (0938) 4348, covers the whole canal in excellent detail, and gives all the information that walkers are likely to need.

Information

Wales Tourist Board Information Centre, Vicarage Garden Car Park, Welshpool. Tel: Welshpool (0938) 2043.

Walk 31   ☒

Oxford Canal

Oxfordshire

Tackley - Lower Heyford   4½ miles

The Walk

This relatively short walk is a celebration of the rural wanderings of the beautiful Oxford Canal. Sadly it is only south of Banbury, along the mellow valley of the river Cherwell, that towpath conditions allow a continuous walk of any substance. In reality it is four walks in one as the seasons change to seduce the eye with a myriad of nature's wonders that, other than the canal itself, still remain largely beyond the touch of man.

Start Point

Heyford Station, 12 miles south of Banbury. OS ref: SP 483247.

Access

Train, bus or car (free parking available at the station). South Midland's X59 (Oxford-Banbury-Coventry) service passes within ¼

mile of both Heyford and Tackley stations. Tel: Banbury (0296) 62368 for bus information; Oxford (0865) 722333 for train times.

Directions

1. Catch a train from Heyford Station to Tackley Halt - there are two useful services each morning (ex. Sunday).

2. Leave Tackley Halt by the gate on the left just beyond the platform and follow the path uphill.

3. At the T-junction turn left and follow the path round to the right and across a backwater of the river Cherwell. Pigeon's Lock on the canal is on the other side of the buildings that are now visible across the field.

4. Follow the footpath signs behind these buildings, across the Cherwell again and round to the left to Pigeon's Lock.

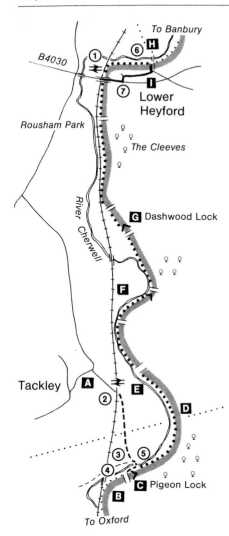

5. Join the towpath at the lockside and proceed north (left) for 3½ miles.
6. Leave the canal at (lift) bridge 205, cross it and proceed into Lower Heyford village.
7. Turn right onto the main street, then left by the "Bell" and right onto the B4030. Heyford Station is on the right down the hill.

Points of Interest

A Tackley
Tackley, a typical stone-built Oxfordshire village, is worth the diversion. The church, manor, village stores and one of the pubs encapsulate an unspoilt village green. In addition to its collection of car memorabilia, the "Gardiner Arms" is known for its baps with the choice of around 40 different fillings!

B Oxford Canal
Conceived in 1768 as the link in the 'Grand Cross' of canals connecting the rivers Thames, Mersey, Severn and Trent, the Oxford Canal was not completed in its entirety from the Coventry Canal to Oxford until 1790. Banbury had been reached from the north twelve years earlier. The canal's incessant meanderings thus far, as it clung closely to the contours act as a reminder that James Brindley was its original surveyor and engineer. By the time the first load of Warwickshire coal made its way into Oxford, canal technology on the southern Oxford, influenced by a modicum of thrift, had progressed somewhat. In particular locks and bridges were constructed to more economic specifications and even the waters of the river Cherwell were twice crossed 'on the level'. Commercial traffic on the Oxford finally ceased in the early Sixties; the records of boats unloading at Oxford tell their own tale - 223 in 1942, 24 in 1952, a mere 16 in 1956. Today the waterway has become, despite periodic water shortages, one of the most popular cruising routes and forms with its erstwhile commercial rival the Grand Union (formerly 'Junction') Canal, an extended circular cruise via the Thames and London.

C Pigeon's Lock
Pigeon's Lock, like all those south of Banbury, was constructed, in the interests of economy, with a single gate top and bottom. Its rise and fall of 8ft 4in typifies the tendency for deeper chambers favoured between Banbury and Oxford. The name derives from the house overlooking the lock which was once "The Three Pigeons", a canalside inn frequented by the working boatmen plying the Oxford cut. If they planned it right they could stop overnight at "The Pigeons", work down to Oxford and be back for another night in the tap-room or bar-parlour.

D Akeman Street
The line of the Roman road known as Akeman Street is crossed by both the track down to Pigeon's Lock and the canal itself. The original purpose of the Roman network of roads was military, to move the advancing legions and to secure the parameters of the conquered territory. Administrative and commercial considerations followed with Akeman Street forming a direct link, via Alchester (near Bicester), between the Fosse Way at Cirencester (Corinium Dubunnorum) and Watling Street at St. Albans (Verulamium).

E The River Cherwell
The canal from Tackley to Lower Heyford - and beyond in both directions - follows the valley of the river Cherwell. Initially both pass through the sylvan delights of what is left of one of Britain's ancient forests, Wychwood, before opening out to rolling pastures to the east and water meadows to the west. Often only the ridge of the lightly wooded towpath separates the two - the natural habitat of the patient heron, which casts a malevolent eye on both canal and river, and the cheeky squirrel playing catch-me-if-you-can. As part of an old packhorse route, the 3-arched bridge across the river near the lonely Northbrook Lock predates the canal; the canal bridge therefore is an appendage which successfully blends in with its neighbour . . . oh, that today's architects and planners had such an eye for the obvious!

F The Railway
The railcar which carries you from Heyford to Tackley travels along a line with its own unique history. Built from Oxford to Banbury by the Great Western Railway in 1850, it was part of Brunel's controversial 'Broad Gauge' empire, whose 7ft between the rails was at odds with all the other railway companies' 4ft 8½in gauge. Converted to standard gauge as early as 1869, today the line is in the fore-front of another battle. Opponents of the M40 motorway extension from Oxford to Birmingham say that the line has more than enough capacity to cater for the transport needs of the area, and that there is no justification for a new road to cut a contentious swathe across some of the finest countryside in the South Midlands.

G The Towpath
Towpaths existed to enable working boats to be horse-drawn before - and even after - the advent of the motorised boat. And it was here on the southern Oxford Canal that the use of the horse continued long after it had vanished from most other waterways. The last of the owner-boatmen, the so-called 'Number Ones', Joe Skinner, was still plying these waters with his mule-drawn boat

Friendship (now an exhibit at the Boat Museum, Ellesmere Port) during the Fifties.

H Lower Heyford Lift Bridge

Following the almost primaeval quality of The Cleeves, the canal opens out and civilization reappears in the form of extensive moorings and the Black Prince hire-base, before it swings eastwards to the sole lift bridge on the walk. The economic considerations already alluded to meant that, wherever possible, lift bridges rather than fixed stone bridges were used south of Banbury. This particular one, being constructed of iron, is in itself unique to this canal.

I Lower Heyford

Our walk began by Flights Mill back at Pigeon's Lock and ends by Heyford Mill, both of which used the water-power of the Cherwell centuries before the canal-builders descended upon this peaceful valley. Lower Heyford too has nestled above the valley of the Cherwell since long before the bridge replaced the 'ford' in the 13th century. The village, complete with olde worlde pub, gathers itself around a small square; it is a place where the artefacts of the 20th century seem curiously incongruous. Close your eyes and a fleeting step back in time could just transform this very square into the bustling 19th century market place it once was. The 14th century church on the other hand keeps itself in the background, its porch adorned with a sundial with the inscription: NIL NISI CELESTIO RADIO.

J Upper Heyford

Further on up the valley Lower Heyford's other half, Upper Heyford, is host to the United States Air Force. Though this is beyond the confines of this particular walk, the F11 fighters don't always see it that way. So be prepared for your peace to be occasionally shattered . . . the curious inter-mingling of American and Oxfordshire accents hereabouts might also come as a severe aural shock!

Sustenance

Both Tackley and Lower Heyford boast good hostelries and the traditional village stores.

Counter Attractions

● Rousham Park, Lower Heyford. Gardens open daily, 10am-6pm (4.30pm, October-Easter). House open Wed, Sun and Bank Hol. April-Sept, 2pm-5.30pm. Tel: Steeple Aston (0869) 47110. Admission charge. Castellated house built in 1635. Remodelled c.1730 by William Kent - the gardens remain

the only surviving example of his landscape design with temples, statues and hanging woods above the Cherwell.
● Blenheim Palace, Woodstock. Open daily 11am-6pm, mid March-end October. Park open daily 9am-5pm. Tel: Woodstock (0993) 811325. Admission charge. An Italian palace in an English park being the cumulative skills of Vanburgh and 'Capability' Brown; the home of the 11th Duke of Marlborough and the birthplace of Sir Winston Churchill. Includes Churchill Exhibition, Arboretum, Butterfly and Plant Centre. Adventure Playground and Narrow Gauge Railway.

Encore

If you are in a walking mood then the featured walk could be tackled in reverse and extended on down to Shipton-on-Cherwell (another 2½ miles), where, between Enslow and Shipton, the Cherwell and the canal flow as one for about a mile. The X59 bus service stops off at Shipton twice a day.

Information

Tourist Information Centre, Banbury Museum, 8 Horsefair, Banbury.
Tel: Banbury (0285) 59855.

Walk 32
Peak Forest Canal
Greater Manchester
Strines - Romiley   5 miles

The Walk

A hundred foot high aqueduct would qualify as the highlight of most towpath trails, but on this modest 5 mile stroll Marple's spectacular aqueduct has to vie with a 16 lock flight, a tunnel with an unusual horse path, and some dramatic Pennine hill scenery, so interest seldom lapses!

Start Point

Romiley railway station.
OS ref: SJ 942908.

Access

By train (local services, daily, between Manchester Piccadilly, Marple and New Mills - Tel: 061-832 8353), bus (Greater Manchester services - Tel: 061-226 8181) and car - Romiley is on the A627, 4 miles east of Stockport. There is no station car park but street parking is available nearby.

Directions

1 Catch a train from Romiley station to Strines - the service is hourly Mon-Sat. but less frequent on Sun, so check times on 061-832 8353.

2 Leave Strines station by "Way Out" sign, descend steps and turn left under bridge. Proceed down cobbled lane, cross river and continue to main road.
3 Go directly over B6101 and follow lane up to canal. Just short of aqueduct turn left between fence posts to reach towpath.
4 Follow towpath for 3 miles to Hyde Bank Tunnel.
5 There is no towpath through the tunnel. Take path over the top which turns into a lane past Hyde Bank Farm. Beyond farm bear left down lane beneath stone bridge to rejoin towpath.
6 Leave towpath down steps at aqueduct. Turn under aqueduct and follow Green Lane until it joins Stockport Road. Turn right back to station.

Points of Interest

A The River Goyt
The tiny unstaffed railway station of Strines snuggles at the foot of the wild country of Mellor Moor. The line, once shared by the Midland and Great Central railway companies, is currently the main route between Manchester and Sheffield, but will soon lose

the canal essays an utterly rural course. One's gaze is alternately drawn onto the rooftops of the Goyt valley or over to the gaunt outline of the moors.

C Marple Junction
The towpath changes sides at bridge 19 and lines of moored boats herald Marple. Bridge 1 of the Macclesfield Canal spans the junction, beyond which stands a handsome stone warehouse. The canalscape is most appealing: stone is used throughout, cobbles

that status when a new link at Hazel Grove causes express trains to be re-routed via Stockport. A steep cobbled lane descends to the valley floor, passing a stone built mill with an ornate dovecote islanded in the centre of the mill pond. The high chimney of a nearby works dominates the view. Indeed the valley of the river Goyt is punctuated by mills and factories that have taken advantage of its inherent power. The river itself rises 1,800 feet up near the "Cat & Fiddle Inn" on the Macclesfield-Buxton road. At its confluence with the river Tame at Stockport it becomes the river Mersey.

B The Peak Forest Canal
A rutted lane climbs up from the Marple - New Mills road and passes under a small aqueduct carrying the canal along its 500ft. contour. The Peak Forest Canal, as hauntingly lovely as its name suggests, is divided into 'Lower' and 'Upper' sections, running from Marple northwards to Dukinfield and southwards to Whaley Bridge respectively. The distinction was brought about by cash flow problems during construction, and instead of the planned lock flight at Marple a less expensive tramway provided a temporary link. Actually, the canal, promoted to bring limestone down from the Derbyshire Peak, was almost immediately a roaring success. It contrived to flourish well into the railway years by astutely selling out to the Manchester, Sheffield & Lincolnshire Railway. Trade on the upper section ceased between the wars but continued on the rest of the canal until 1959. Subsequently the lower section fell into decay but was happily re-opened as part of the 'Cheshire Ring' in 1974. As far as Marple

abound, and there's an air of well kept confidence about the place in accord with the junction's strategic position on the 'Cheshire Ring'.

D Marple Locks
The sixteen locks of the massive Marple flight carry the Peak Forest Canal 200ft. down towards the valley of the Goyt. The top four chambers must be unique in their parallel proximity to the neat front gardens of a row of houses; below lock 13 the towpath passes through a short separate tunnel of its own; by lock 9 a lovely stone warehouse has been tastefully converted into offices; the railway tunnels beneath locks 4-6; and down, down descends the canal, escaping from Marple's suburbs as woods close in to accentuate the gradient.

E Marple Aqueduct
Marple aqueduct is not alone in its juxtaposition to the adjoining railway viaduct - the same phenomenon occurs at Chirk on the Llangollen Canal. The two immense structures bridge a steeply wooded ravine carved by the Goyt; the canal is 97 ft. above the river, the railway 135ft. Just past the northern end of the aqueduct a stepped path leads precipitously down through the trees, offering a clearer view of the design of the aqueduct with its unusual cylindrical hollowed sections, built so to lessen the weight resting on the piers.

F Hyde Bank Tunnel
On the far side of the aqueduct the canal enters a narrow cutting with a stone retaining wall. This was originally Rose Hill tunnel until opened out in 1820, but you don't have to walk too far to see a real tunnel. The canal runs through woods on a shelf high above the Goyt. Huge stone buttresses support a retaining wall on the towpath side. The portal of Hyde Bank tunnel then swallows up the canal and walkers have to follow the path taken by boat horses in days gone by. The diversion is entrancing. Climbing abruptly the path meets the route of the "Valley Way" and together they pass a farm where you can buy milk fresh from the cow or indulge in a carton of home produced cream. Beyond the farm the horse path goes under an elegant stone bridge, carrying the driveway to an adjacent house, and crosses the north-western portal of the tunnel to rejoin the towpath opposite Oakwood Mill. The walk's attraction barely diminishes as the towpath crosses a pair of sturdy aqueducts to reach the outskirts of Romiley.

Sustenance

Marple's busy town centre is only a couple of minutes walk from bridge 18 and here can be found numerous pubs, cafes and shops. At Romiley the "Duke of York", a John Smiths house offering bar lunches Mon-Sat, could be a fitting end to your outing.

Counter Attractions

Lyme Park - National Trust Elizabethan house and deer park. Located on A6, 2 miles west of Disley. House open Apr-Oct, afternoons ex Mon. Gardens open daily all year. Tel: Disley (06632) 2023.

Encore

The Peak Forest Canal is accompanied by parallel rail routes (though not always the same one) throughout the 14 miles from Dukinfield to Whaley Bridge. Therefore two more relatively short linear walks will, added to that featured here, be enough to familiarise you with the whole canal. They are: Dukinfield (nearest station Guide Bridge adjacent to Ashton Canal, bridge 25) to Romiley and Disley to Whaley Bridge. Tel: 061-832 8353 for details of rail services.

Information

Tourist Information Centre, 9 Princes Street, Manchester. Tel: 061-480 0315.

Hyde Bank Tunnel on the Peak Forest Canal.

Opening the gates - Tilstone Lock on the Shropshire Union Canal

Autumn woods beside the River Don near Conisbrough

Winter conversation on the Trent & Mersey Canal

Ocean bound through Cheshire pastures on the Weaver Navigation

Walk 33
Rochdale Canal
Yorkshire
Todmorden - Hebden Bridge   4½ miles

The Walk

This is a walk of almost unparalleled Pennine beauty, a natural beauty edged with that rugged and uncompromising facade that is uniquely Yorkshire. The Leeds & Liverpool Canal might justifiably claim to be 'the mightiest of them all', but in its heyday the 33 broad miles of the Rochdale Canal must surely have instilled in the observer a sense of wonder. The walk, along the young valley of the river Calder, encompasses much of the longest restored section and whets the appetite for further exploration of what was - and might yet again be - the most successful of the trans-Pennine waterways.

Start Point

Hebden Bridge Railway Station.
OS ref: SD 995268.

Access

Bus, train or car. Hebden Bridge is served by good MetroBus links within Yorkshire (Tel: Halifax (0422) 26313) and a frequent MetroTrain service between Leeds and Manchester (Tel: Bradford (0274) 733994), Hebden Bridge Station has its own free car park.

Directions

1 Catch a train to Todmorden. The service is fairly frequent.
2 Alight at Todmorden and take the road almost opposite the exit (Rise Lane) that swings down to the right of the "Queen Hotel".
3 Turn right onto the main road at the T-junction.
4 Turn right at the canal bridge to view Todmorden 'Library' Lock.
5 Proceed north-east under the road bridge and continue along the towpath to Hebden Bridge.

6 Cross the lock at Hebden Bridge and proceed back along offside path (Hebble End Aqueduct) and follow this up the hill to view the aqueduct and the river Calder.
7 Return to the lockside and follow the towpath (now changed sides) through Hebden Bridge as far as the next bridge, beyond which leave the towpath by the cottages and head back up to the road.
8 Turn left - the station is a short distance up the hill.

Points of Interest

A The Rochdale Canal
The construction of this, the first trans-Pennine waterway to be completed, was a mighty undertaking. In a relatively short distance it links Lancashire and Yorkshire; from Sowerby Bridge and its junction with the Calder & Hebble Navigation it rises through 36 broad locks to a short summit 600ft. above sea level before dropping a further 56 locks through Rochdale to Castlefield

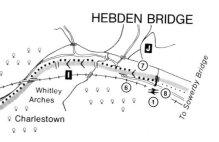

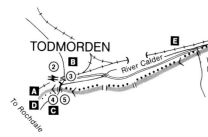

Junction and the Bridgewater Canal in Manchester. Three of the greatest canal engineers, James Brindley, John Rennie and William Jessop, had a hand in its conception and construction and the end result, even after years of dereliction, remains a lasting testimony to the skills of these embryonic canal surveyors and engineers. The last barge travelled the full length of the canal in 1937, though local traffic continued at the Manchester end until 1950. Until recently, however, only the 1¼ miles of the 'Rochdale Nine', a vital part of the popular 'Cheshire Ring' cruising route through Manchester, has remained navigable. But through the efforts of the Rochdale Canal Company, the Rochdale Canal Society and the active support of local authorities, restoration of the remainder has become more than a likelihood - the Todmorden-Hebden Bridge section being one of the first to taste again the passage of boats.

B Todmorden

Calderdale's cross-Pennine valleys meet at Todmorden, a millstone grit town with textiles in its blood, nestling in a gently sloping vale. The transport revolution went hand in hand with industrial change and with the coming of the canal Todmorden took full advantage of both. Mechanisation evolved faster in the cotton-spinning industry and the town, with strong Lancashire leanings (until 1888 it was mostly in Lancashire), switched from wool to cotton as its raw material. The canal also brought prosperity to one of Todmorden's best known sons, John Fielden, who in turn bestowed the Unitarian Church, the Town Hall and Dobroyd Castle on the town. Fielden himself is best known for his campaign to secure the 'Ten Hour Act' in 1847 which sought to improve factory conditions by making it illegal to have to work more than a ten-hour day and 58 hours a week.

C Todmorden 'Library' Lock (No. 19)

The plaque on this restored lock not only commemorates its re-opening in 1982 but also recognises the stalwart support given to the Restoration Scheme by both Calderdale Council and the West Yorkshire County Council. Restoration along the whole length of the canal has involved the active participation of other local authorities viz: Greater Manchester, Manchester City, Oldham and Rochdale - a united approach that assures the canal's future as a living linear amenity.

D The Calderdale and Rossendale Ways

The 50 mile Calderdale Way, "not so much a footpath, more a way of life", crosses the canal on the southern outskirts of Todmorden. More detailed information of what a Dutch organisation voted as one of Europe's "finest walks" can be found in Walk 7, the Calder & Hebble Navigation. The canal towpath beyond 'Library' Lock also accommodates one of the series of Rossendale Way walks (No. 8) details of which are available from the Planning Section, Stubby Lee Hall, Bacup, Lancashire.

E The Valley of the Calder

Todmorden's rows of tightly terraced houses and the bric-a-brac of assorted industry are soon left behind. The gaunt, almost satanic, church atop the valley is an ever-present

Glistening cobbles and a newly restored lock on the Rochdale Canal.

sentinel. Rail, road, river and canal fill the valley floor, the railway keeping itself aloof on an impressive viaduct visible from Lobb Mill Lock (No. 16) and the river, still in its infancy, chortling along just beyond the towpath, a convenient recipient of the canal's overspill via the towpath itself. 'Calder' means 'rapid water' so it is hardly surprising that, augmented by Colden Water and Hebden Water, the river that the canal crosses on the 4-arched Hebble End Aqueduct at Hebden Bridge, is beginning to come of age. The valley is punctuated on the one hand with the remnants of the textile industry and, on the other, a steeply wooded hillside and the constant trickle of water. Just beyond Holmcoat Lock (No. 14), a small graveyard, seemingly minus a church, inspires a mental diversion from the almost compulsory canalside sewage farm alongside.

F Callis Mill
Here by Callis Lock (No. 13) is the headquarters of the Rochdale Canal Joint Restoration Scheme, a Community Project funded by the Manpower Services Commission. Their success thus far in restoring the canal is evident everywhere you look, an achievement all the more astonishing when you take into account that the young workforce is self-taught. Dozens of lock gates have been made in the workshops here, including those for the restored locks on the Huddersfield Narrow Canal (see Walk 19). Fortunately the Canal Company was able to produce original drawings for most of the locks, some of which were found to have useful - and invariably correct - annotations such as, "these gates would have been better 1 inch wider at the top".

G The Pennine Way
If by now you have decided that towpath walking is not for you there is an alternative just above Callis Lock where the Pennine Way crosses the valley; by turning left here you could be in Scotland in a week or so. The Way was Britain's first long-distance footpath, a more detailed account of which can be found in walk 25, on the Leeds & Liverpool Canal.

H The Manchester and Leeds Railway
In railway terms the line that accompanies the canal from Todmorden and crosses it via the Whitley Arches was one of the pioneers of the Railway Age. Surveyed by George Stephenson in the late 1820s the line was eventually opened in 1841 and at the time boasted the longest railway tunnel in the world, the 2285yd. Summit Tunnel.

Stephenson once wagered his reputation on the strength of the tunnel's linings, asserting that nothing could destroy it; the accident in 1984 when a petrol tanker caught fire in the tunnel and sent burning gas shooting from the ventilator shafts perhaps proved him right.

I Stubbing Wharf
The final approach to Hebden Bridge is dominated initially by the older - and originally more important - hamlet of Heptonstall high up on the ridge to the left. But as you watch the tower of the old church appear to set behind the hill don't miss the canalside community around Stubbing Wharf. Here perhaps more than anywhere else the imagination can run riot as it pieces together a past scene busy with boats working their way through the two nearby locks (Nos 11 and 10), their weary crews availing themselves of the handy hostelry. Not far away are the canalside remains of a canopied warehouse, another piece of the jigsaw that recreates images of another time.

J Hebden Bridge
Millstone grit personifies this rugged Yorkshire terrain. Yet there is another softer side to this stony facade and when the sun shines down on Hebden Bridge it reveals a softness and warmth that is nothing short of seductive. It is a town steeped in history from the building of the 'bridge' in 1510 that gave it its name, to the Battle of Heptonstall in 1643; from being at the forefront of the textile revolution in the 19th century to being the 20th century's 'Pennine Centre'. The coming of the canal and then the railway put Hebden Bridge on the textile map of the Pennines and much of the town's obvious and accessible history reflects this once thriving industry. There are the remains of early cotton mills and, still inhabited, several of the so-called 'double-deck' houses built into the steep hillside. On the canal itself the original wharf has been restored as a public amenity, a fine example of a thoughtful and aesthetic approach to preserving and building on the past.

Sustenance
Both Todmorden and Hebden Bridge abound in good pubs and restaurants. The former seems to have a penchant for Indian restaurants while the latter boasts a gem of a cafe, "The Cabin", where you can buy tea by the pint! En route the "Woodman Inn" near Callis Lock is both accessible and inviting.

Counter Attractions
The area positively bursts with potential attractions and the Information Centre at Hebden Bridge (see below) is a superb starting point in itself.
● Automobilia, Billy Lane, Old Town, Hebden Bridge. Open daily (ex Mon) April-Sept, noon-6pm. Sat & Sun only Oct-Mar. Admission charge. Tel: Hebden Bridge (0422) 844775. A fascinating collection of old cars and motor cycles, concentrating on Austin/Morris vehicles. Licensed restaurant on site specialises in Austrian food.

Encore
The towpath is walkable in both directions from the extremities of the featured walk, with good rail and bus connections at convenient points along the route. The $3\frac{1}{2}$ currently unrestored miles of the Mytholmroyd to Sowerby Bridge section, through Luddenden Foot and Friendly take the walker into less dramatic terrain. At the end is the only tunnel on the Rochdale, albeit a short offering, and the link with the Calder & Hebble Navigation at Sowerby Bridge.

Information
Tourist Information Centre, 1 Bridge Gate, Hebden Bridge, West Yorkshire. Tel: Hebden Bridge (0422) 843831.

Walk 34
Shropshire Union Canal
Staffordshire
Brewood - Wheaton Aston   **4 miles**

⊠

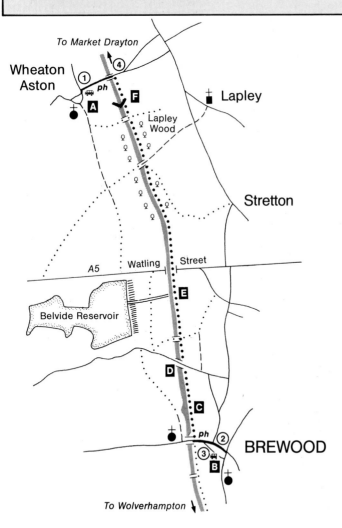

The Walk
Walking the former Birmingham & Liverpool Junction section of the Shropshire Union Canal between Wolverhampton and Nantwich is not easy. Not that the towpath is poor, for the most part it's in good condition. The problem is that the canal cuts across the social grain of the countryside it traverses and consequently there are few parallel public transport services. However, the walk featured here manages to illustrate just about all the characteristics of this characterful waterway and part of the fun is the ride out from Wheaton Aston on the idiosyncratic Green Bus Service.

Start Point
Wheaton Aston village.
OS ref: SJ 852127.

Access
Bus (Midland Red/Green Bus services from Wolverhampton, 3 or 4 per day Mon-Sat. Tel: Wolverhampton (0902) 20018) and car - Wheaton Aston is 2 miles NE of Ivetsey Bank on the A5, 7 miles west of the M6 at Junction 12.

Directions
1 Catch Green Bus Service 471 from stops in Wheaton Aston to Brewood market place. Currently there are convenient departures for walkers at 9.40 Mon-Fri and 13.20 Mon-Sat, but check on Cheslyn Hay (0922) 414141 before you go.
2 Leave Brewood market place along Bargate Street, continuing past Lloyds Bank until you reach the canal.
3 Access to the towpath is down steps opposite the "Bridge Inn". Turn right under bridge 14 and follow the towpath for 3 miles to bridge 19.
4 At bridge 19, opposite the "Hartley Arms", leave the canal and turn left back into the village to complete your walk.

Points of Interest
A Green Bus Co.
Warstones of Great Wyrley, near Cannock, operate their distinctive Green Bus Services over a wide variety of routes north of Wolverhampton. Small independent bus companies of this sort tend to acquire 'cast-me-downs' from the large networks, put out to grass on less strenuous duties. On our research trip the 9.40 from Wheaton Aston was a venerable double-decker with one of those 'half-cab' fronts, a rear door, side corridor on the top deck, and a rubicund

conductor who sold us our tickets from a rack of many colours, clipping them with a bell punch. Even the more commonly used saloons date from the early Sixties and rattle their way down the dusty lanes to Brewood.

B Brewood
Brewood retains an ancient air of calm. Doubtless because it has had the luck to be a soundproofing mile away from the cacophonies of the A5, and few of the hurriers along that artery ever bother to find their way along the little byways to 'Brood' as the locals call it. These winding lanes lead to a pleasing market place (though no market alas) looked over by the Gothic fantasies of Speedwell Castle, built in the 18th century from the winnings of a racehorse called 'Speedwell'. The parish church of St. Mary & St. Chad dates from the 13th century. Inside are alabaster monuments to the local Gifford family. After the Civil War Battle of Worcester, Charles Gifford was with Charles II on his flight from the 'Royal City'. Riding quickly northwards they came to nearby Boscobel where the King spent the wet day of September 4th, 1651 hidden in a coppice disguised as a woodman. Two days later, after an abortive attempt to cross the guarded river Severn, Charles II and a local man, Colonel Carless, who is buried in Brewood churchyard, hid within the trunk of a hollow oak in the grounds of Boscobel House while the Roundheads beat the woods.

C Canal Wharf
The canal wharf at Brewood remained important to the prosperity of the village for longer than is usually the case. The railway never came to Brewood, so until the development of reliable road transport, coal was still brought in by narrowboat for distribution around the village and outlying communities, and agricultural produce was taken to the wharf for shipment. Today the wharf remains busy and largely unaltered, seeing continued use as the base for a hire boat firm.

D The Shropshire Union
The Shropshire Union Canal Company was formed in 1845 as an amalgamation of several earlier concerns. What is now known as the Shropshire Union Canal - from Autherley Junction, near Wolverhampton, to Ellesmere Port on the banks of the Mersey - is made up of three constituents: The Chester Canal of 1778; the Wirral Line of 1795; and the Birmingham & Liverpool Junction Canal opened between Autherley and Nantwich in 1835. This last was the final major canal to be built in Britain (with the notable exception

of the Manchester Ship Canal) but already the Railway Age had dawned and narrow-boats carrying 25 tons at 3 mph could hardly compete with goods trains steaming along at 25 mph with a payload in the hundreds of tons. Nevertheless the 'Shroppie', as it is affectionately known, continued as a commercial link until the demise of the last cargo carrying narrowboats in the 1960s.

E Stretton Aqueduct
Emerging from Brewood cutting the canal heads in a north-westerly direction past the huge headbank of Belvide Reservoir from which a feeder comes in on the far bank. Presently, Telford's famous aqueduct of 1832 is reached, and you can look down with disdain upon the 20th century traffic hurtling along what was once the Roman's Watling Street; that highway which echoed to the relentless tread of the legions from Dover, through London, to Wroxeter on the banks of the river Severn. The histories of Watling Street and Holyhead Road are intertwined and often confused. The ubiquitous Telford was commissioned to re-engineer the London-Holyhead coaching route and the resultant improvement on the turnpikes was opened in 1830. Numerous canal writers have fallen into the trap of assuming that Telford's aqueduct crosses his own road at Stretton. Sadly, historical accuracy defies romance, because Telford's road threaded the Black Country north of Daventry, not rejoining the Roman road until Oakengates, some ten miles to the west of Stretton. The aqueduct is a sturdy, yet elegant structure consisting of a cast iron trough resting on brick abutments and stone columns.

F Wheaton Aston Lock
Beyond Stretton Aqueduct the canal is quickly enveloped by the bosky shadows of Lapley Wood cutting. The towpath, though wide, can be a little glutinous here as the cutting has penetrated the water table. Eventually the woods recede to reveal the one and only lock in 24 miles of canal between Autherley and Tyrley, near Market Drayton. By the time this canal was planned at the end of the Canal Era, experience had shown that boats could be worked faster through lock flights of several chambers rather than single locks spaced at irregular intervals. In the summer months a shop by the lock sells gifts to passing boaters.

Sustenance
Taylors bakers have branches in both villages and you can pick up the basis of a fine picnic in either. Both villages are also fortunate to boast pleasant cafes: "Trevett House Carvery" in Wheaton Aston is open daily (ex Mon) for breakfasts, morning coffees and lunches; in Brewood, "Studio One" in Church Street is a craft shop which offers coffees, light lunches and teas. Brewood has lots of pubs to choose from and Wheaton Aston has two.

Counter Attractions
Chillington Hall. 2 miles south-west of Brewood. A Georgian house with grounds landscaped by Capability Brown. Open Thursday afternoons May-Sept. Admission charge. Tel: Brewood (0902) 850236.

Encore
Unless you are prepared to cover long distances, walking the towpath of the former Birmingham & Liverpool Junction section of the Shropshire Union Canal is fraught with lack of public transport. A few short circular walks suggest themselves though. At Gnosall, on the A518 8 miles west of Stafford, a lane crosses above Cowley Tunnel offering a 1½ mile 'figure of 8' walk between bridges 32 and 34, car parking being available adjacent to the latter. Two miles to the north, at the interesting former junction of Norbury, a walk along Shelmore embankment combined with the parallel path at the edge of Shelmore Wood makes a satisfying 2 mile circuit. Lastly, the towpath between Tyrley and Market Drayton is part of the 4 mile Market Drayton Nature Trail, descriptive leaflets to which are available, price 30p from: Shropshire Trust & Nature Conservation, Agriculture House, Barker Street, Shrewsbury. Tel: (0743) 241691.

Information
Tourist Information Centre, Greengate, Stafford. Tel: (0785) 3181.

Walk 35
Shropshire Union Canal
Cheshire
Calveley - Tarporley   7 miles

The Walk

If, south of Nantwich, the Shropshire Union resembles nothing so much as a Roman road, then, northwards to Chester, the 'Shroppie' appears to have been engineered on an off-day by the 'Rolling English Drunkard' of Chesterton's poem. The truth is, of course, that these disparate sections were built at different times by quite separate companies which were taken over by the Shropshire Union in 1845, thus forming $2/3$ of what we now know today as the Shropshire Union Main Line. Thus, in contrast to the grouping of locks in flights and the use of 'cut & fill' techniques evinced in the previous walk, here the canal adheres closely to the contours, descending through irregular locks off the Cheshire Plain down into the valley of the Dee. In fact, throughout, this is perhaps a surprisingly scenic walk with the tiny River Gowy a constant and entertaining companion until one leaves the canal astern and makes the acquaintance of the Sandstone Trail.

Start Point

Tarporley Post Office.
OS ref: SJ 555625.

Access

Bus or car. Crosville C84 links Chester with Nantwich, Crewe and Newcastle-under-Lyme, hourly, daily - Tel: Chester (0244) 381515. Tarporley is on the A51, 15 miles south-east of Chester. There are two handy car parks off the High Street.

Directions

1 Catch a Crosville C84 bus (see Access) from the stop by Tarporley Post Office (opposite the Church) and book to the "Davenport Arms" at Calveley.

2 Alight from bus, cross the railway and join the canal at bridge 104, proceeding westwards for 4 miles to Wharton's Lock.

3 Cross the lock and climb the stile with yellow Sandstone Trail way-marker. Proceed around the left hand edge of the field to the road.

4 Cross stiles and minor road and follow yellow way-markers through three fields.

5 Go over stile and follow minor road to left for $1/2$ mile.

6 At T junction, cross road and climb stile into field (stepping stones are thoughtfully provided across the muddy ground by the cattle trough). Keep to the right hand hedge and follow yellow way-markers from field to field.

7 A signpost points the way to Tarporley, leaving the field to the right across two stiles and through a kissing gate. Keep to the left hand edge of this new field. Yellow arrows reassure you of your progress.

8 Cross the stile at the top end of the field and turn left as arrowed. After 50 yards bear right through a kissing gate and across an elaborate stile through the arch of a tree. Proceed up shallow cleft as way-marked.

9 Stiles lead across the new Tarporley by-pass (under construction at the time of writing). Once across the new route, simply follow the yellow arrows across the fields to reach Tarporley High Street.

Points of Interest

The Chester Canal
Watching enviously the development of the Trent & Mersey Canal to the east, the businessmen of Chester decided, early in the 1770s, to promote their own canal to link with the 'Grand Trunk' at Middlewich. Their enthusiasm was not shared by the directors of the Trent & Mersey, who feared that trade could be directed away from the northern section of their canal should such a link be constructed. Consequently the Chester Canal, the building of which began in 1772, headed southwards to Nantwich. This quiet Cheshire market town was reached seven years later. The trouble was, of course, that hardly anybody desired to carry any commodity between these two points and the canal quickly lapsed into a moribund state. Like a sad spinster, hardly expecting suitors to beat a path to her door, the Chester Canal sat on the shelf until the developing routes of the Ellesmere Canal Company to the north and west saw, by 1805, it becoming part of a through route. Even better times lay ahead, for in 1835 the Birmingham and Liverpool Junction Canal opened between Nantwich and Wolverhampton, creating a new route from the Black Country to the ports of the Mersey Estuary - the Chester Canal had become a main line at last, 56 years after its opening ceremony.

A Calveley Wharf
Calveley is a hamlet on the Chester-Nantwich road consisting of little more than a pub and a cheese warehouse. In the early days of the railway era, the Shropshire Union Company actually proposed converting their canal southwards from here to Wolverhampton into a railway. Instead, the wharf became a trans-shipment point between the two transport modes, extensive sidings filling the now cindered wasteground between the forgotten platforms of the long vanished Calveley Station and the linear moorings along the canal. One of the wharf buildings remains busy as a useful shop selling groceries and gifts to boaters. The broad beam canal sets uneventfully out westwards from Calveley, traversing the final vestige of the Cheshire Plain.

B Bunbury Locks
All of a sudden the landscape stirs from its lassitude and begins to pitch and roll, forcing the canal builders into the construction of a 'staircase' lock of two chambers at Bunbury. A staircase lock is one where adjacent chambers share common gates; here this

technique would have been adopted to make the most of a confined space. Beside the paired chambers stands a well preserved row of stables now used for boatbuilding and repair. In horseboat days, Bunbury was a change-station where fresh horses would take over from their exhausted colleagues on the 'flyboats' which completed the 80 mile Birmingham-Ellesmere Port journey in less than 30 hours. The horses, driven at a canter on these important services, were changed at roughly 20 mile intervals. An adjacent wharf building houses another gift shop. Bunbury village itself lies a mile or so to the south along a minor road bordered by big and prosperous Cheshire farmhouses and out-buildings. If you decide to divert that far you will find a notable parish church, an irony in a village which had close and often necessarily closet connections with the Methodist John Wesley.

C The Railway
Twice each night in the small hours the Holyhead Boat Train, once the famous "Irish Mail" rushes across the short iron span (cast on the Roodee at Chester) which carries the Crewe-Chester railway over the canal at the foot of Bunbury Locks. The line was opened on 1st October, 1840 as part of the 'Grand Junction' system. Though crossing nothing more than peaceful countryside punctuated by sleepy stations, often far from the villages they purported to serve, the line's status as a main line was never in doubt; an interesting parallel to the canal's history. Local railcars still supplement the Holyhead expresses but the last intermediate station, Beeston & Tarporley, was closed by - you've guessed it - Beeching in 1966.

D Tilstone Lock
It really is astonishing how hilly the landscape has become in such a short distance. The canal shimmies deftly between banks rising steeply from the narrow valley of the Gowy. Presently Tilstone Lock is reached, couched in the most gorgeous of settings. Lockside, an old brick-built watermill, dating from 1838, has been tenderly restored for residential use. Its now dry mill pond a declivity of mace and reed. A curious circular building was once used as a lengthsman's hut, the round roof is topped by a chimney that would not look out of place on a steam locomotive. Beneath the white-washed span of bridge 106, your breath is taken suddenly away by the sight of Beeston Castle perched on its uncompromising outcrop some two miles to the west: its brooding dominance increases as you

proceed westwards.

E Beeston Locks
The hideously ornate "Wild Boar Motel" mars the southern horizon, an object lesson in the dangers of overkill, but you can always look the other way upon hills reminiscent of the Downs, close-cropped by North, rather than South-Country sheep. In any case, you soon reach Beeston Stone Lock, so called to distinguish it from the lower of the two locks, which is built of iron. Constructed on running sand, Beeston Iron Lock was engineered by Thomas Telford in 1828 as a final solution to conquer the instability of previously conventionally engineered chambers. It is unique on the canal system.

F Beeston Wharf
Another of the numerous boathire bases which nowadays, at least in summer, make the Shroppie busier than even in its commercial heyday, occupies Beeston Wharf. It includes a little shop selling waterway books and curios. On Wednesdays and Fridays tannoy voices are conveyed on the wind from beyond the railway embankment where a busy cattle market bustles with live-stock and farming folk. Beneath the adjacent hillside, ribboned by a foreboding iron fence, hides a strategic oil reserve; a melancholy house with its windows shuttered waits for a national emergency before coming into its own. But let's not cloud this lovely walk, for beyond the wharf the canal is quickly lost in pockets of woodland bounded by pastures rarely bereft of Friesian milking herds.

G Wharton's Lock
Wharton's Lock lies almost within arrow shooting distance of Beeston Castle. Had Beeston Crag been fortunate enough to stand above the Rhine or perhaps beside the Loire, it would have been a world famous beauty spot - in England we tend to underplay such things. There is a less spurious German connection here, for during the Second World War a stray bomb, unleashed by a passing Luftwaffe bomber, blew the lock cottage to smithereens. There was also once a mill astride the Gowy at this spot. Another mill, restored not unlike that at Tilstone, survives beside the next bridge, but our route now leaves the canal and joins the Sandstone Trail.

H The Sandstone Trail
Millions of years ago, Cheshire was a desert. During a period of dramatic earth movements a ridge was created from the fractured rocks. A 30 mile long public right of way has been

surveyed following this ridge from the Mersey southwards to the Shropshire border, offering walkers a slice of Cheshire off the beaten track. To reach Tarporley our route lies along part of the trail, crossing typical Cheshire milking pastures carpeted with grass rich in nutrients which give the county its reputation for fine milk and cheese. Though the towpath has been left behind, this tranquil end to your walk comes as no anticlimax.

Sustenance

We found to our cost that early closing day in Tarporley is Wednesday - some establishments take this so literally that they don't open at all. Nevertheless, Tarporley has a number of pubs, a fish & chip bar and an Egon Ronay recommended tearoom adjunct to a dress shop (though male readers may find this latter somewhat intimidating!). By the bus stop in Calveley stands the "Davenport Arms", a Greenall Whitley house offering bar food. The next convenient watering hole lies at Beeston where you have the choice of the Lock Gates Cafe or beyond the railway, the "Beeston Castle Hotel" (Bass and bar food). "The Shady Oak", by bridge 109, $\frac{1}{4}$ mile beyond Wharton's Lock, has pleasant waterside gardens and a sophisticated bar menu.

Counter Attractions

● Bunbury Mill - $\frac{3}{4}$ mile south-west of bridge 105. Open Easter-Sept., Sat, Sun & Bank Hol. Mons., 2-5p,. Small admission charge. Restored water-powered mill.
● Beeston Castle - $\frac{3}{4}$ mile south of canal from bridge 108. Open daily, but note afternoons only on Sun and closed Mon-Sat for lunch 1-2pm. 13th century fortress offering wonderful views from the ruined battlements.

Encore

North of Chester and onwards to Ellesmere Port lies the third constituent of the Shropshire Union Canal Main Line, the Wirral Line of the Ellesmere Canal opened in 1795. Built to wide beam dimensions it has more in common with the Chester Canal than the Birmingham & Liverpool Junction. Its 8 lockless miles extend across the flat base of the Wirral Peninsular and though scenically unexceptional are not without interest to the true canal fan; especially with the Boat Museum to explore at journey's end.

Information

Tourist Information Centre, Beam Street, Nantwich. Tel: (0270) 623914.

Walk 36

South Yorkshire Canal
South Yorkshire

Doncaster - Conisbrough   8 miles

The Walk

The modern day Great North Road - A1M - as it passes to the west of Doncaster, leaps a deep wooded gorge through which runs the river Don. Few of the drivers hurtling across the chasm realise that the waterway below them is Britain's most recently modernised commercial navigation - the South Yorkshire Canal. So this walk sets out to become familiar with the reticent course of what was, prior to modernisation, known as the Sheffield & South Yorkshire Navigation, a transport route with ten times the capacity of the A1M, but one sadly neglected by bad timing and the 'depression' following modernisation. But waterway politics apart, this is an invigorating walk, encompassing industry and agriculture, woodland and quarry; a journey of oscillating moods that is more an adventure than a modest towpath stroll.

Start Point

Conisbrough railway station.
OS ref: SK 509995

Access

Train, (half-hourly service Mon-Sat on Sheffield - Doncaster line, also Sunday trains Tel: Doncaster (0302) 20191) and car - Conisbrough is on the A630 4 miles west of its interchange with the A1M; free car parking at station.

Directions

1 Catch train to Doncaster. Conisbrough station is unstaffed so you will have to buy your ticket from the guard or at the Doncaster end.
2 Turn left out of railway station along Trafford Way. Bear left at roundabout signposted "Wakefield A638". Cross bridge over railway and canal. Turn down steps on left signposted "Waterbus".

3 Follow path parallel to navigation past lock control tower, across old power station arm and continue along perimeter fence. The way here tends to be narrow and uneven but persistence pays dividends.
4 Cross bridge over unnavigable channel and proceed along embankment path.
5 At stile leave embankment and bear right to gate between farmhouse and outbuildings. Continue through farm.
6 Descend to stile on left and follow narrow path beside river. Presently this leads to another stile, cross this to embankment path and proceed to A1M viaduct.
7 Cross stile and follow path through trees.
8 Continue past Sprotbrough Lock, go under bridge and then turn right up stone steps at waterbus stop. Turn right again across bridges over navigation and weir stream then follow pavement to right uphill.
9 Follow road through Dolomite quarry. Take care of traffic.
10 Where quarry road veers to left under railway, proceed along waterside path, which presently begins to climb up through woods.
11 The path descends again to river then passes beneath railway bridge. Continue up it as it climbs back up through the woods and emerges to join broader track. This immediately forks, choose the lower route to the right and follow beneath viaduct.
12 Beyond viaduct bear right off the track down path through the woods.
13 The path reaches the outskirts of Conisbrough. At the bottom of a residential road called Milner Gate it becomes a lane known as Windgate Hill, continue downhill to "The Castle" pub.
14 Turn right and proceed down lane past squash club for a final look at the river. Return to squash club and turn right up Burcroft Hill. At main road turn right to station.

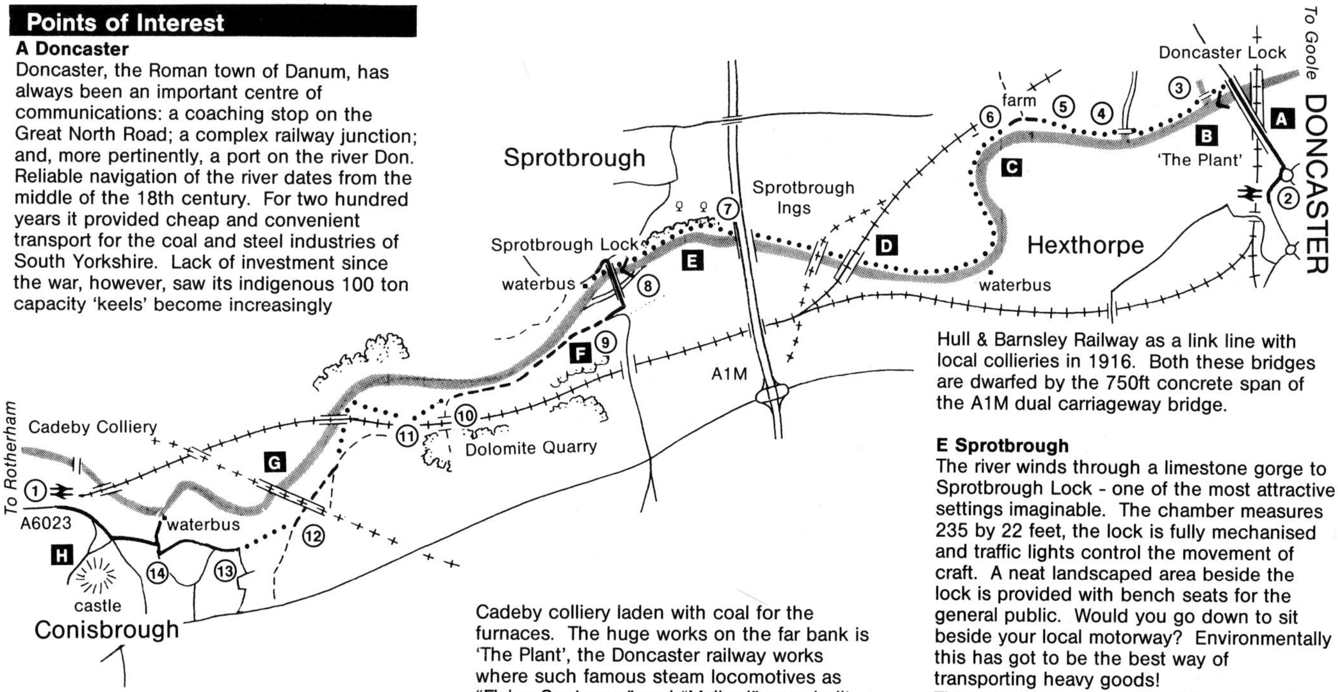

Points of Interest

A Doncaster

Doncaster, the Roman town of Danum, has always been an important centre of communications: a coaching stop on the Great North Road; a complex railway junction; and, more pertinently, a port on the river Don. Reliable navigation of the river dates from the middle of the 18th century. For two hundred years it provided cheap and convenient transport for the coal and steel industries of South Yorkshire. Lack of investment since the war, however, saw its indigenous 100 ton capacity 'keels' become increasingly

[Map labels: To Goole, DONCASTER, Doncaster Lock, ③, ④, ⑤, ⑥, farm, A, B, C, 'The Plant', ②, Sprotbrough, Sprotbrough Ings, ⑦, Hexthorpe, D, waterbus, E, Sprotbrough Lock, waterbus, ⑧, F, ⑨, A1M, Cadeby Colliery, G, ⑩, ⑪, Dolomite Quarry, ⑫, To Rotherham, ①, A6023, waterbus, H, ⑭, ⑬, castle, Conisbrough]

outmoded and obsolete when faced with containerisation and the spread of the motorway network in the region. After two decades of delay, government authorised modernisation in 1978. Ironically the modernisation scheme, completed in 1983, coincided with the retrenchment of South Yorkshire's traditional heavy industries, which might have been expected to benefit thereby. Nevertheless, if you make this walk on a weekday it will be disappointing if you don't encounter at least some of the canal's current traffics, which include: sand, stone, chemicals and steel. Doncaster Lock, with its neat stone control cabin - a feature of all the modernised locks - is your first view of the canal as you cross the railway bridge. On summer Sundays and Bank Holidays a waterbus service operates upstream to Mexborough.

B The Plant

Doncaster power station was in the throes of demolition when we researched this walk, and tied up in the old basin were a large number of laid up barges. Until 1981 this would have been a busy spot, with a steady stream of keels coming downstream from

Cadeby colliery laden with coal for the furnaces. The huge works on the far bank is 'The Plant', the Doncaster railway works where such famous steam locomotives as "Flying Scotsman" and "Mallard" were built.

C Hexthorpe

A charming group of farm buildings reach down to the riverbank. There is a peculiarly Flemish feel about the landscape; barely a mile out of Doncaster and it could be mistaken for a remote reach of the river Somme. Suddenly the river turns sharply to the south. The angle here was even more acute before modernisation saw part of the far bank cut away. A little further on you can see the pilings and mooring bollards of a former petrol jetty which received supplies by tanker barge from the Humber estuary refineries. Adjacent to this is a jetty still in use, a waterbus stop handy for a popular Doncaster recreation park.

D Viaducts

Three bridges span the Don along Sprotbrough Ings. The first dates from 1910 and carries a line opened by the Great Central Railway enabling goods trains to bypass the congested tracks of Doncaster station; it is of lattice girder construction and rests on brick columns. The second railway bridge is no longer in use. Supported on cylindrical steel columns, it was built by the

Hull & Barnsley Railway as a link line with local collieries in 1916. Both these bridges are dwarfed by the 750ft concrete span of the A1M dual carriageway bridge.

E Sprotbrough

The river winds through a limestone gorge to Sprotbrough Lock - one of the most attractive settings imaginable. The chamber measures 235 by 22 feet, the lock is fully mechanised and traffic lights control the movement of craft. A neat landscaped area beside the lock is provided with bench seats for the general public. Would you go down to sit beside your local motorway? Environmentally this has got to be the best way of transporting heavy goods!

There were once two mills at Sprotbrough which harnessed the flow of the Don to power their machinery. A minor road swoops down into the valley and crosses the navigation and weir channel. Prior to 1850 a ferry plied the river here. Just past the waterbus landing stage there is a group of old buildings, one of which was once an inn where Sir Walter Scott is reputed to have stayed whilst writing "Ivanhoe". He could not have chosen a more delightful environment.

F Quarries

Hidden in the woods of the bluntly named Levitt Hagg (sounds like a character from a Scott novel!) are several worked-out quarry faces and abandoned lime kilns. Stone chippings from here were used as a surface for the towing path in the days of horse drawn keels. Beyond the railway lies a huge dolomite (magnesium limestone) quarry. The wetlands bordering the southern bank of the river are used as a nature reserve by the Yorkshire Conservation Trust.

G Conisbrough Viaduct

On the far bank, a newly built jetty provides stone traffic for the navigation and limestone spoil tips create a Dr. Who like landscape as the river passes under two railway bridges. The first, more modest affair, carries the busy Sheffield-Doncaster line which you journeyed along from Conisbrough. The second is the spectacular Conisbrough Viaduct with a central girder section sandwiched between 21 slender blue brick arches. This route, now disused, dates from 1909. Promoted by local collieries, it was known as the Dearne Valley line and later became affiliated with the Lancashire & Yorkshire Railway.

H Conisbrough Castle
As the path begins its descent to Conisbrough, wide views open out towards the keep of the Norman castle and the headstocks of Cadeby mine; man's contribution to the landscape separated by eight centuries. Until 1973 there was a lock at Conisbrough and a passenger ferry which crossed to the far bank upstream of the weir. Like Sprotbrough there was a riverside mill here too.

Sustenance
This is not a walk well endowed with cosy waterside inns. One might wisely stoke up with 'Traveller's Fare' before setting out from Doncaster station, for the next watering hole (unless you're prepared to climb up to Spotbrough village to patronise an uninspired roadhouse) is "The Castle" public house near the end of the walk.

Counter Attractions
● Conisbrough Castle. Unique 12th century buttressed keep, the setting for Sir Walter Scott's "Ivanhoe". Open daily.
● Cusworth Hall Museum. Country house with historic collections illustrating bygone South Yorkshire. Open Mon-Thur & Sun p.m. Admission Free. 3 miles north of Doncaster. Tel: Doncaster (0302) 786925.

Encore
The towpath is a largely unheard of phenomenon on the South Yorkshire Canal, and so alternative walks are scarce. Happily though, the final non commercial section into Sheffield itself retains a towpath and has a character all of its own. A 7 mile linear walk from Ickles Lock, Rotherham to Sheffield Basin, using the frequent parallel rail service in one direction would be an ideal introduction to this forgotten length of urban waterway.

Information
Tourist Information Centre, Central Library, Doncaster. Tel: (0302) 734309.

When coal came by keel to the power station - former activity at Doncaster on the South Yorkshire Canal.

Walk 37

Staffordshire & Worcester Canal

West Midlands

Kinver   8 miles

The Walk

Unexpectedly, considering the proximity of the West Midlands conurbation, the Staffordshire & Worcestershire Canal is a beautiful waterway; the surprise is akin to finding a rare wild flower in a municipal park. Opened in 1772, it was one of the early undertakings of the Canal Age and shows all the hesitancy of those pioneering times. There is a modesty of scale about the canal's locks, bridges and other engineering features which delights the eye. This walk is based on the pretty little town of Kinver and incorporates part of the Stourbridge Canal too.

Start Point

Kinver Lock
OS ref: SO 849835.

Access

Bus (West Midlands PTA Service 257 runs hourly, daily from Dudley and Stourbridge. Tel: Brierley Hill (0384) 77752) and car -

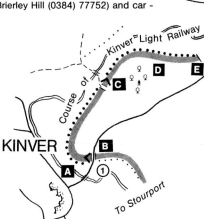

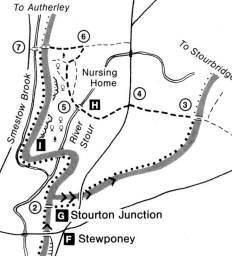

Kinver is 4 miles west of Stourbridge; nearest public car park to the canal is on Mill Lane, but space is limited and additional parking is available further into the village.

Directions

1 Proceed northwards along towpath for 2 miles to Stourton Junction.
2 Cross bridge 33 and follow Stourbridge Canal towpath up to bridge ¹/₂ mile beyond top lock.
3 Immediately through bridge turn left off towpath up onto lane and follow for ¹/₂ mile to main road.

4 Cross main road and enter gates of nursing home opposite, follow bridleway downhill to bridge across river Stour.
5 Beyond bridge bear left uphill, continuing past front of sanatorium (ignore "Private - Staff Only" signs this **is** a public right of way!). Beyond house turn right downhill at T junction and proceed through stable block.
6 Turn left along lane for ¹/₂ mile to canal.
7 Follow towpath back to Stourton Junction and then retrace steps to Kinver.
*NB 2 miles of walking can be saved by catching the bus back from Stewponey.

Points of Interest

A Kinver
Kinver is a jaunty little town which attracts its fair share of visitors; most of whom are bound for Kinver Edge, a wooded outcrop rising to 500 ft. topped by an Iron Age fort and the curious ruins of rock houses hewn out of the soft sandstone. The town name derives from Kine Fare, or cattle fair, but in the 17th and 18th centuries a flourishing iron industry stood along the banks of the Stour, temporarily changing the nature of the community. Fine views of the town and surrounding countryside can be had from the parish church of St. Peter, itself a distinctive landmark for miles around.

B Kinver Bridge
Kinver bridge has a characteristic Staffs & Worcs name and number plate, partially hidden by a pipe on the south facing parapet; note the use of the old spelling Kine Fare. At the outset of the walk the surroundings are rather untidy as the towpath passes the derelict buildings of a former marina, but such distractions are rapidly left behind and the arboreous character of the canal and the sanguine quality of the exposed sandstone establishes itself.

C The Hyde
Soon the Hyde is reached with its attractively situated lock and adjoining keeper's house - home made cooking is usually available here during the boating season. Above the lock a solitary house is all that remains of a once extensive iron foundry. The works predated the canal and there were twenty furnaces here. A slitting mill powered by the waters of the Stour cut iron plate into thin strips for blacksmiths and nail-makers.

D Kinver Light Railway
The canal makes an arc around pastures bounded by a fir plantation. Some stately beech trees separate the towpath from the

abandoned trackbed of the former Kinver Light Railway. This delightful country tramway operated for barely thirty years. Opening in 1901, it linked Kinver with the urban tramways of the Black Country.

E Dunsley Tunnel

The canal builders, their way barred by an outcrop of rock reaching down to the river, were forced to build a short tunnel at Dunsley. The result is an exciting, albeit brief adventure for walkers as, doubtless emboldened by the brevity of the bore, a towpath was incorporated, a rarity in 'first generation' canal tunnels.

F Stewponey

Stewponey doesn't find its way onto the OS map but it is thought that this curious name derives from 'stewpons', or fish ponds. When the canal was used commercially, Stewponey was the hub of the Staffs & Worcs system. The toll house survives, as do the former stables and carpenter's workshop. The last regular traffic through here was coal, down to Stourport power station, which finished in 1949.

G Stourton Junction

At Stourton Junction the Stourbridge Canal ascends through a flight of four locks. It is a pretty junction, encircled by trees, with a lofty wooden signpost ensuring that boaters take the route of their choice. The Stourbridge Canal dates from 1779 and was an important connecting route with the Birmingham Canal Navigations. The canal actually became derelict after the demise of working boats, but in 1962 the Inland Waterways Association held its annual National Boat Rally at Stourbridge, a campaigning event which brought about the impetus of restoration completed in 1967.

H Prestwood Hall

Your route follows the old carriageway of the former Prestwood Hall estate. A bridge over the river Stour, winding across parkland, creates an attractive scene. The history of the estate goes back to the reign of Richard III in the 13th century. In more recent times this was the home of the Foleys who owned one of the first ironworks in the district. Prestwood Hall was burnt down in the 1920s but the derelict stable block remains and some glum modern buildings are used as a sanatorium.

I Devil's Den

Deep in woodland, and keeping company with the Smestow Brook, the canal rounds a sharp bend and comes upon a curious cave

Autumn woods beside the Staffs & Worcs Canal near Kinver.

cut out of the rock at water level. Known as Devil's Den, this is thought to have been used as a boathouse for a punt used by the owners of Prestwood Hall. Shortly beyond the Den the canal turns to cross the Stour on a low slung aqueduct of typical Brindley design. The Stour rises on the Clent Hills to the south-west and pursues a wide arc before joining the river Severn at Stourport.

Sustenance

The "Vine Inn" at Kinver Lock is a very pleasant canalside pub offering a wide range of food. The centre of Kinver has a number of cafes and pubs and plenty of shops. The "Stewpony Hotel" does bar food, whilst the friendly little shop at the crossroads is open daily and can always supply fresh sandwiches. Plus don't forget that you may be able to get some home cooking at Hyde Lock.

Counter Attractions

Severn Valley Railway. Steam trains between Kidderminster and Bridgnorth operate weekends Easter - October and weekdays during the high season. Tel: Bewdley (0299) 403816.

Encore

Lack of parallel transport is the bane of the Staffs & Worcs and yet there are sections of outstanding beauty and interest which cry out to be explored. Of particular impact is that part of the waterway extending northwards from Wolverley to Caunsall, including two picturesquely situated locks, Cookley Tunnel and the famous overhanging rock at Austcliff.

Reference to OS Landranger maps 138 and 139 suggests that a number of adjacent public footpaths could be combined with the towpath between these points to provide an enjoyable 4-5 mile circuit.

Information

Tourist Information Centre, Market Street, Kidderminster. Tel: (0562) 62832.

Walk 38
Stratford-on-Avon/ Grand Union Canals
Warwickshire

Bearley - Hatton   **10 miles**

The Walk

We had some difficulty in compiling an itinerary for a walk along the Stratford Canal. Parallel public transport never coincided with the ingredients of an interesting walk. But ultimately, after two false starts, we devised the route featured here which incorporates the canal's major engineering structure - the aqueduct at Bearley (or Edstone) - plus numerous examples of the split-bridges indigenous to the canal, and several of the distinctive barrel-roofed lock cottages common to the central section. As a bonus two miles of the northern section of the Grand Union are featured too, including the unique towpath tunnel at Shrewley. Entirely rural throughout, taking a sinuous course through quintessential Warwickshire, this is one of the loveliest towpath trails imaginable.

Start Point

Hatton Railway Station. OS ref: SP 224664.

Access

Train, (local services Birmingham Moor Street-Leamington Spa, hourly, Mon-Sat, Tel: Leamington (0926) 22302) or car - free car parking at the station for rail users. Hatton Station is 2 miles southwest off the A41, 5 miles west of Warwick.

Directions

1 Take the train from Hatton to Bearley. The service is roughly bi-hourly, Mon-Sat, details are available from the Leamington number

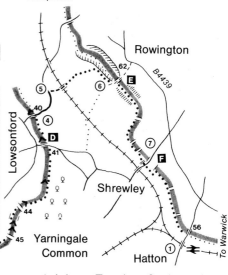

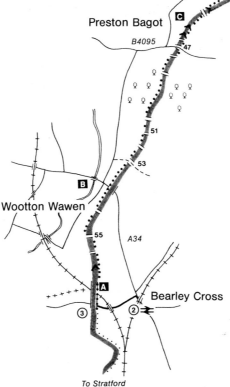

quoted above. There is no Sunday service.
2 Leave the platform at Bearley and descend to the road, turning left along the pavement to the crossroads. Turn left along road signposted "Little Alne".
3 Steps lead up to the towpath from the eastern side of the aqueduct. Join towpath and proceed north for 6 miles to bridge 40.
4 Turn right off towpath and follow minor road for ¹/₂ mile to east.
5 Turn right off road up bridle way. After bypassing the farm, this becomes a clearly defined track crossing the railway and proceeding through the fields to the Grand Union Canal at Rowington.
6 Go over the stile, across the lane and descend to the towpath at bridge 62 of the Grand Union Canal.
7 Keep to the towpath as it passes through its own tunnel at Shrewley. Beyond the tunnel go directly across the street and follow the lane right to the other end of the tunnel. Then proceed along towpath to bridge 56 and Hatton Station.

Points of Interest

The Stratford Canal
Work began on the Stratford-on-Avon Canal in 1793. It took 22 years to build and had an independent life of only 40 years before being taken over by the Great Western Railway in 1856. It runs for 25 miles from King's Norton, where it meets the Worcester

Wootton Wawen Aqueduct on the Stratford Canal.

& Birmingham Canal on the south-western outskirts of Birmingham, to Stratford and its junction with the River Avon. There is a junction with the Grand Union Canal at Lapworth dividing the Stratford Canal into Northern and Southern sections. After the railway takeover, traffic gradually deserted the canal. By the 1930s, the southern end was bereft of trade and virtually derelict. Robert Aickman, founder of the Inland Waterways Association (see Walk 43) encountered it as a boy; an experience which later had much to do with his championing of the waterways. In the face of abandonment, the Southern Stratford was transferred to the National Trust during 1958. It was subsequently restored by volunteers and prison workers, being reopened by the Queen Mother on 11th July 1964. But the two decades of National Trust ownership have not always been harmonious ones, and the canal is currently up for grabs should any institution with sufficient funds to maintain it in a navigable state be found.

A Bearley Aqueduct
The aqueduct looms across the fields as you walk along the road from Bearley Station, a structure - given the modest rolling countryside - barely less imposing than the famed Pontcysyllte. Its iron trough, over 150 yards long, rests on 13 brick piers. The 'sunken' towpath offers walkers a fish's-eye view of passing boats as well as wide vistas across the charming Warwickshire landscape. The aqueduct spans the minor road; a tributary of the River Alne; and the twin-track Birmingham & North Warwickshire Railway which was opened in 1907 - comparatively late in the Railway Age. Traces of an earlier branch opened in 1876 from Bearley Junction to Alcester can be seen running beside the stream to the west. Now the existing railway is under threat of closure south of Hampton in Arden. Its loss would be sad and would somehow diminish the impact of the aqueduct.

B Wootton Wawen
Continuing northwards past an isolated lock, the Stratford Canal runs through a wooded cutting to reach Wootton Wawen, a village of more than passing interest marred only by the ceaseless traffic on the A34. Another, though shorter, iron-troughed aqueduct, dated 1813, carries the canal over this trunk road and has been collided into by several

highsided lorries in recent years. A steep, unofficial path leads down beneath the aqueduct from its southern end giving access to the nearby pub and village. On the way in, one passes a former paper mill, once powered by the Alne; crosses the river upon a balustraded stone bridge adjacent to several ornamental weirs in the grounds of the huge 17th century Wootton Hall; and arrives at the venerable Parish Church of St. Peter, parts of which date from Saxon times. Back on the canal, and immediately beyond the aqueduct, is a busy boat-hire base.

C Preston Bagot
After Wootton Wawen the canal loses itself in the old Weldon (or Arden) region of Warwickshire, a gently undulating landscape once densely forested and comparatively ignored by the passage of time. Doubtless, Shakespeare would have made something of the canal. Certainly a later literary figure, Quiller-Couch in his delightful story "True Tilda", published in 1909, included a description of a journey by narrowboat down the southern section of the canal. Throughout this length, lanes and footpaths criss-cross the canal by way of the distinctive split-bridges which consist of brick abutments and seemingly fragile cantilevered

iron arches broken in mid-stream so as to permit the passage of a tow-line in horseboat days. Most are still guarded by diamond-shaped cast iron load warnings erected by the GWR who took over the canal in 1856. At Preston Bagot, one comes upon the first of the delightfully unusual barrel-vault roofed lock cottages, unique to the middle section of the canal which was opened in 1813.

D Lowsonford
The canal climbs steadily across Yarningale Common through a series of locks encountering another, albeit diminutive, iron trough aqueduct. One barrel-roofed cottage has been incorporated into a luxurious modern home. Almost throughout, trees border the water, suggesting that summer might be a very claustrophobic season to walk this way. It was at Lowsonford that E. Temple-Thurston met the man on a bridge parapet, frightened of returning home to tea, now that his wife of 51 years had died.

E Rowington
The bridle way crosses the Birmingham-Leamington railway line, once the premier GWR route to the north, but less busy now that inter-city trains are largely diverted via Coventry. Nevertheless, it is interesting to

contrast the grandeur of the railway's engineering with the modesty of that on the Stratford Canal. Similarly impressive construction techniques can be found on the Grand Union Canal. In climbing the Avon Valley, the Warwick & Birmingham Canal (as it was originally known), dating from 1800, cut boldly through Rowington Hill and used the resultant spoil to cross the adjoining valley on a high embankment.

F Shrewley Tunnel
Emerging from the arch of bridge 59, one is confronted with the unusual sight of two portals, one to the right and considerably higher than the other. This is no ocular phenomenon, but rather the unique Shrewley Tunnel where the towpath rises steeply to cross the village street, passing through its own tunnel in the process. Once past the village you follow the old boat horse track to rejoin the canal at the south end of a 433 yard bore. Returning to Hatton, there is ample evidence, embossed in concrete pilings, of the Grand Union's 1930s improvements to the canal, a modernisation plan which included the complete rebuilding of the Hatton flight of 21 locks to the south.

Sustenance
There are pleasant pubs with food at Bearley Cross ("The Golden Cross", Flowers) and Wootton Wawen ("The Navigation", Whitbread). At Preston Bagot the canalside "Haven Tearooms" are Egon Ronay recommended but closed on Mondays. There is a canalside pub, "Fleur de Lys" at Lowsonford and at the western end of Shrewley's main Street, "The Durham Ox" is a freehouse where children are welcome.

Counter Attractions
Hatton Craft Centre, 1/2 mile east of Hatton Station. Old farm buildings renovated to house an expanding community of craftsmen and small businesses. The general public are at liberty to walk round and see the various craftsmen at work and are given the opportunity to buy anything that catches their eye. There are numerous places to visit in the Warwick & Stratford area, ask for details at the Tourist Information Centres listed below.

Encore
On the northern section of the Stratford Canal under British Waterways Board control, the towpath is in appalling condition so a cohesive walk in this vicinity is virtually out of the question. On the southern section,

currently looked after by the National Trust, the towpath is in surprisingly good condition considering the limited resources available to this department of the Trust. An alternative shorter walk on the southern section can be taken between Stratford itself and Wilmcote using the train in the outward direction. This includes the interest of the Wilmcote Flight and Stratford Basin, but lacks the distinctive Stratford Canal characteristics. The ultimate towpath trail combining the Stratford on Avon and Grand Union Canals would be from Stratford to Leamington including the Hatton Flight and stately aqueduct over the Avon at Warwick. But at 20 miles, this would be an ambitious day's walk for the fittest only. If it does appeal to you, then there is a bi-hourly train service between the two towns Mon-Sat together with a limited Sunday service in summer (Tel: Leamington (0926) 22302) or alternatively Midland Red connects the two towns as well (Tel: Leamington (0926) 492212.

Information
Tourist Information Centre, High Street, Stratford-on-Avon. Tel: Stratford (0789) 293127.
Tourist Information Centre, Jury Street, Warwick. Tel: Warwick (0926) 492212.

Walk 39

Thames & Severn Canal
Gloucestershire
Sapperton - Stroud   8½ miles

The Walk
If ever a canal cried out for restoration it is the Thames & Severn; not that its unrestored state affects the walker, it is just a pity that those who get their pleasure from boating rather than walking are missing out on such a gem. It is no exaggeration to say that this is a unique walk for there can only be one 'Golden Valley' in the Cotswolds. But along-side its undoubted scenic attributes there is a bonus in the shape of a Thames & Severn 'roundhouse' and another rarity, an inland 'port'.

Start Point
Stroud Bus Station. OS ref: SO 849052.

Access
Bus, train and car. Stroud is on the Cheltenham-Gloucester-Swindon-London main line - enquiries to Gloucester (0452) 29501. Bus and coach connections are excellent: Stroud (04536) 3421 for information. There is a large multi-storey car park next to the bus station.

Directions
1 Catch a bus (service 22) to Sapperton -

there are three morning services.
2 Alight at Sapperton School and walk up the hill towards the church.
3 Turn left down the lane just before the church, cross the stile and continue downhill keeping well to the left.
4 Cross over the stile on the left hand fringes of the slope and then cross along the top of Sapperton Tunnel's portal.
5 Follow the towpath for 3½ miles to Bell Lock at Chalford.
6 Cross the A419 and rejoin the canal by walking through the car park opposite and turning right - it has changed sides.
7 Leave the towpath again at the site of Chapel Lock and follow the path up to the road side for a short distance before rejoining the canal.
8 Leave the towpath after Bourne Lock and follow the path (later to become a works road) between the stone wall and the river Frome to the left.
9 Cross the Frome and continue up to the road and past the "Ship Inn".
10 Rejoin the towpath by following the 'public footpath' sign on the left just beyond the pub - quite unexpectedly the canal reappears in 1/4 mile on the left, the towpath having changed sides - continue along the

towpath for 2½ miles.

11 Leave the towpath at the A46, just above Wallbridge Upper Lock and turn right.

12 Cross the road and turn left at the junction.

12 Turn left down Merry Walks at the traffic lights, the bus station is 100 yards on the right.

Note: The towpath vanishes from time to time, as does the canal, but in all cases - except those detailed above - the route is obvious.

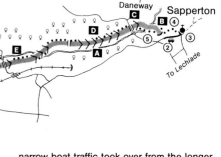

gradually other lengths succumbed until in 1933 it was finally abandoned. The Stroudwater Navigation had no such problems and remained open until 1954 when the inevitable decline in traffic took its toll.

B Sapperton Tunnel

Walking down from the church it is hard to believe that over two miles of underground canal breaks out of the hillside down there in the wooded valley of the Frome. The western portal of the tunnel has lost most of its castellated glory and the attendant lengthman's cottage is in a sorry state, possibly beyond reclamation. Much of the canal's problems centred around this area where alternate strata of fuller's earth and inferior oolite were points of weakness; two rock falls (around 1916) eventually severed the through

route. But such problems are in the past and the softness of the setting overcomes the melancholy of this place with its secluded timeless quality.

C Daneway

Almost immediately west of the tunnel mouth, the line of the canal crosses over the culverted river Frome, a constant companion now until Stroud. Daneway is ¼ mile away where, like Woolroad on the Huddersfield Narrow (see Walk 19), a trans-shipment basin with attendant wharves and warehousing was set up while the tunnel was still being worked on. The "Daneway Inn" was originally built to house the 'navvies' working on Sapperton and first became an inn, the "Bricklayers Arms", in 1807. Today its car park all but obscures the site of Daneway Bridge Lock, the last of 28 in the climb up from Stroud to the summit level. From the bridge itself the Daneway settlement remains much as it was, the main 'absentee' being the sawmill. Besides being a reservoir, the basin was where boats would 'lay-up' while waiting to work through Sapperton - navigation being on a strict alternate four hourly basis in each

direction, day and night. Leaning wistfully on the bridge's parapet, the imagination soon recreates a bustling scene with locks, wharves and basin and *the raison d'être*, the working men and boats.

D The Locks

Derelict locks tumble down the spectacular wooded valley in quick succession, their stone chambers overrun by the decay of time as they are ensnared by a profusion of Triffid-like vegetation. Evidence of two attempts to solve the water shortages of the summit level still remain: there are several wide pounds that acted as mini-reservoirs between the locks and most of the chambers themselves were shortened by some 20 feet as the narrow boat traffic took over from the longer Thames barges for which they were designed. The lonely brick and stone Whitehall Bridge was the arbitrary line to the east of which the canal was abandoned in 1927.

E Puck and Twissel's Mills

The Frome meanders along to the south, its clear waters gaining momentum as we head west. The valley opens out then narrows again around the isolated settlement by the former Puck Mill. The private residence by Puck Mill Upper Lock was once the "Oak Inn", though it is hard to imagine the community it served. Up a side valley, behind the railway viaduct, is the tiny hamlet of Frampton Mansell but perhaps another answer is in the leakage problems in the short pound between the two Puck Mill locks which was in constant need of attention from, no doubt, thirsty 'navvies'. Another, more dramatic, mill setting is just around the corner where Twissel's (also known as Baker's) Mill overlooks an attendant reservoir. Its water storage function is now less relevant, it is instead a uniquely bewitching place with waters, mill buildings and abundant wild life encapsulated in a time trap of trees.

Points of Interest

A The Thames & Severn Canal

The bus ride from Stroud to Sapperton gives tempting glimpses of the canal, particularly west of Chalford. As the bus climbs along the southern edge of the Golden Valley it is clear that, scenically at least, this is no ordinary canal. The idea of linking the Thames and the Severn goes back to the early 17th century, but it was not until 1779 that the first link in the chain, the Stroudwater Navigation, was completed. The longer - and technically more difficult - link, the Thames & Severn Canal from Stroud to Inglesham (near Lechlade) on the Thames, was completed some ten years later. The main problem was the summit level which crossed "some bad rocky ground" and was thus prone to leaking. This caused a series of prolonged closures in the 1890s culminating in Gloucester County Council's efforts early in this century to 'restore' the canal. It reopened in 1904 but just seven years later the last boat passed over the summit and

Restored roundhouse at Chalford on the Thames & Severn Canal.

F Chalford

A plate-less mile post stands between river and canal opposite the solid brick facade of the old Chalford Waterworks before Golden Valley Lock on the outskirts of Chalford. All the buildings here and around the next two locks, Red Lion and Bell, have strong canal connections. All too had adjacent inns taking their names from (or giving them to) the locks; the remains of wharves and mills punctuate this aptly named 'Golden Valley', the soft Cotswold stone of the weavers' cottages completing the richness of the setting. Chalford's housing staggers down the valley's sides but is almost paled into insignificance by the cluster of interesting buildings beyond the site of Chapel Lock. But first, as at Bell Lock, the canal is culverted here and has a plated milestone built into the culverted arch: WALBRIDGE 4 INGLESHAM $24^{3}/_{4}$. From the building beyond, James Smart, a coal merchant, ran his fleet of barges - trading as recently as 1933. Then there is Chalford's most interesting feature, its conical-roofed roundhouse built about 1790/1 as a lengthman's cottage and one of five such buildings unique to the Thames & Severn. The ground floor was a stable (with access from the road) with the top two storeys providing living accommodation with access from the towpath.

G Brimscombe Port

The old 1850 turnpike (now the A419), the railway, the canal and the Frome share a parallel course along the valley almost to Brimscombe Port. The railway recrosses by Bourne Mill and its adjacent lock, a hybrid in that its dimensions, 16ft. 1in. x 90ft., allowed Thames barges to reach Brimscombe *and* the wide Severn trows could get through to the company's boatyard, Birds, by Beale's Lock. The high stone wall beyond Bourne (see direction 8) was the boundary wall of the hub of the canal's activities, Brimscombe Port. Sadly, there are few remains of this extensive (90ft. x 250ft.) trans-shipment basin capable of accommodating up to 100 vessels. The complex included a foundry, mills, an island coal wharf, a boat gauge and a forge in addition to the various offices and ware-housing facilities. All that is left is the lengthman's cottage and the salt store to the right about 100 yards before the "Ship Inn". It is thus difficult to imagine the importance

of such a complex - the car park and buildings of Benson International Systems are scarcely the foundation for such mental exercises.

H For Hope and Ham

Most of the mills of the Stroud Valley were originally built for the manufacture of woollen cloth but with the eventual superiority of the Yorkshire mills many turned their hand to silk production. One of the last 'active' silk mills was Hope Mill, the site of which lies north of the lock with the same name; to the east of the lock was the canal's most famous boat-building yard Abdela & Mitchell. Here were born all manner of craft, from small sailing boats to longer steam screw and paddle river launches, many of which were exported to South America. Boats were normally 'got out' by water but abandonment of the canal in 1933 quickly led to the company's demise. Half-a-mile further on is Ham Mill, again close to a like-named lock. It was to here in 1933 that the last load of coal was brought in the barge "Dorothy". The railway remains close at hand and, though it survived the Beeching

butchery, many of its stations and halts - such as the one here by Ham Mill - fell under the axe.

I The Stroudwater, Thames & Severn Canal Trust

It is places like Brimscombe Port that make restoration of this canal seem something of a pipe dream and yet there is an active Canal Trust dedicated to this end. Indeed, in 1982, the Trust created something of a 'first' with a nationally televised Appeal for funds towards their efforts. It is, therefore, heartening to see that the rot has been contained and that in some places, particularly between Ham Mill and Stroud, the channel has been dredged to a navigable depth. An unusual cast iron lattice-work footbridge, each of its rivets fashioned into a flower, and built, it is believed, at the time of Queen Victoria's Golden Jubilee, has also been refurbished by the Trust. At Bowbridge Lock too, there is evidence of the Trust's work in the shape of a restored circular weir.

J Wallbridge

The setting west of Brimscombe is largely rural but defies comparison with the Golden Valley. Now that Stroud is close at hand, the river and railway sort themselves out, the one crossing under the canal, the other over on an impressive brick-clad viaduct designed by Brunel. The turnover bridge just before the latter, provided access to the Midland Railway yards on the left; on the other side, a little way up the track and within the precincts of the Stroud District Council depot, are the remains of a two-storey building, once the LMS's carrier's stables. Here the horses were bedded down upstairs while hay etc. was stored below. The unmistakable sights and sounds of urbanisation drift near but are never obtrusive. Wallbridge Warehouse with its large, almost flamboyant, brick facade dominates the cut and gives definition to Stroud's Wallbridge Wharf. The wharf was second only to Brimscombe in importance to the canal and initially competed directly with the Stroudwater's Wharf a few hundred yards to the west where the two canals unite.

K Stroud

Five valleys converge at Stroud, a fact which directly led to its importance as an industrial and commercial centre for the area. By 1824 these valleys boasted over 150 mills, most of which produced quality cloth - Stroudwater Scarlet, used for military uniforms, was, and still is, world-renowned. As elsewhere, the cloth industry declined though never ceased; many mills were demolished while others were adopted by more modern industries such as engineering and woodworking. Nevertheless, Stroud remains a country town with many interesting buildings, some dating from Tudor times, along its narrow, often steep, streets. Like most Cotswold towns, it is well worth exploring.

Sustenance

The Golden Valley was once alive with alehouses. Many of them found alternative 'accommodation' but there are enough still selling their wares to ensure that the walker is well fed and watered. In Stroud, there is a wide selection of shops, restaurants and cafes including "Mother Nature", an excellent vegetarian restaurant, its 'front' a health food shop selling similar wares over the counter.

Counter Attractions

● The Prinknash Pottery and Abbey, near Upton St. Leonards, Gloucester. Open Mon-

Sat, 10.30am-4.30pm. Admission charge. Telephone Painswick (0452) 812239. The Abbot of Gloucester entertained Henry VIII and Anne Boleyn in Prinknash Abbey, the home of Benedictine Monks from Caldy Island. The Monks' Pottery and Tearooms are open to the public . . . but only *male* visitors may visit the monastery itself.
● The Pack Age Revisited, the Albert Warehouse, Gloucester Dock, Gloucester. Open daily (ex Mon) 10am-6pm. Tel: Gloucester (0452) 32309. A unique collection devoted to the history of the consumer society - a treasure trove of tins, cartons, packets, display cards, posters, hoardings, boxes and bottles dating from the 19th century. Certain to stir many a childhood memory.

Encore

The western end of the Stroudwater Canal is not exactly rife with public transport options. However, between Stonehouse and Stroud, the opposite is the case - there are both good rail and bus connections. A seven mile circular walk along both the canal and the old Stonehouse-Nailsworth railway, now a pedestrian/cycle trail (the two cross at the site of an interchange wharf at Bridgend) is dominated by a series of mills - a sawmill, two flour mills, two wool mills and a cloth mill. By far the most impressive is Ebley Mill, arguably one of the finest buildings of its type.

Information

Tourist Information Centre, Council Offices, High Street, Stroud. Tel: Stroud (04536) 4252.

Walk 40

Trent & Mersey and Staffs & Worcs Canals

Staffordshire

Great Haywood   **6 miles**

The Walk

Two famous canals , some of the most glorious countryside in the Midlands, no less than seven historic bridges, and the opportunity to visit Shugborough Hall and Staffordshire's County Museum, make this a memorable walk. It commences at Seven Springs on the edge of Cannock Chase, and includes some two miles of forest and hill walking combined with the towing paths of the Staffs & Worcs and Trent & Mersey canals which the famous engineer, James Brindley, designed to meet at the junction of Great Haywood.

Start Point

Seven Springs, Cannock Chase. OS ref SK004204.

Access

Car or bus. Car park at Seven Springs just off A513, 5 miles East of Stafford. Adjacent

bus stop for Midland Red 'Chaserider' services, approx hourly, daily. Tel: Stafford (0785) 42997.

Directions

1 Three tracks leave the car park area; take the right hand one, bearing right again after about 100 yards. Paths cross the main track at frequent intervals, leading temptingly off up bracken-covered slopes to copses of birch and pine or into deeper woods of conifers, but ignore these and keep to the main track.
2 The track reaches a clearing with picnic tables. Stepping stones lead across a rippling brook, follow these and bear right following the track signposted 'The Punchbowl'.
3 A signpost points to Mere Pool, Punchbowl, and Milford; take the last route of these up a steep track onto Oat Hill.
4 Descend slope and turn left.

5 Bear right and descend to road.

6 Cross main road by entrance to Shugborough Hall and follow unclassed road (pavement on left hand side) over railway and River Sow to Bridge 106 on the Staffs & Worcs Canal.

7 Turn right under canal bridge and follow towpath for 2 miles to Great Haywood Junction.

8 Turn right under Great Haywood's slenderest of slender roving bridges onto the Trent & Mersey Canal towpath; follow this as far as Haywood Lock.

9 Detours can be made to Great Haywood village and/or over Essex Bridge to Shugborough Hall, museum and farm park. Otherwise continue along towpath for 1 mile to Bridge 72.

10 Through Bridge 72, turn right up onto the road and go left along the road (pavement on right hand side) under railway, over river, across main road and up to the land back to Seven Springs.

Points of Interest

A Cannock Chase
Cannock Chase consists of twenty six square miles of open heathland and conifer plantations rising to 800 feet above sea level, of inestimable recreational value to the 4 million benighted inhabitants of this part of the heavily industrialised West Midlands. The fact that the soil is poor has protected the Chase from agricultural development. The original deciduous woodlands were largely cut down in the 16th century for charcoal burning. Today's plantations date from the 1920 acquisition of approximately a quarter of the Chase by the Forestry Commission. Fallow deer are among the residents in this wild landscape.

B Oat Hill
The woods recede, and from 550 feet up amidst the bracken of Oat Hill you can look clearly down on the Staffs & Worcs Canal meandering between the railway and the river along the Sow Valley towards the blessedly distant high-rise horizon of Stafford.

C River Sow
The River Sow rises near the Shropshire and Staffordshire border, is joined by the Penk below Stafford, and meets the Trent at Shugborough. At Milford it is crossed by a handsome stone road bridge and, slightly to the West, a typical Brindley canal aqueduct.

D Staffs & Worcs Canal
James Brindley's Staffordshire &

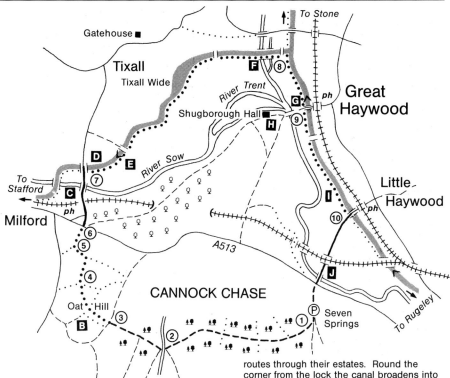

Worcestershire Canal was completed in 1772 as part of his plan for a 'Grand Cross' of canals linking the four great estuaries of Thames, Mersey, Humber and Severn. It is 46 miles long linking Great Haywood, where it meets with the Trent & Mersey Canal, with Stourport on the river Severn. It is typical of early canals, taking the easiest way through the landscape, clinging to contours, lacking the confidence with which later canal builders cut and embanked their way directly across the countryside.

E Tixall
Just before you reach the picturesque Tixall Lock you can glimpse to the right the grandiose western portal of Shugborough railway tunnel which attempts to disguise the main London to Glasgow line's progress through the parkland of Shugborough. 18th and 19th century landowners had little enthusiasm for the passage of new trade routes through their estates. Round the corner from the lock the canal broadens into a lagoon known as Tixall Wide which, it is said, similarly placated the landlord of Tixall Hall when the canal was built. The Hall, where Mary Queen of Scots was imprisoned, has long gone, but a decorative Tudor gatehouse and crescent-shaped stable block remain.

F Great Haywood Junction
Two more Brindley aqueducts, characteristically carrying the whole weight of the puddled clay canal bed within sturdy low-slung masonry frames, take the canal over the river Trent and a mill stream to Great Haywood Junction spanned by its famous roving bridge, a miraculous combination of functional engineering and architectural beauty. Considering that this is one of the key junctions on the inland waterways system, one which once saw narrowboats carrying goods to all points of the compass, there has been little adverse affect on the landscape. The tiny, gothic-windowed toll house is open during the summer months as a gift shop specialising in traditional roses & castles canal ware.

Leaping into the unknown - bosky moorings on the Trent & Mersey Canal at Great Haywood.

during the winter months too - telephone for details or see local notices. Admission charge. Tel: Little Haywood (0889) 881388.

Encore

Another Trent & Mersey possibility lies at Shardlow, near Derby, the canal's southern terminus and a virtually unspoilt example of a canal era inland port. The Arkwright Society have produced a local history trail which guides you around the port's most interesting features. One of the warehouses has been converted into a waterways museum. Copies of the trail leaflet are obtainable from: The Arkwright Society, Tawney House, Matlock, price 25p plus SAE.

Information

Tourist Information Centre, Greengate, Stafford. Tel: Stafford (0785) 3181.

G Essex Bridge

From Bridge 73 on the Trent & Mersey, a lane leads under the railway between two terraces of Georgian cottages to the centre of Great Haywood village. In the opposite direction the trees recede to confront you with the marvellous 14-arch, 16th century, Essex Bridge, which replaced an earlier, much longer, wood and stone structure extending to 43 arches; a route used by medieval hunting parties to cross the marshy ground up on to the Chase. Huge cutwaters demand to be lingered over while you view, upstream is the confluence of Trent and Sow and downstream are the ruined abutments of a former carriageway to Shugborough (an iron bridge which took it over the canal survives).

H Shugborough

Home of the Anson family since 1624, the present Shugborough mansion dates from the 17th & 18th centuries, and is of neo-classical style. The house belongs to the National Trust and is open to the public. Former stables house the Staffordshire County Museum, with a fascinating exhibition of the county's domestic, social and industrial past. A third attraction is the estate farm where rare breeds and old farming implements are preserved. The grounds are studded with monuments and follies; two visible from the towpath are the Tower of the Winds and the Triumphal Arch: both copies of Athenian originals.

I Trent & Mersey Canal

Built primarily to bring raw materials to, and export finished products from, the Potteries, the Trent & Mersey Canal was opened between Preston Brook near Runcorn and Shardlow near Derby in 1777. This is a particularly picturesque length of the canal, with deep woods on the one side, and the widening Trent Valley bounded by the heights of Cannock Chase on the other.

J River Trent

You cross the river Trent for the second time upon a 6-arched brick bridge which retains its cobbled roadway. A plaque reveals that it was erected in 1887-8 by public subscription and the 'liberality' of one Joseph Weetman.

Sustenance

Unprepossessing refreshments can be had at Milford in the shape of cafe grub, hamburgers, 99s etc. Great and Little Haywood both have a brace of unostentatious pubs, but our recommendation (when open, see below) is the eatery adjoining Shugborough museum.

Counter Attractions

Shugborough. Opening times: House, museum, gardens and farm, Mar-Oct., Tue-Fri, Bank Hol. Mon, Sat & Sun afternoons. The museum and gardens are likely to be open

Walk 41
○

Trent & Mersey and Macclesfield Canals
Staffordshire/Cheshire

Kidsgrove   **5 miles**

The Walk

'Kit Crew' is a famous spectre in canal circles, a ghost reputed to haunt Harecastle Tunnel which takes the Trent & Mersey Canal 1¾ miles beneath a ridge of gritstone on the northern edge of the Potteries. This walk includes: a visit to the northern portal of the tunnel, the curious junction at Hardings Wood where the Macclesfield Canal meets the Trent & Mersey, a cross country interlude of field and woodland paths, and the impressive flight of duplicated locks at Red Bull.

Start Point

Kidsgrove railway station.
OS ref: SJ 838544.

Access

Train (station served by local services between Manchester & Birmingham and Crewe and Derby. Tel: Stoke (0782) 411411); bus (stops on nearby Liverpool Road served by PMT Tel: Stoke (0782) 48284) and car (car parking on station forecourt).

Directions

1 Head east from the station forecourt, following the path past the signal box, which leads down steps to the canal. Turn left along the towpath.
2 Cross the junction roving bridge and turn immediately left onto Macclesfield Canal towpath.
3 Cross footbridge and follow towpath over aqueduct for 1 mile to Hall Green Lock.
4 Turn left up steps immediately beyond bridge 93 and follow path between houses, turning left on reaching the road. Continue to main road.
5 Cross main road and bear left to "Bleeding Wolf" pub. Turn right down Bleeding Wolf Lane. Bear right at end of lane onto path between hedges.
6 Turn left across stile just before end of

footpath and walk parallel to hedge to next stile.
7 Go straight across field to gap in hedge by concrete gas main marker.
8 Bear diagonally across field, gradually descending to top left corner. Cross miniature footbridge over marshy ground and turn left along well defined path to larger footbridge over stream.
9 Proceed along path through wood. At top

end of wood climb stile and continue directly across field to church. The wrought iron gate doesn't open, so bear right along perimeter wall to stile.
10 To view church turn left to entrance gate, otherwise turn right to stile by tree and turn left onto canal towpath. Proceed 1½ miles along Trent & Mersey towpath back to Hardings Wood.
11 Cross bridge 133 and retrace earlier route continuing past station steps to view Harecastle Tunnel. Then return to station.

Points of Interest

A Orange Water
The first surprise, on reaching the towpath, is the peculiar orange colour of the canal water. This phenomenon also occurs at Worsley on the Bridgewater Canal near Manchester. In both cases the strange colouring is caused by the seepage of chemicals from ironstone strata beneath the canal bed.

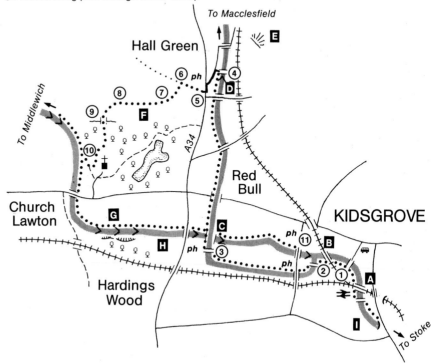

B Hardings Wood Junction

The second surprise, at Hardings Wood Junction, is that the Macclesfield Canal, bound northwards, leaves the Trent & Mersey from its southern bank! A quick glance at the map will explain matters. For here, as perhaps not too coincidentally as nearby Hazelhurst on the Caldon Canal (see Walk 8), one route leapfrogs the other in order to achieve the required contour. Historically, in fact, the canal you follow to Hall Green was built by the Trent & Mersey Company, though oddly an inscription stone on the junction roving bridge at Hardings Wood proclaims "Macclesfield Canal MDCCCXXVIIII". At any rate, the route you're about to take is nowadays generally referred to as the Macclesfield Canal, and as if in proof of this the first bridge encountered is numbered 97 in the Macclesfield sequence. Once through the bridgehole the towpath traverses a barren isthmus of wasteland between the two canals. Some peculiarity in the lie of the land convinces you that the canal is climbing!

C Aqueducts

Pool Lock Aqueduct carries the 'Macclesfield' over the Trent & Mersey and it is fascinating to look down on the senior route to watch boats working through the duplicated chambers of Lock 42. Like the roving bridge at the junction, an inscription on the aqueduct (best viewed as you return along the towpath below) is dated 1829. Only a few yards further on Red Bull aqueduct, of even loftier proportions, carries the canal over the A50 trunk road.

D Hall Green Lock

Regarding Hall Green Lock today, the ridiculously shallow chamber appears unnecessary, but it was built for the express purpose of separating the precious waters of the Macclesfield Canal to the north and the Trent & Mersey to the south. Known as 'stop' locks, these diminutive structures are often a feature of junctions between the canals of different companies. Northwards from Hall Green the Macclesfield runs for some 26 miles to Marple near Stockport. It was completed in 1831, one of the final generation of narrow beam canals. The influence of Thomas Telford is apparent in the canal's bold progress on embankments and in cuttings along the edge of the Peak District. Today it is a popular cruising route for holidaymakers; part of the famous Cheshire Ring.

E Mow Cop

Views of Mow Cop abound throughout this walk. The folly-topped hill is part of a gritstone escarpment rising to over a thousand feet. The castellated ruin, known as Wilbraham's Folly, is a typical example of 18th century landscaping. On these heights, one Sunday morning in May 1807, the first open air camp meeting of the Primitive Methodist revivalists was held.

F "The Bleeding Wolf"

Far from being a boring link between the two waterways, the walk between Hall Green and Church Lawton has a pastoral appeal all of its own. The stiles are generally well maintained and although the fields are pastureland for milking herds, the walker feels under no threat, as is sometimes the case on public footpaths over farmland. How the memorably named "Bleeding Wolf Inn" came to be so called is an interesting legend. In the 13th century, King John, hunting in the forest that covered the Cheshire Plain, was attacked by a savage wolf. At the height of the struggle a passing forester came to the King's rescue, killing the beast with his long hunting knife. As a reward the King offered his saviour all the land he could walk over in a week. There are few wolves in the woods today, only a charming footbridge over a sinuous stream which emanates from the lake in the grounds of nearby Lawton Hall, finding its way via the rivers Wheelock, Weaver and Mersey to the Irish Sea.

G Red Bull Locks

The locks at Red Bull are only part of a series - 26 altogether in 7 miles, known colloquially as Heartbreak Hill - all of which were duplicated in the 1830s to enable traffic to be speeded up in the face of competition from the new fangled railways. The double chambers remain a bonus to this day, although occasionally they are closed for maintenance whilst the extra chamber at Lock 43 has been removed altogether. The towpath, bounded by a sturdy stone wall, climbs past the double locks against a background of mature trees which screen the parallel railway. Just beyond Lock 44 one of the original 1819 cast iron mileposts indicates that it is 63 miles to Shardlow (near Derby where the Trent & Mersey joins the river Trent) and 29 to Preston Brook (near Runcorn where the canal joins with the Bridgewater Canal). The Trent & Mersey Canal was opened in 1777, sponsored by the pottery manufacturers of North Staffordshire who needed a more reliable alternative to transport by packhorse; both for the carriage of incoming raw materials such as clay from Cornwall (brought by ship around the coast to Liverpool) and the export of finished goods to the growing markets of Europe and North America.

H Section Office

Canal maintenance is nowadays the responsibility of the British Waterways Board, an undertaking quite separate from the regional water authorities. The entire system of over 2,000 miles of navigable waterways is divided into areas known as 'sections'. Red Bull is the headquarters of the Potteries Section and the smartly whitewashed office stands beside the canal above Lock 44.

I Harecastle Tunnel

Nearing Harecastle Tunnel the water grows an ever more brighter orange. A tiny cabin houses the tunnel keeper who, along with his colleague at the other end, controls the progress of boats through the single-line bore. Boats take some ¾-hour to pass through the tunnel, an extraordinary adventure for amateur navigators who might have only a matter of hours experience. The present tunnel dates from 1827 and was engineered by Thomas Telford. The abandoned portal of James Brindley's original tunnel is visible to the right. Craft were propelled through this claustrophobic corridor by 'leggers' who lay on their backs, literally walking a boat from one end to the other; a feat which took three hours!

Sustenance

There are four pubs en route (all marked on the map) which offer food as well.

Counter Attractions

Little Moreton Hall, one of the most celebrated examples of a moated, half-timbered manor house in England, is on the A34 Congleton road 4 miles north of Kidsgrove. This superb National Trust property is open Mar-Oct. Sat & Sun afternoons; Apr-Sept. daily afternoons. Tel: Congleton (02602) 2018 for further details. The hall can also be reached by footpath from bridge 86 on the Macclesfield Canal, 1 mile north of Hall Green.

Encore

Whilst we're on the edge of the Potteries, it's worth considering trying out the towpath between Longport (south of Harecastle Tunnel) and Stoke. There are handily placed railway stations at either point (Tel: Stoke (0782) 411411 for service details). Not as overtly industrial as in the past, particularly since the demise of Shelton Bar steelworks and the advent of the International Garden Festival, this is nevertheless a stirring 3½ mile urban walk of particular interest to those with an enthusiasm for industrial archaeology.

Information
Tourist Information Centre, Central Library, Bethesda Street, Hanley, Stoke-on-Trent. Tel: (0782) 21232.

Walk 42

Weaver Navigation/ Trent & Mersey Canal

Cheshire

Acton Bridge   9 miles

The Walk

An unlikely encounter with a ship gliding through Cheshire milking pastures could be the highlight of this unusual walk along the towpath of one of Britain's lesser known river navigations. As a bonus, the longer walk option includes a length of the Trent & Mersey Canal as well.

Start Point

Acton Bridge railway station.
OS ref: SJ 599745.

Access

Train (hourly service Mon-Sat to/from Crewe and Liverpool. Tel: Crewe (0270) 255245), bus (Crosville service Frodsham - Northwich bi-hourly Mon-Sat. Tel: Chester (0244) 315400), and car - station car park on B5153 5 miles NW of Northwich).

Directions

1 Turn right outside the station and proceed along Hilltop Road signposted "Acton Cliff".
2 Bear right along Acton Lane signposted "Runcorn & Warrington".
3 Turn left onto main road (pavement on far side) and continue to swing bridge.
4 Join lane running parallel to river.
5 Just short of the sluice channel turn right over stile and climb track up to Trent & Mersey Canal. For a shorter 6 mile option continue along lane to Dutton Lock and read on from direction 10.
6 Cross stile onto towpath and turn left under bridge 211, following towpath 1¾ miles to

Preston Brook Tunnel. Retrace steps to field path at direction 7.
7 Climb stile and go straight across field (keeping brick barn to your left). Join road opposite half-timbered farm house and turn right, bearing left at next farm and continuing downhill to fork in lanes.
8 Follow footpath signposted "Acton Bridge and Delamere Forest". Cross stile and go straight on with steep grassy bank to your right. Head for the white footbridge.
9 Turn left across bridge and proceed to lock.
10 Cross lock (walkways provided over gates) and turn right along river path for 1 mile to Pickerings.
11 Turn left up pathway lined with poplar trees. Go over footbridge and join road.
12 Turn left onto lane and follow back through village for 2 miles to railway station.

Points of Interest

A Acton Bridge
The existence of a non-conformist chapel and the absence of a parish church give clue to Acton Bridge's 19th century origins. It is an isolated place, unmentioned in guidebooks, with little traffic disturbing its no through road. In fact there are more horses than motor vehicles and it's pleasant to find a village smithy flourishing near the railway station.

B Swing Bridge
Every once in a while thundering traffic on the A49 trunk road is brought to an abrupt standstill at the flashing lights which guard

the huge girder swing bridge over the Weaver. Few of the motorists bother to switch off their ignitions, but they should exercise patience, for it takes some time for the ships, which twice a week on average trade up the river, to pass. Acton swing bridge was built in 1932 and weighs over 600 tons. It is constructed on a buoyancy tank, and so finely balanced that less than one unit of electricity is required to swing it.

C Weaver Navigation
The Weaver is a foundryman dressed in game-keeper's garb, a workaday river winding its way through remote, roadless countryside, a waterway known to few outside the close-knit communities who earn their living on and beside it. It has contrived to connect the salt, and later chemical industries of the Northwich area with the Mersey ports for centuries. The fact that it still does is a tribute to the foresight of its owners and engineers down the years, who constantly sought to modernise its locks, bridges and other infrastructure. One only has to look up the hill at the moribund Trent & Mersey Canal, unaltered since construction and consequently unused by commerce, to judge their achievement. The head of navigation is at Winsford, 11 miles and 3 sets of locks upstream from Acton Bridge, but nowadays commercial craft trade only as far as Anderton where, incidentally, the Weaver is dramatically linked to the Trent & Mersey by a famous boat lift (see Counter Attractions).

D Trent & Mersey Canal
After the Weaver, the Trent & Mersey seems tiny. The narrowboats which traded along here until their demise in the 1960s carried only a modest 25 tons. Small wonder this and other 'narrow gauge' canals lost their trade. But in its late 20th century guise as a pleasure cruising route, part of the popular Cheshire Ring circuit, the Trent & Mersey fulfils a role scarcely considered when it was planned by James Brindley as a link between the Potteries and Mersey ports in the 18th century. In fact, as the first milepost you encounter shows, you're only 2 miles from the northern terminus of the canal at the far end of Preston Brook Tunnel, whilst the other end of the canal is at Shardlow, 90 miles away on the banks of the river Trent.

E Dutton Dock
Dutton Dock is the base for a number of smartly turned-out hotel boat pairs. These craft cruise the canals during the summer months offering a unique style of floating holiday. Such a relaxing way of seeing the

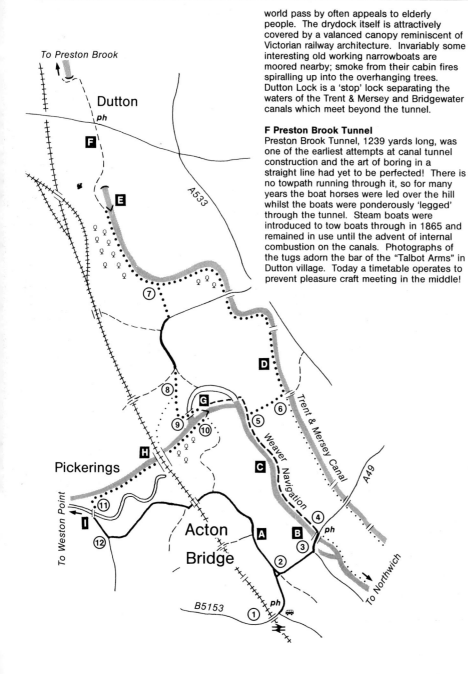

world pass by often appeals to elderly people. The drydock itself is attractively covered by a valanced canopy reminiscent of Victorian railway architecture. Invariably some interesting old working narrowboats are moored nearby; smoke from their cabin fires spiralling up into the overhanging trees. Dutton Lock is a 'stop' lock separating the waters of the Trent & Mersey and Bridgewater canals which meet beyond the tunnel.

F Preston Brook Tunnel
Preston Brook Tunnel, 1239 yards long, was one of the earliest attempts at canal tunnel construction and the art of boring in a straight line had yet to be perfected! There is no towpath running through it, so for many years the boat horses were led over the hill whilst the boats were ponderously 'legged' through the tunnel. Steam boats were introduced to tow boats through in 1865 and remained in use until the advent of internal combustion on the canals. Photographs of the tugs adorn the bar of the "Talbot Arms" in Dutton village. Today a timetable operates to prevent pleasure craft meeting in the middle!

G Dutton Locks
A substantial towpath bridge of handsome proportions spanning the sluice channel leads to Dutton Locks. There are two chambers, the smaller being split by intermediate gates so that shorter craft can save water. The larger, electrically operated chamber measures 13 by 67 metres and can be used by vessels of up to 1,000 tonnes capacity. Two pairs of semi-detached cottages house the lock-keepers and their families. Benches are thoughtfully provided to take the weight off your feet and a Red Ensign flies proudly from a mid-chamber mast. The railway-like semaphore signals which once controlled movements in and around the locks are now unused. There is an uncanny quietness about Dutton Locks, broken only by occasional bursts of activity at the advent of a vessel.

H Dutton Viaduct
The twenty massive stone arches of Dutton railway viaduct dominate the landscape for miles around and it is a slightly sobering experience to pass beneath. It was built in 1837 as part of the Grand Junction route from Birmingham to Warrington. Today it carries the busy Euston Liverpool/Glasgow electrified railway, and those with an interest in railways as well as canals won't fail to be fascinated by the parade of trains along this line, which is seldom out of sight throughout the walk.

I Pickerings
Reedy, silted remainders of the Weaver's old meandering course lead to the remote community of Pickerings. Before the river was linked to the Manchester Ship Canal downstream at Weston Marsh, the salty tide made its presence felt here, and there is a haunted ambience to the place; a sense of activity departed. There was once a lock here, its red sandstone chamber still discernible, and the keepers' cottages, similar to those at Dutton, are now private premises.

Sustenance
Smile, you're in Greenall Whitley land, and could do worse than repairing to the quaintly named "Hazel Pear" beside the station; a good choice of bar food is available and there's a children's playground and bowling green.

Counter Attractions
Anderton Lift. Located $^1/_2$ mile off the A533, $1^1/_2$ miles north of Northwich, a viewing area is provided for visitors to this astonishing

engineering structure. Currently sadly out of use, it dates from 1875 and consists of two water filled tanks which raise or lower narrow beam craft through the 50 foot disparity in height between the Weaver and Trent & Mersey. The viewing area is always open and there is no admission charge. There are hopes that a more sophisticated celebration of this now unique structure will be provided in due course.

Encore

The riverside path continues beyond Pickerings downstream to Frodsham, so there is potential here for an extended one-way walk using the Crosville bus service linking Frodsham, Acton Bridge and Northwich. A circular walk, again combining the Trent & Mersey, could be devised between Acton Bridge and Barnton. Southwards from Northwich the Weaver enters the picturesque Vale Royal but the towpath is unfortunately not continuous all the way to Winsford.

Information

Tourist Information Centre, 57/61 Church Street, Runcorn. Tel: (09285) 76776.

Dutton Dock on the Trent & Mersey near Preston Brook.

Walk 43

Worcester &
Birmingham Canal

Worcestershire

Tardebigge   **5 miles**

The Walk

A nostalgic walk this, retracing, as it does, Robert Aickman's walk from Bromsgrove Station to Tardebigge after the War when, for the first time, he visited L.T.C. Rolt aboard his home, the narrow boat "Cressy". Their meeting was destined to be the spark that, within a matter of months, led to the formation of the Inland Waterways Association. "I caught a train to Bromsgrove and, taking a footpath marked on the one inch Ordnance map, I walked over the fields

to Tardebigge where the Rolts were then living on a boat called Cressy. It all has rather a dreamlike quality for me . . ." *Our* start point has to be just around the corner from Bromsgrove Station for, sadly, today's rail service does not cater for regular - or even nostalgic - stops at Bromsgrove.

Start Point

The "Dragoon", Aston Fields, near Bromsgrove Station.
OS ref: SP 969695.

Access

Bus or car. There is a free public car park next to the "Dragoon". A regular Midland Red West service links Aston Fields with

Stourbridge and Redditch - both of which have a regular rail service. Information from Bromsgrove (0527) 72265.

Directions

1 Proceed north from the "Dragoon" (ie away from the shops) and turn first right, St. Godwald's Road.
2 Keep left at the top of the hill following the signs to Stoke Cross and Tardebigge.
3 Turn right almost immediately, signposted to Stoke Pound and Upper Bentley.
4 Turn left off this road just after it crosses a small stream and enter the field.
5 Follow the left-hand edge of the field up to the stile in the top left corner; cross this and again follow the field's left-hand edge to its top left corner.
6 Cross into the field on the left and follow its right-hand edge up to the canal.
7 Cross the canal bridge (No. 52) and turn left onto the canal towpath.
8 Leave the towpath at lock 50 and walk up to the edge of the reservoir on the right.
9 Return to the towpath at lock 52 and proceed to Tardebigge Top Lock, No. 58.
10 Cross the lock to view the commemorative plinth.
11 Re-cross the lock and leave the towpath following the signpost to the church.
12 Return to the towpath via the path back downhill from the entrance drive to the church.
13 Turn left onto the towpath and head back towards and past Top Lock as far as the 2nd bridge (No. 55).
14 Cross the bridge and proceed to the T-junction.
15 Turn left at the T-junction.
16 Take the 2nd turning on the right; this is St. Godwald's Road and leads directly back to Aston Fields.

Points of Interest

A The Railway

Travelling northwards by canal or rail one is left in little doubt that Birmingham is on a hill. The canal climbs out of the Severn basin up to the Lickey Hills by way of the Tardebigge flight, the railway builders following 30 years later built the Lickey Incline; at 1 in 37 the steepest gradient on any British main line. Heavy trains are still banked up the incline by a pair of diesels, but this overbridge must have been a dramatic spot in steam days when as many as four banking engines would be used. One of the most famous bankers, specially built for duty, was an 0-10-0 nicknamed 'Big Bertha'.

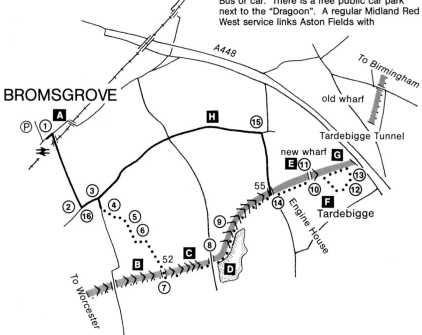

BROMSGROVE

Tardebigge top lock and alehouse in working boat days.

B The Worcester & Birmingham Canal

The Worcester & Birmingham was conceived as a short cut from the Midlands to the river Severn, a route that would save some 30 miles on the existing Staffs & Worcester/Stourport link. The Canal Company's initial optimism in planning a broad canal was short-lived. The two barge locks at Worcester's Diglis Basin were as far as that idea went, though all tunnels and bridges were built broad. In addition to its links with the Severn and the Midlands network at Birmingham, junctions with the Stratford Canal at Kings Norton, an extension to the Dudley Canal at Selly Oak and the Droitwich Junction Canal at Hanbury all provided additional traffic. Despite competition from the railways, the canal continued to carry commercial traffic into the 1960s and, as pleasure boating increased, it soon became a major constituent of two popular cruising routes, the Stourport and Avon Rings. The canal has two features of particular note: the 2726yd. Kings Norton Tunnel (also known as Wast Hill or Westhill) and the longest lock flight in Britain at Tardebigge.

C The Tardebigge Flight

Walking through the fields from Bromsgrove, Robert Aickman might well have wondered if he was going the right way, for the line of the canal is not immediately obvious until the top of a humpbacked bridge suddenly appears on the skyline. From bridge 52 the Tardebigge flight falls away through the gently folding hillside and down 16 locks; Aickman's climb took him past the remaining 14, each with its own distinctive charm. Some have attractive lock-side cottages, one of which has a convenient coal-shute by the towpath . . . it's a long wait these days for a convenient coal-carrying boat. In 1808 an experimental boat lift was built at the top of the flight but this proved unsatisfactory and was replaced by the present deep lock - reputedly the deepest narrow lock in the country, but there are a few lock-keepers on other flights who would dispute that.

D Tardebigge Reservoir

The best views of the locks are to be had from the rim of Tardebigge Reservoir; from here the problems of climbing such an escarpment can be put into perspective - after all haven't these hills kept the encroaching Birmingham at bay? The reservoir was originally built to store water for and return it to the summit level. An underground culvert went to the red-brick Engine House (now a bistro) by lock 57 from where it was pumped up to just above the top lock. Today the canal is fed from reservoirs in Birmingham.

E Aickman and Rolt

Above the top lock a brick plinth bears a cast bronze plaque that commemorates the historic meeting in 1946 (sic) between Tom and Angela Rolt and Robert Aickman aboard "Cressy" which eventually led to the formation of the IWA. Aickman recalls the occasion thus, "I walked with my map from Bromsgrove Station and my host began well by saying that I was the first visitor who had the initiative to do so". His 'initiative' stemmed from his reading of Rolt's masterpiece, "Narrow Boat", and he determined to meet with the man who unknowingly had stirred something within. Ironically the euphoria of those early years turned sour and five years later the two were at loggerheads. Coincidentally, whilst researching these walks we were working on an unpublished Aickman manuscript which appears to set that first meeting, in 1945. Our suspicions were encouraged by the discovery of a Christmas card from the Rolts to Aickman bearing a photograph of "Cressy" moored at Tardebigge and dated 1945!

F Tardebigge Church

The slender 135ft. tower of Tardebigge Church is a notable landmark, not least from the canal. In 1775 the original church's tower fell through the roof and damaged the whole building beyond repair; the present church is thus the 18th century replacement. At one time the Warwickshire/Worcestershire county boundary actually divided the nave and the chancel of the old church. It is a steep climb up the hill so there is every excuse to have a breather and enjoy the view across to the Malvern Hills and, just below, Tardebigge new wharf. On the way down, the path leads towards the mouth of Tardebigge Tunnel which claimed the lives of many of those who lie in the church's graveyard; in 1842 alone three 'leggers' were drowned while working boats through.

G Tardebigge Tunnel and Wharves

The 568yd. tunnel, one of four on the 14 mile summit level, cuts through red sandstone and was completed in 1810, three years after the line from Birmingham had reached the northern end. This delay resulted in two Tardebigge wharves - the old wharf, now a hire-base, and the new wharf, now a BWB maintenance yard. By 1946 there was no trade at either of the Tardebigge wharves, a far cry from the days when boats loaded wheat and agricultural produce at the new wharf bound for Birmingham, and returned with coal and limestone from which lime was produced in wharfside kilns for building and agricultural purposes.

H Around Tardebigge
Before the coming of the canal most parishes in this part of Worcestershire were not villages in the proper sense, consisting rather of scattered farms and cottages. The canal and its immediate environs created a focus and most of the habitation around the wharves dates from the early 19th century. Some of the older and more scattered areas are on the way back to Bromsgrove. Old, thoughtfully restored cottages along Dusthouse Lane, with whimsical names such as "Pipkin" and "Withybrook", and the half-timbered Stonehouse Farm contrast sharply with more recent and instantly forgettable 'infilling'.

Sustenance
Besides the "Dragoon" at Aston Fields there is a take-away and a reasonably good selection of shops, including a butchers that specializes in home-made pies etc. The "Tardebigge Inn" $1/4$ mile east on the old A448 does good food and is a unique experience in itself.

Counter Attractions
● Avoncroft Museum of Buildings, Stoke Prior, Nr. Bromsgrove, Worcs. Open daily, Mar-Nov, 10.30am-5.30pm (closed Mon, Mar & Nov). Admission charge. Tel Bromsgrove (0527) 31886. An open-air museum with many historic and important buildings rescued from destruction; includes a reconstruction of an Iron Age hut.
● The Patrick Collection, 180 Lifford Lane, Kings Norton, Birmingham. Open mid May-Oct daily 10am-5.30pm (Sept & Oct closed Mon & Tues). Admission charge. Tel: 021 459 9111. A new motor museum which will not be fully completed until 1987 (times may change then). The collection includes 150 motor vehicles including an Austin 10 which was restored by two of the coachbuilders who produced the car in 1934.

Encore
In total contrast to the featured walk the $5^1/2$ miles from Kings Norton to Gas Street in Birmingham puts the canal in its historical perspective. The canal crosses some glorious countryside but only as a means to an end - and that end was the industrial Midlands. Between Kings Norton and Gas Street is the Cadbury Works at Bournville, one of the regular and most recent users of the canal; at Selly Oak there was a link with the Dudley Canal though this has now been heavily disguised with a hotch-potch of more modern industry. There are good rail and bus connections between Kings Norton and Birmingham but no access on or off the canal between the two.

Information
Tourist Information Centre, 47-49 Worcester Road, Bromsgrove, Worcs. Tel: Bromsgrove (0527) 31809.

Acknowledgements
The authors and publishers are grateful to the following for their valued help in the preparation and production of "Towpath Trails" - Harrad Jackson; The Matthews Wright Press; Waterways Museum, Stoke Bruerne; British Waterways Board, Press Office; Cromford Canal Society; John Harker & Co; John Masters; Pauline & Colin Burgess; Rita & Walter Bickerston; Glynn & Val Edwards; Mike & Carol Golds; Kathryne Harvey; Barbara & John Lower; Marcus Potts; Hugh Potter; Christine Richardson; Jos Weaver; Tim Wheeldon; Lindy Wood; Kay Bowen; Joy Hales; Janet Hoult; Felix Pearson, Suzanne Shilton, Jackie Pearson & Lesley Fearn.

Photographic credits
All photographs are by the authors with the exception of - Robert Aickman collection: pages 25 & 123; Harry Arnold: pages 3, 61, 81, 87 & 95; British Waterways Board: pages 32 & 96; The Boat Museum: page 76; Michael Dolphin: page 34; Clive Durley: page 10; Hugh McKnight: pages 45 & 47; Derek Pratt: pages 2, 62, 63, 73 & 92; Roy Westlake: page 110.

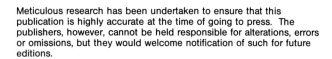